Hugh Lunn was born in wartime Brisbane just months before Pearl Harbor and began his adventures at Annerley Junction where his parents ran the 'Lunns for Buns' cake shop. Caught between a tough brother Jack and younger sisters Sheryl and Gay, he teamed up with the unlikely Dimitri Egoroff, becoming Jim's 'left-hand man'.

As a teenager Hugh began his newspaper career on the *Courier-Mail* in 1960 before heading for Fleet Street, via China and Russia. He worked on the London *Daily Mirror* and was a Reuters correspondent in Vietnam, Singapore and Indonesia. He has won seven national awards for feature writing, including three Walkley Awards.

Hugh's first memoir, *Vietnam: A Reporter's War*, was an *Age* Book of the Year and was subsequently published in New York. *Over the Top with Jim*, his next memoir, became the biggest selling book ever about an Australian childhood. He has written eleven books, of which *Working for Rupert* is the latest.

GW00458761

Working for Rupert

Other memoirs by Hugh Lunn:

Over the Top with Jim
More Over the Top with Jim
Head over Heels
Vietnam: A Reporter's War
Spies Like Us

Working for Rupert

Hugh Lunn

HODDER

A Hodder book

Published in Australia and New Zealand in 2002
by Hodder Headline Australia Pty Limited
(A member of the Hodder Headline Group)
Level 22, 201 Kent Street, Sydney NSW 2000
Website: www.hha.com.au

Copyright © Hugh Lunn, 2001

This book is copyright. Apart from any fair dealing for
the purposes of private study, research, criticism or
review permitted under the *Copyright Act 1968*,
no part may be stored or reproduced by any process
without prior written permission. Enquiries should
be made to the publisher.

National Library of Australia
Cataloguing-in-Publication data

Lunn, Hugh, 1941- .
Working for Rupert.

ISBN 0 7336 1532 5 (pbk.).

1. Lunn, Hugh, 1941- . 2. Journalists - Queensland - Biography.
3. News Corporation - Employees - Biography.
4. Australian (Canberra, A.C.T.) . 5. Queensland -
Social life and customs - 1965- . I. Title.

994.306092

Cover design and digital imaging by Scooter Design
Text design and typesetting by Bookhouse, Sydney
Printed in Australia by Griffin Press, Adelaide

Contents

1 Meeting Rupert

My first meeting with Rupert Murdoch was completely unexpected. It came a few months after I began work on his newspaper, the *Australian*, thirty years ago in 1971. From then on, for the next seventeen years in his company, I was always aware that Rupert might bob up, unannounced, anywhere at any time.

And so he did.

This man who everyone in News Ltd—and probably Australia for that matter—invariably referred to merely as 'Rupert', but only when he wasn't there. When Rupert was present, strangely, nobody seemed to call him anything. No Australian journalist was going to feel comfortable calling someone 'Mr Murdoch', especially when everyone in News Ltd called everyone else—including the Chairman, Ken May—by their first name. But what to call this man who controlled all our destinies? He was too much of an unknown, and much too powerful, to be called 'Rupert' to his face. At least without being asked. And he didn't seem to ask.

Not being able to begin or end sentences with a name—any name —made people uncertain, uneasy... unimportant. Sentences necessarily started off-kilter, with hesitation, or a sort of sigh...and trailed off into the ether. Often with a rising inflection, so that we sounded as if we were seeking permission rather than answering questions.

Looking back, Rupert's presence made our opinions sound less than strongly held.

I only began working for Rupert Murdoch through a series of unusual circumstances. It wasn't as if I had sought him out, or he had sought me out. I hardly knew anything about him, except that he was ten years older than me and he had founded Australia's first national daily newspaper, the *Australian*, in 1964, just before I left Brisbane's *Courier-Mail* to work overseas. I was 23 and Rupert only 33.

Rupert was very young to be turning the country's newspaper industry upside down. The experts on the *Courier-Mail* at that time predicted that the *Australian* wouldn't last six months. Australian newspapers had always been State-based, for who wanted to read about car accidents and robberies in other States? Being young and inexperienced, I believed them. Yet the experts were proved wrong: the *Australian* was still hitting the streets nationally when I got back home to Australia in 1971, though no one, except perhaps Rupert himself, would have called it a success. It was losing millions of dollars every year; it sold very few copies for a daily newspaper, not even reaching six figures most days; and there was no room for expansion because it attracted few advertisements, which meant it was a very thin paper. Being a national paper, there were no classified ads to ensure people bought the *Australian* to find a house or a plumber, and so there was none of the usual huge cash flow from these pages. Our editors always referred jealously to the classified pages in the State-based metropolitan papers as 'rivers of gold'.

On my return, aged 30, after seven years of self-imposed exile abroad, I could see that one reason the *Australian* had survived until 1971 was that it was the only newspaper in the country that wasn't stuck deeply in our colonial past. Thus it was the only paper that actively opposed Australia's involvement in the Vietnam War. The Australian government of that time—and for the foreseeable future—

was committed to blindly following the United States anywhere. Even to partaking in chemical warfare. Even to sending teenage male conscripts to their death, or, worse, their destruction. Even to the annihilation of a faraway ancient civilisation. And all with the support at that time of virtually every powerful person, corporation and institution in the country (though they might deny it later).

Except. Except for Rupert.

Rupert, who alone in our media dared propagate—in the national newspaper he had founded—a contrary view. An extremely unpopular view. Was he the first media proprietor to dare damn a war in which the Anzacs were fighting? This Rupert Murdoch was clearly a renegade, a man from out of left field or, in cricket terms, from behind square leg. In a country that judges people by the size of the city they come from, Rupert had arrived in Sydney out of Melbourne via Adelaide, where he had been running his family's afternoon paper, the *News,* since 1953. So he landed in Australia's biggest city as an outsider, young and underestimated, a man without the views of the class who judge.

Rupert had arrived from one of those powerless and distant places that the Australian Broadcasting Corporation refers to dismissively in inter-office memos as 'the BAPH States': Brisbane, Adelaide, Perth and Hobart. Places dismissed, ignored, laughed at by the nation's elite, or, to use the modern term, 'marginalised'. But then even the Dutch and the French were written out of Australia's history books because they had explored and landed on the coasts of the BAPH States...154 years before the arrival of Captain Cook in Sydney.

Having spent thirteen months in Vietnam as a war correspondent for Reuters, London, I was impressed by the *Australian*'s anti–Vietnam War stance, especially since the *Sydney Morning Herald* (at that time owned by Sydney's aristocratic Fairfax family) was still, incredibly, writing editorials headed 'The Winnable War' four years after the US had realised that the game was up, that the game was definitely up following the Tet Offensive of January–February 1968. This Rupert seemed to know what I knew: that in Saigon the truth was a lie. That the Americans had no chance whatsoever of achieving victory over Ho Chi Minh despite their CBUs; their WBLCs; their M16s; their Hueys; their B-52s; their Free Fire Zones; their H and I; their Beehive rounds; their F-111s; their six-barrel machine-guns; their 2,4-D and 2,4,5-T; their Agent Blue, Agent Green, Agent Pink, Agent Purple, Agent White, or even their Agent Orange. It was that simple: if you were there. There among the disposable olive-green plastic zip-up body bags. There when five hundred teenage American soldiers were dying each week. I mean living there—not living in Paddington discussing the war with a gob full of onion dip, the only deadly weapons in sight the two-pronged forks from the fondue set, with feet dug deep into a beige shag-pile carpet. I mean standing in mud and hiding in holes. I mean talking to dead Americans. Eating turkey combat rations instead of Chicken Maryland and bread sticks. Head rocking under the weight of a helmet. Chest not protected by a flak jacket. I mean, testicles achingly vulnerable in khaki cotton pants above the thin aluminium floor of a helicopter. Wearing dead man's boots. Being defoliated. Carrying a black M16 rifle no longer needed by yet another dead 18-year-old American. I mean, knowing what it means to piss red. Knowing that just because you're shot, it doesn't mean you will die; knowing that what is most frightening in war is the getting dead.

Good on you, Rupert, I thought. People are listening to you, mate. This was why the *Australian* was still going: it was being read by few, but an important few. Particularly academics.

No one was listening to me. The publishers of the Fairfax family's *Sydney Morning Herald* took no notice when I tried to tell them what I knew. In Sydney, March 1968, immediately after witnessing the Tet Offensive, I headed for the Fairfax Building and caught a lift to the 17th floor to see the Managing Director, Sir Angus McLachlan. A waiter in starched white shirt and black bow tie wheeled in a trolley for afternoon tea as I told Sir Angus the unadulterated opinion of a 26-year-old Australian Reuters correspondent on six weeks post-war leave from London: 'Every reporter in Vietnam who goes out into the field—into "Indian country" as the Americans say—knows that we cannot win in Vietnam. They know that the US military has already lost the war and that it knows it has already lost.'

Sir Angus seemed quite interested in this information but more interested in the scones. I returned to London knowing that Australian newspapers were very happy in their ignorance: except for 'young Rupert'.

Like Rupert, I had come out of a BAPH State newspaper, except that I was from Brisbane. And we had another experience in common. Arriving in Swinging London—me in 1965 and Rupert a couple of years later—we both headed for the same place: the British national daily broadsheet the *Sun*. We had different motives, of course, for knocking on the door. I was looking for a job and using every contact I had in a confident quest to work on Fleet Street; Rupert wanted to buy the joint.

I had been given the name of an editor to contact at the *Sun*, but by the time I got there he had been moved six miles away from Fleet Street. He nervously touched his pencil-thin moustache, clearly embarrassed to have to explain his situation to a young man. He had, unfortunately, been demoted to Gardening Writer. Then, only the previous week, he had been demoted again. Now his job was to answer the letters to the Gardening Writer—he waved his hand carefully above a shoebox stacked with hand-written envelopes, as if the box were filled with red-back spiders. So I didn't get an interview with the *Sun*.

The *Express* had 'enough Australian reporters'; the *Telegraph* had 'a long list of experienced reporters waiting to join our staff'; the *Times* was so English that they didn't reply to my job application. At the *Daily Mirror* the news editor, Roland Watkins, greeted me with a handshake, saying: 'Congratulations on being the one millionth Australian reporter this year to apply for a job with the *Mirror*.' But when he heard I was from Brisbane he immediately offered me casual work six days a week at eight pounds a day: well above the Fleet Street minimum rate. 'What a coincidence! The best journalist we've ever had was from Brisbane, and his name was Hugh as well! Hugh

Curnow. It was a great shame Hugh had to return home for family reasons. We still miss him.' (Three years later, in March 1968, Hugh Curnow, Peter Burke and Noel Buckley were killed when a helicopter spun out of control on a natural gas platform in Bass Strait between Victoria and Tasmania and cut through a group of journalists.)

Rupert had more luck at the *Sun* than I did. He bought it, very cheaply, from the people who owned the hugely successful London *Daily Mirror*. The *Mirror* owners made a big mistake selling to Rupert Murdoch—an aggressive young newspaperman who knew the industry front page to back. But others had made the same mistake too: in 1960 Fairfax sold a failing newspaper, the Sydney *Mirror*, to Rupert. It was a mistake Rupert himself was never to make when he became the magnate. When Rupert unloaded metropolitan papers in Australia—and he only did so in order to obtain bigger, more influential and more profitable papers—they ended up in the hands of his former editors. Or, once, he sold to an extremely rich businessman from outside the industry who was trying to block a Rupert takeover.

The *Sun*'s problem in London was that it was up against an array of top Fleet Street national morning newspapers—the *Mirror*, the *Express*, the *Mail*, the *Telegraph*, the *Sketch,* the *Guardian* and, of course, the *Times*—and so was losing circulation daily, as well as a fortune. But Rupert knew what he was doing. He turned the staid broadsheet into a small, bright tabloid that looked very much like the *Mirror*, which at the time was said to be the biggest selling English-language paper in the world. Newspaper sellers on street corners complained it was now difficult to tell which paper was which. And, since the *Mirror* was outselling the *Sun* six to one, the advantage was all Rupert's: the *Sun*'s circulation doubled in a year. Rupert was smart enough, too, to bring the great Australian cartoonist Rigby to London, and sometimes the *Sun* ran Rigby's cartoons right across the top half of the front page—something no other London paper dared do.

Rupert also hired some of the *Mirror*'s best London staff, including a reporter I worked with, a 40-something Londoner known to all as 'Mac'. Mac worked six days a week as a casual at the *Mirror,* and had been doing so for twenty years when I started as a casual there. Clearly, Mac was their gun reporter but still he sat off to the right-hand side of the reporters' room next to the glass-enclosed Features section where another Australian reporter worked, a tall, broad-shouldered, fair-haired bloke who wore, surprisingly, short-sleeved white shirts. Mac pointed to this reporter through the glass and said his name was John Pilger. I was surprised he knew the Aussie's name. Mac didn't mix much. He had the mien of a man who wanted to be alone: staring into his typewriter or his notes while thinking, never talking across the reporters' room like others, always untidy in braces and a blue suit that crumpled as he leaned back in his chair for hours.

Mac obviously wasn't interested in promotion. It showed in the way he wore his clothes, the way he spoke to bosses as if they weren't present, the fact that he remained a casual employee. One day I asked Mac why he didn't take a full-time job on the *Mirror* like everyone else. 'Don't be silly,' Mac replied. 'I wouldn't work for this lot.' But Mac did sign up for the full-time executive job of news editor on the *Sun* once he had met Rupert. A persuasive man, Rupert, as I was to find out myself.

Since Mac and I were both six-day-a-week casuals at the *Mirror*— and since he had the best reporter's contact book in London—I constantly sought his advice. Londoners, he explained, didn't know what a 'suburb' was. A singlet was known locally as a vest. Sandshoes were called 'plimsolls'. And as for Durex, it was a condom in England, not clear sticky tape like it was back home in Australia. Mac explained this last item after I had called out across the *Mirror* newsroom: 'Does anyone know where I can get some special white Durex for Christmas? I need to get my presents for home in the post quite soon.'

'You mean Australians give their family white Durex for Christmas?' said an English reporter.

'Yes,' I said, 'It's the Durex with Christmas bells on.' There was silence in the newsroom. 'Two little bells tied with ribbon. Mistletoe in between. And green, glossy, spiny-edged holly, and small red berries. On one side, that is; there's nothing on the sticky side.'

At that point Mac stepped in and saved me. But he couldn't always help. When a 76-year-old pensioner lost his precious blue-and-yellow South American parrot called 'Romeo', Mac gently advised me not to begin my story: 'Romeo, Romeo, wherefore art thou Romeo?' as planned. 'They like their news straight here. Just write that Romeo, an expensive South American parrot, has escaped from his distraught, aged owner,' said Mac. He was right: they ran it on the front page. Next day an observant reader rang to say he had spotted Romeo in a shrub in central London. A photographer and I jumped in a car and raced around to Russell Square, a fenced park full of huge trees that was enclosed by narrow London terrace houses. By the time we arrived, Romeo was already perched on his aged owner's hand, tethered by a small leather strap on his leg—reunited at last. I had a great idea for a dramatic photo. Forgetting that a bird in the hand...I asked the 76-year-old to shin up a tall, branchless tree, while holding Romeo triumphantly above his head.

Back at the office, I confessed to Mac there was no advance on the story because the pensioner had fallen out of the tree, landed on his back, and Romeo was, unfortunately, again at large somewhere in the city of London. A score of Poms at the scene had abused me.

'What's the story now, Mac?' I asked.

'You are,' he replied.

One of my ambitions was to get a job as a foreign correspondent with Reuters news agency. But Mac advised against it. 'I hear it's a sweatshop round there,' he said, rolling his untidy shoulders. But, as usual, I ignored good advice and one day slipped out of the office, walked the few blocks to 85 Fleet Street and applied for a job. At that time, Reuters almost exclusively hired young men with First Class Honours degrees from Oxford or Cambridge who could speak at least two foreign languages fluently. The Cambridge staff complained that they didn't get a fair go up against the Oxford graduates. Or maybe it was the other way around. Because I spoke no second language, and had left Australia before completing my degree at night at the University of Queensland, my chances weren't good. However, the

Personnel Manager, Charles Farmer, seemed impressed by one thing: the fact that I had managed to worm my way into 'Red China'. Back in 1965, half the world (including Australia) didn't recognise Mao's Communist regime, but I'd got in because of my pink cheeks and my name, which meant Dragon. A few days later, Mr Farmer rang to say I had been selected to sit for the Reuters test. To my surprise he said I would be paid to do it.

On arrival I was handed what I quickly surmised to be the twenty most badly written stories sent in from around the world in the past decade. I was told to rewrite them or leave them untouched, as I saw fit. One, from the Soviet news agency Tass, contained statements by Soviet scientists about photos of the Moon a Sputnik had taken, all translated into English—with some words and phrases in Latin. Another was a New China News Agency story that stretched about ten metres on the continuous telex paper. Right at the end it attacked the Soviet Union, saying they were 'bedfellows' with the Americans, which, of course, was the lead to the story. There was another on a plane crash in thick fog in Germany. A murder in the Caribbean. A coup in Africa...

Next, I was told to write a thousand-word profile on Brigitte Bardot. An hour later I handed my Bardot piece to Reuters' home editor, Jack Henry, an older man who always wore a grey vest. He was in charge of the infamous Reuters test.

'That didn't take long,' Jack Henry said suspiciously from over black horn-rimmed glasses as the tea lady arrived. You couldn't miss the Reuters tea lady. She yelled 'Trolley' at the top of her voice whenever she appeared on the floor and eighty journalists, all carrying filthy mugs, converged on her like a flurry of striking typewriter hammers when all the keys were pressed at once. Some of the English journalists then stirred their tea with rolled up pieces of copy paper (the poor quality paper they typed stories on).

'I've always been a Bardot fan, Jack,' I replied. 'Ever since I saw *And God Created Woman* when I was 18.'

Jack Henry dropped my feature in his ample rubbish bin and told me not to call him Jack. 'Well, Lunn, have you ever heard of Dr Martin Niemöller?'

'No, Jack...sorry mate...no, Henry. Can't say I have.'

'Give me one thousand words on him then.'

Next morning Reuters gave me a job and I said goodbye to the *Mirror* blokes with drinks in their pub, known as 'the Stab' because it was where you got stabbed in the back.

Five days a week I sat inside Reuters' heritage-listed building on the fourth floor at 85 Fleet Street and rewrote any poorly written stories from around the world before they were sent back out to the rest of the world. I strode around London in a camel-coloured fringed suede jacket that I'd picked up expensively in the King's Road, with my long fair hair tied back in a ponytail. I felt almost like a local until Sydney journo Adrian McGregor turned up from Australia. Despite his long shaggy hair, he exclaimed that I looked like Wild Bill Hickok.

After eighteen months in London, at the end of 1966, I was sent out to Singapore as the Reuters correspondent there. Then, in February 1967, aged 25, I was sent to cover the Vietnam War for a year. It was back to Singapore for the rest of 1968, then I became Reuters correspondent in Indonesia for a year, then back to London in 1970.

In Indonesia, for six weeks in mid-1969 I witnessed the Indonesian takeover of the Stone Age people of West Irian (aka Irian Barat or West Papua) in what was called an Act of Free Choice held under UN auspices. Papuans, frightened of the Indonesian military, made furtive contact late at night; they hid blood-soaked letters inside seashells; they left messages in my motel wardrobe; they shoved letters under my arm in the dark and disappeared. As only two reporters— the foreign editor of Holland's *De Telegraaf*, Otto Kuyk, and myself—were covering the entire Act of Free Choice we were the only chance for these Papuans to get their message out to the world. No wonder one letter shoved under my arm was addressed to 'the nicest man in Merauke'. One midnight in the dark I told a Papuan that no one was going to come to their aid, that—despite their hopes that the UN would help them—they were going to become part of Indonesia. He cried on my shoulder. The UN coldly and deliberately handed these 800 000 Papuans to the Indonesians, with the active connivance of the United States and Australia: thus Irian Barat became Irian Jaya (successful Irian).

There were no elections for this Free Choice. The decision was made in each of the eight provincial capitals by small groups of specially selected Papuans who, even so, had to raise their hands while being closely watched, not just by a couple of UN representatives but by Indonesian soldiers in the guise of civilians. And with armoured personnel carriers nearby. At one time three Papuans who carried a sign saying 'One One Vote' were marched away at gunpoint despite my protestations and in full view of the four UN team members. Regardless of my appeals, the UN four neither did nor said anything. Papuans who yelled out *'sendiri'*, for independence, outside one Act of Free Choice meeting in Manokwari were grabbed. Indonesians then tossed them into the back of military trucks and took them away. When I protested, an Indonesian policeman pulled out a revolver and waved it in the air. I ran inside the building and told the UN chief, Dr Ortiz Sans of Bolivia. He replied: 'Our job is to observe what happens inside, not outside.' Meanwhile, the Australian government wasn't saying nothing. Or anything. Which was something.

All I could do was write what I saw and send it out to the world. The stories went out by morse code: there were no phones, but plenty of mobile stone axes. And, when I realised Otto's and my stories wouldn't have any effect, I did one more thing; I taught a dozen Papuans to sing *We Shall Overcome* when we were accidentally left alone in a lifeboat in Tjenderawasih Bay for an hour. They were going to need the pride and the hope of that song, perhaps more than anyone else on earth: *Ohhhh deep in my heart, I do believe, that we shall over-come some day...*

In 1971, after seven years overseas, and now aged 30, I returned—like Ulysses, made weak by time and fate—home to Brisbane where, I noted, cows grazed next to the airstrip at Eagle Farm aerodrome. The more despair I'd seen, the more I'd missed home. I knew that if I didn't return now I never would. I was becoming a Londoner: and what was the use of living and dying far from home? With me came the girl I had met in Indonesia, a Norwegian window dresser whom I referred to as 'Miss Norway' because she was, to me, a beauty queen. And she called me 'James Blond' because of my hair and my job. She reckoned there were handicapped people on every corner in Brisbane, 'and they all sell the [afternoon] Brisbane *Telegraph*.' Her family's house in Norway was, of course, centrally heated, so Miss Norway suffered that winter in our Queensland houses with their doors set the usual two centimetres above the doorsills. To survive, she bought some thin foam rubber material and made herself a dressing-gown which reached out and down stiffly to the bare timber floor. She walked regally around in it, looking like a young 18th-century Nordic queen.

I had no idea then that I was getting closer and closer to a meeting with Rupert.

With my international experience, it would surely be no trouble for James Blond to get a job back on Brisbane's *Courier-Mail* where I had completed my four-year cadetship. The Editor now was none other than John Atherton, who had been at my 21st birthday party nearly a decade before, when he was the ace reporter just returned from representing the *Melbourne Herald* in New York. I was so confident that I didn't even bother taking documentation to the interview.

The redheaded Atherton said his quota of journalists was filled. There was no room for me back on my old paper.

'But I covered the Vietnam War for Reuters—and exposed the Act of Free Choice in West Irian. My articles were quoted in the UN,' I protested.

Atherton was unimpressed. He said the *Courier-Mail* needed people who knew what was happening in Queensland, not overseas. 'Our group has Denis Warner in Melbourne to write on Vietnam, and a man in New Guinea,' Atherton said. Yet, with half of New Guinea being taken over by Indonesia, neither the olde worlde Melbourne

Herald group, nor Fairfax, nor the ABC, nor any photographer, nor any Australian TV station had bothered to cover the six-week Act of Free Choice of 1969. A few arrived for the opening day: which was worse than not covering it at all. Only Murdoch's *Australian* had bothered to send someone for a couple of weeks: its foreign editor, Peter Hastings. And as for Warner, everyone knew exactly what he thought about the Vietnam War—and his experience of the war was totally different from mine.

Atherton suggested the *Courier*'s sister paper, the *Sunday Mail*. This time I went fully prepared. I took along a letter from Reuters congratulating me on my coverage of the Tet Offensive. Plus a letter from AAP in Sydney thanking Reuters for my coverage of the Act of Free Choice. Plus a letter from Reuters pointing out that I had been a copytaster on their world desk in London. The *Sunday Mail* Editor said, 'We do have a couple of vacancies, Hugh, but, unfortunately for you, some bright young men from Sydney have applied.'

American reporters in Vietnam returned home as stars and were paid handsomely to go on their university lecture circuits, yet I had been knocked back by my own newspaper. So I started thinking about Rupert and his gallant little intellectual national paper, even though it was based in Sydney and faced an uncertain future because of an obvious lack of advertising from big business.

Back then, rates of pay for Australian journalists were based on four grades: A, B, C and D. Because of my seven years overseas experience, I was looking for a job as an A grade. David Jack, the *Australian*'s bureau chief in Brisbane, worked from a small cluster of offices a few floors up in Penneys Building, an old rabbit warren above a supermarket in Brisbane's Queen Street. David Jack said they had one vacancy: for a D grade. Too bad.

The blonde Miss Norway wasn't having much luck either. She was from stylish Scandinavia, where even refrigerators and stoves came in bright reds and greens and blues, but when she inquired at the employment department about window dressing the man behind the counter said: 'Migrant? Migrants work in factories. Get a job in a factory.'

Though I had never worked in radio or TV, my next stop was the ABC at Toowong. They gave me casual work as their political roundsman because the previous man, Allen Callaghan, wasn't allowed to cover politics while he served out three-months notice before becoming Media Officer for the Queensland Premier, Johannes Bjelke-Petersen. Stories at the ABC went to both radio and TV. I found it hard to believe that—while they had a beautiful canteen with lines of clean white cups and saucers and silver teaspoons plus a dozen beautiful women to type the bulletins—there was no library. The only information filed was the previous day's stories. I was doing all right until the Prime Minister of Fiji flew into Brisbane and the news editor wanted someone to interview him for TV. He looked around the reporters' room but they were all cadets: Trish Lake, Andrew Olle and Tony Maniaty. Except for 30-year-old me in my cream Singapore tailor-made suit.

'You've worked overseas, Hugh.'

'Yeah, but nowhere near Fiji,' I said. 'And I've never interviewed anyone for TV, either.'

At Eagle Farm aerodrome several camera crews awaited the Prime Minister's arrival. (For some reason, editors think it's news if someone arrives at an airport and, conversely, not news if they stay at home and think. Perhaps it harks back to the days when only important people could afford to fly.) But when he appeared, no one wanted to go first and, since 30 is very old for a reporter in Australia (though young in the US or England), I volunteered while the others all stood and watched in very fear. The only thing I knew about Fiji was that there was some problem with the Indians.

'Now, Mr Prime Minister,' I said as the film camera rolled and I leaned forward with the microphone, just as I had seen the NBC and CBS reporters do in Vietnam, 'how is the problem with the Indians?' The Prime Minister turned his grey head and looked disdainfully at me with my ten centimetre wide, royal blue Thai silk tie and long auburn sideburns that were becoming curly.

'What problem is that?' he asked.

'Well...it's the, er, it's the problem you have...with the, er, Indians.'

'Which Indians?' the Prime Minister said.

Back at the ABC everyone was invited into the theatrette to watch a reporter squirm his way through his first TV interview, and then they offered me a B grade. Reluctantly, Miss Norway and I decided we would have a better chance in Sydney. After all, wasn't that where all the bright young men came from?

In Sydney, the response from the *Australian* was much different from the one I'd had in Brisbane. An urgent telegram arrived at the hotel from the news editor of the brand new *Sunday Australian*, Chris Forsyth. This paper was Rupert's latest baby. Just as everyone was predicting his daily *Australian* would fold, Rupert had expanded. 'Know who you are,' said the telegram. 'Can start immediately as A grade?'

I was about to become a Sydneysider.

Rupert's offices always seemed to be in the oldest, most depressed part of a city, and Sydney was no exception. When I saw Chris Forsyth at News Ltd in Surry Hills I told him I already had a flat lined up for rent in Macleay Street, Potts Point.

He looked surprised. 'Not here, mate. We don't want you bloody here! We've got wall-to-wall famous journos here. Evan bloody Whitton, Adrian bloody McGregor, Phil bloody Cornford, Tony bloody Stephens... You're what we're looking for in bloody Queensland. You've been a foreign correspondent in lots of strange places, haven't you? We ran your stories from Vietnam and from West Irian. Well we need a foreign bloody correspondent in Queensland! Someone who can tell our readers what the hell is going on up there. You know: why their elected Premier is a peanut farmer born in New Zealand with a Danish name who only gets nineteen per cent of the bloody vote. Simple bloody things like that.'

We shook hands, and that was it. No test. No letter of appointment. No terms. No conditions. No form to fill in. No pension scheme. No two-hour medical examination like at Reuters. I could see that here they just wanted to get the paper out. And I liked that.

I was surprised to hear the *Australian* had published my West Papua stories because Rupert's infant paper was the only metropolitan daily in Australia that could not buy the Reuters service. His paper was too new to get into the Reuter news-sharing arrangement that the other papers had set up decades before. Thus the *Australian* for many years had to rely on the American wire service UPI, which showed little interest in such places as West Papua. But, I found out later, when they needed to the *Australian* got Rupert's *News* in Adelaide, which was in on the Reuters deal, to telex copies of my Reuters stories to Sydney. I didn't mind the breach of copyright. At least they were interested in what had happened to the Papuans; interested enough to pinch my stories: though I later discovered they'd once re-christened me 'Hug' Lunn on a front page.

It was May 1971, and, back in Brisbane from Sydney, I found myself once again in Penneys Building. David Jack cleaned out a tiny room at the back for me. It had a sliding door to save space, and the two sports writers sat outside this door: one on each side like guards. The other dozen reporters were working for the *Australian,* but I was separate: the sole Queensland representative of the *Sunday Australian*, writing stories that I hoped would not be written by anyone else before Sunday. I was a little taken aback on the first day when I went to see the woman who ran the office, Hazel O'Rourke, and asked for a free copy of the *Australian* to be delivered to my house each morning: standard practice around the world so that reporters read the paper before coming to work. Hazel said that she would wait for a few weeks before arranging my free paper: 'You reporters. I organise it, and the next thing you're gone. My son Dennis, he's a filmmaker, he says to always wait a few weeks before you deal with a reporter.'

As luck would have it, on the day I started in Penneys Building,

Miss Norway, who hadn't been able to get any work until someone told her she'd never get a job in Brisbane until she wore stockings to the interview, landed a job right next door in the middle of town writing stylish window price tickets for Brisbane's most up-market jewellery store, Prouds.

A few months later, a couple of men with dark suits and very short haircuts swept into the building and straight through to David Jack's office. They asked David, as bureau chief, for three reporters on the roster 'to go' because of the recession (unemployment had leapt from two per cent to an amazingly high three per cent). David told me later that when he hesitated he was asked whether he wanted to be one of the three. David pointed to three names, then changed his mind about one because he'd remembered that this reporter had just built a house for his wife and kids. He pointed to another name instead. 'The four then,' said one of the grim reapers. These men also told him to remove the 'Butter eaters make better lovers' slogans that someone had stuck on the opaque glass doors to the offices. Rupert, they said, didn't like stickers and posters plastered over office walls. It didn't happen in Adelaide.

I was shocked. I'd never in my ten years of journalism seen reporters sacked. Some of those gone were the best reporters in Brisbane: people who had deliberately chosen to work for an aggressive, radical paper in a conservative land; like the tough, hard-working political roundsman Ian Miller. I was impressed with Miller. Reuters would have loved him. He was always writing something down left-handed and upside down, on a piece of paper held up against a wall, any wall. From noon on his copy flowed to meet the *Australian*'s incredibly early deadlines. When the *Courier-Mail* reported an anti-government march through the city as a series of 'nasty incidents', in the *Oz* Miller described exactly what he saw: the police bashing marchers; how, when, who and where. Even so, two journalists union officials came around especially to say that there was absolutely nothing they could do. As it turned out, three of the four sacked reporters ended up working, very successfully, for Rupert again years later as his empire expanded to envelop them.

A few months after this incident, a rumour went around that Rupert was coming to town from overseas. It seemed to put everyone into a panic, something else I'd never experienced. Everyone was agog. But I knew the rumour was true when all the butter stickers, and all the lovers, disappeared from the office overnight.

Luckily for us, Rupert's Brisbane newspaper, the *Sunday Sun*—his Queensland headquarters—was a long way away. It was in a white building a few kilometres down the road in the very depressed area of Fortitude Valley, known locally simply as 'the Valley'. It was an area strongly associated with Brisbane's two fingered up yours salute, known here as 'two to the Valley'. So, when Rupert hadn't appeared in our office by 5.00 p.m. we were all confident he'd never find us in this hidey-hole. 'He couldn't find us with a map,' someone joked, nervously. Besides, Rupert had a huge empire to worry about, without bothering about us in our tiny, distant bureau. Rupert's London *Sun* was now one of the three biggest selling daily papers in the UK. He also owned the biggest selling UK Sunday paper, the *News of the World* (better known to Brits as the *Screws of the World* because of its enthusiasm for sex stories and scandals). It sold six million copies a time. I'd found out for myself how popular it was during a transport strike in 1970 when I walked out of the Reuters doorway with a copy under my arm to read over lunch in Fleet Street, and someone offered me ten shillings for it: more than ten times its cover price. I took the money, and for the first time realised Rupert's profit potential.

By 5.30 p.m. it was pretty dark in the Brisbane office and, with no sign of Rupert, everyone adjourned to the nearby Majestic Hotel for a drink. David Jack came around to my little room to let me know. I told him I had to finish writing the seven days of TV comment for the *Sunday Oz*. He told me to do it later. I said I'd catch up with him there. I was desperate to establish myself in my new job and to show I could get a lot done. So David elected to wait for me to finish, saying he might as well get stuck into some work back in his office.

Sometime after six, the world was very dark and I was aware that David Jack was back standing over my desk in the small rear office. I was determined to meet my self-imposed deadline and so typed on furiously without looking up: to let him know that I definitely wasn't going to the pub until I'd finished. Anyway, I didn't like standing in pubs, and I hated the taste of beer, so I hadn't been keen on going in the first place. David said my name a couple of times, but that only made me more determined to keep going. I pounded the keys on the ancient Imperial typewriter even harder. 'I just have to get this done,' I said, without looking up.

'That's what I like to see,' said another voice; a soft, radio announcer type voice. I looked up curiously and standing next to David was a man in shirt and tie: an immaculate blue-and-white, thick-striped body shirt and a wide navy-blue tie. His arms were folded. He was carrying no baggage: no briefcase, no clipboard, no notebook, no newspaper, not even a pen that I could see. He was travelling very light. He had a very satisfied, loving look on his round, pale face and a real twinkle in his brown eyes, as if he were looking at a favourite nephew. His dark hair had started to thin. He looked more relaxed, more buoyant, more happy and more trim than I had expected. But it was him. It was the famous Rupert. How had he found us in this warren hidden above a supermarket and a cafeteria in an old building the inside of which was so complex that the bald lift driver had been killed the previous week when he accidentally stepped into the lift well? Nowadays I still wonder why Rupert had bothered visiting we unhappy few. And why was he travelling alone and unassisted?

Rupert, who looked much younger than his 40 years, held his hand out as David Jack absolutely gleamed at our good fortune. What filled my thoughts at that moment, as Rupert and I shook hands, was that David had named his black dog Rupert. In a country where journalists called the Prime Minister 'Billy', and the Premier 'Joh', why were we so uncertain before this brilliant businessman?

Rupert's handshake wasn't as hard as I had expected. I was, I suppose, ready to have my hand crushed. Instead, the skin of his hand was soft, even softer than mine. He was altogether a much gentler man than I had imagined. He spoke softly; looked, stared even, into my eyes and wasn't stiff at all. In fact he was charming. 'I'm very pleased to see you both still so hard at work,' Rupert said. 'There's nothing worse for me than walking into a newspaper office and finding nobody on the job.'

David Jack looked as though he was going to kiss me then and there.

The three of us chatted while standing in my tiny room: a little about politics but mainly about Rupert's high hopes for his newspaper. All I could remember in a jumbled mind afterwards was that Rupert said: 'The main thing to remember with a newspaper is never be without the story.'

Then Rupert said he was going to walk back down to the Valley, and he was gone as quickly as he had appeared.

2 All window-dressing

The biggest surprise on my return to Australia in 1971 was the way university students dressed. When I'd left Australia in 1964 most blokes went to uni lectures in long trousers, white shirts and ties. Just seven years later they dressed like hippies.

It was said this was because of rebellion associated with anti–Vietnam War protests: perhaps a spin-off from the belief that US soldiers in Vietnam dressed other than in uniform. Well, when I was there, no US soldiers wore bandannas around their heads. Unlike in Hollywood films. None that I saw were on drugs either: they were high on just staying alive. All wore steel helmets, or else got abused by a fat sergeant. They drank Coke rather than sniffed it. They did write pithy phrases on the camouflage cloth of their helmets, which was probably the precursor of the message T-shirt.

It was strange coming home after four years in Asia because there were now large gaps in my knowledge. People were surprised that I'd never heard of *Sergeant Pepper's Lonely Hearts Club Band*. And I was surprised too. Everyone in Australia, it turned out, was an expert on the Vietnam War: even though they didn't know that a C-130 was a Hercules; an M16 wasn't an AK47; or that the plane wasn't an

F-one-one-one, it was an F-one-eleven. Most Australians—except, perhaps, for readers of Rupert's *Australian*—knew for certain that the Americans were winning the Vietnam War: they could not imagine otherwise. It meant nothing to them when I said I had been there in the jungle eating American ice-cream and drinking their chocolate milk and watching them lose. At a party, a doctor from Chermside Chest Hospital insisted that the Americans were fighting the Chinese Army in Vietnam. I assured her that if even one People's Republic of China soldier were found in Vietnam the Americans would hold the biggest press conference ever seen.

Soon after I joined the *Australian*, there was a huge anti–Vietnam War march down Queen Street, Brisbane, following a rally at the Roma Street Forum. Since I couldn't write my opinion in the paper—I wasn't well known enough to be a weekly columnist—I offered to speak at the rally. Not that I was a public speaker. But once, while on R & R leave at Songkhala, Thailand, I'd given a talk to three hundred US Peace Corp workers. The Peace Corp three hundred wanted to know all about the war they had escaped by volunteering for peace. I drew a map of Vietnam on a blackboard to mark in places they might not know: Khe Sanh, Nui Dat, Con Thien, Dong Ha, Pleiku, the Elephant's Ear. It was only when these Americans living and working in Thailand asked me to mark Saigon on the map that I realised how little was known.

But the protest march organisers in Brisbane weren't interested.

It's still the most amazing thing I have seen in my home town: standing on the footpath outside Penneys Building in 1971, looking up Queen Street to see ten thousand tightly jammed locals sweep around the corner from Albert Street like an unstoppable tidal wave of thought. The march was small by Melbourne's standard, but for someone used to only trams rolling down Queen Street this mass of Brisbane civilians defying the law was as unexpected as anything I had seen in the war itself.

I had suggested to organisers that, for maximum impact, the protesters dress up in suits and ties so office workers would relate to them. But most were in sandals or thongs, carried shoulder bags with long fringes hanging down, were bearded and wore kaftans or loose trousers. To the office workers in their bell-bottomed suit pants and beehive hair-dos, looking down from their walled cells at these free, shouting spirits, the marchers looked like—were—outlaws.

Water bombs rained on the demonstrators from a great height. Shoppers called them 'beatniks'. The demonstrators, having filled the block, sat down (illegally) on the road, whereupon a man ran in among them and danced around with a sign saying 'RED RATS'. It was fully five minutes before one of the protesters punched him right on the nose after being double-dared to do it. Blood dripped on Queen Street outside Christies in what was once a Safety Zone for tram travellers headed for the Valley.

The Vietnam War, in its dogged, persistent fashion, had followed me all the way home.

The marchers turned back up Adelaide Street. As they passed Prouds, Miss Norway happened to be sitting in a window arranging wristwatches. She watched as a Queensland policeman walked up to a long-haired, bearded young man standing on the corner by himself. The young man carried no sign; in fact, he wore a grey suit. The policeman kicked this young man in the shin as hard as he could, but instead of collapsing in pain, the young man laughed. Then, for the policeman's benefit, he pulled up his trouser cuff to reveal a wooden leg.

Just because you work for a newspaper doesn't mean you can have your say. Except for a select, specially chosen few, reporters are paid to write what they're told to write about. So I didn't even get to write about this demonstration. I was too busy in 1971 doing what I was told: writing for the *Sunday Australian* about riding an express delivery truck 2500 kilometres to Darwin; watching an illegal vasectomy operation (ouch); covering the Springbok Rugby state of emergency ('paint 'em black and send 'em back') and the infamous police charge outside the Tower Mill Motel; describing Brisbane's first freeway; and interviewing the Bee Gees on their return to where it had all started at Brisbane's Humpybong State School. Meanwhile, discussion of the Vietnam War was left to the all-knowing ignorant. Come to think of it, it still is.

At the Bee Gees' press conference at the old Lennons Hotel in Brisbane, every time I got them talking nostalgically about how in their childhood they used to sing in that very same room, 'The Rainbow Room'—'It all looked so glamorous back then, now it looks so small'—a radio type would butt in: 'Has your latest LP got a red rocket next to it?' Then, unfortunately, the Bee Gees would remember that a press conference is really just a commercial: that radio and TV are selling mediums. When Maurice Gibb started to talk about singing on the dirt track between races at the Redcliffe Speedway when he was 11 years old—'We got the pennies the public threw on the track. We picked up five quid one night'—a Sydney reporter asked if they'd cuddled a koala bear? He didn't seem to realise that the Bee Gees were back home in Brisbane. I almost got them talking about the meaning of their whimsical song *I Started a Joke*, but got interrupted again.

Oh, if I'd only seen that the joke was on me.

Still, it was great to be back under the blue-blue, clean, safe skies of Australia, instead of the chemical white air of everywhere else I'd been in the world; dropping in at my father's cake shop for a pie and peas (though I did occasionally crave a Singapore beef chilli rice wrapped in a banana leaf for 20 cents); getting a home-cooked tea after work from Mum, instead of combat rations; going to the cricket and sitting under the shade of the Moreton Bay figs at the Gabba with my mate Rod Lesina, even though he smoked; watching footy again. Footy, footy footy...how I'd missed it. Never heard a score for four years in Asia. Or I could zap down to the old Gold Coast with Dimitri (Jim) Egoroff for a surf.

Jim and I had sat next to each other for eight years at primary and secondary school after he arrived in Australia in 1950 as a Russian refugee from China, so we could always have a great time anywhere, doing anything. I loved listening to Jim's unique brand of English, which often broke into Russian, whereupon he would say: 'What the bloody hell am I talking Russian to you for, Lunn?'

One day, soon after returning from my seven years abroad, Jim turned up at my place during a thunderstorm: 'It's raining dingoes, Lunn,' he said. 'Isn't that what you say?'

People who have read my books ask if Jim is real. American writer Jack Olsen captured Jim—who now lives in San Francisco—in 1998 in his *Hastened to the Grave* (St Martin's Press, New York):

> Dimitri Nicolayevich 'Jim' Egoroff turned out to be a Russo-Australian with a Crocodile Dundee accent whose dark hair, black moustache, straight black eyebrows, and muscular arms put Fay in mind of a Cossack warrior; or of a Mexican huckstering velvet paint-ings in a Tijuana bazaar: she couldn't decide which...

When at first I had been unable to get a job in Brisbane in 1971, Jim and I had decided to start manufacturing freezers in opposition to Kelvinator. At this time, three decades ago, shopping hours were restricted and every suburban butcher displayed a sign advertising whole sides of lamb. Thus, everyone wanted to buy meat cheaper in bulk, freeze it, and avoid running short. To get in on this new tech-nological revolution we rented a large factory with a mezzanine floor: in retrospect, a factory big enough for Kelvinator itself. Once inside, Jim produced what he called his 'little beauties'—two beakers of chemicals; one black, one brown—saying: 'I'd be very nice to me if I were you.' His brown face glowing in the semi-dark, Jim poured a little of each into the bottom of a twenty-litre ice-cream can. The liquids mixed and settled on the bottom.

'The surge is coming, Lunn,' said Jim as the mixture started to make a faint hiss. There was gas; then foam; then brown froth; and suddenly millions of tiny brown bubbles rose quickly to the surface, stopping just short of the top, and quickly set hard. Jim tipped the can on its side and jumped up and down on it in his red thongs, making only a slight distortion. 'Lord and behold, Lunn! You couldn't believe me.'

This, Jim said, was the quickest and cheapest way to brace and insulate the walls of a freezer. 'While Kelvinator are stuffing glass wool, Lunn, we will of have them stuffed. I can't deprive my earthly joys.'

By the time our prototype was built and beautifully spray-painted eggshell white by Jim, I had started working for Rupert; and Jim had disappeared. Thus our freezer was left glowing, lonely, tiny, and gorgeous, in the middle of the cavernous dark shed like a nice thought in a criminal mind. Trying to track Jim down, I left a message on the noticeboard at one of his favourite haunts, the Primitif Coffee Lounge in the Piccadilly Arcade, asking him to contact me, and received an aerogram from the Canberra Rex Hotel, saying, 'If I don't see you through the week I will see you through the window.' When he returned, Jim apologised in a joke version of the Latin: 'Me a Cowboy; Me a Cowboy; Me a Mexican Cowboy.' Since I now had a job, we decided to call it quits: Jim would keep the freezer because it was his design.

To help pay my bills, for the first twelve months with Rupert I made extra money on Saturdays by covering the athletics in summer and the club Rugby Union in winter for the *Sunday Australian,* using the alias 'Len Nyster'. Miss Norway was also doing well, keeping the windows handsome at Prouds Jewellers on the corner of Adelaide and Edward streets for the thousands of people who walked past every hour. Prouds sold watches, crystal vases, grandfather clocks, engagement rings, brooches and expensive cutlery sets. Miss Norway also did extra jobs on her days off, including the windows in Katies dress shop in Queen Street. Fascinated Aussie men would gather in the street outside Katies to watch this blonde Norwegian in an orange miniskirt remove the clothes, and then the arms, from the dozen dummy models so she could re-dress them. As she did this, Miss Norway (who had picked up most of her Australian by watching *Aunty Jack* and reading Bazza McKenzie comic strips) would say out loud in her heavy accent for the benefit of the audience: 'I'll rip your bloody arms off!' And laugh! She called roos 'bush kangaroos' and I wondered why until I found out that *Skippy* had been a very popular show in Norway in the 1960s.

Miss Norway spoke perfect French, called a halo a glory, and often accused me of 'swimming beside the boat' when I made excuses. She would sometimes make endearing errors, like calling her toes her teeth: 'I will have to clean my toes.' She called wrinkles 'skrinkles', and when I got a cold she bought 'Wicks Waporub'. She knew to call people 'Aussie-cobber-digger-mate' but sometimes got her Bazza quotes wrong: 'Look at him,' she said of Rugby League tough-guy John Sattler to the crowd in the outer at Lang Park, 'he's built like a shit brickhouse!'

Knowing some of the local lingo could lead to frightening experiences: like when council workmen carrying picks and crowbars stepped out and stopped Miss Norway and a couple of Norwegian friends on a lonely dirt road in the bush. The biggest worker poked his unshaven head in the window. 'What's the score?' he demanded.

The three Norwegians froze in their seats.

'What's the score?' he said again, louder this time. A Norwegian faintly protested: 'We are not making bad trouble.'

'We are not coming the raw prawn,' said Miss Norway.

The Norwegians didn't know that the men merely wanted to know the score on the first day of the first cricket Test at the Gabba.

One day that first summer, Miss Norway was annoyed by all the big Aussie flies in the kitchen. 'Bloody big flies—go away,' she said, waving her arms furiously over the lunch she was preparing. A mate of mine was visiting and he said, 'Do you want to know how to get rid of flies from your kitchen?' Miss Norway swung around, eager to hear such fantastic information.

'Put a bucket of shit in the lounge.'

'If you're driving past, please do,' Miss Norway replied.

She was amused by our Christmas traditions in Brisbane—

particularly the custom of putting a bottle of beer on the rubbish bin for the garbageman.

My brother Jack was so well known as a *Courier-Mail* reporter that people kept introducing me, now that I was back in town after years abroad, as 'Jack Lunn's brother'. So much so, that whenever Miss Norway was asked at a function who she was, she would flick her straight blonde hair and reply drolly: 'I'm Jack Lunn's brother's girlfriend.'

Instead of being in the exclusive Queensland Club, or the Brisbane Club, or Tatts, I ended up a card-carrying member of the Norwegian Club. I went to their Saturday night dances at Stones Corner, their picnics, their meetings, and I even ended up in a multicultural Australia Day pageant at Lennons Hotel: since Miss Norway had been selected by the club to promenade in her full-length, colourful national costume. Miss Norway knew a hell of a lot about fashion, but when we were in Jakarta in 1969 I'd warned her that it was no use bringing her mini-skirts to Australia. I said she'd be arrested if she wore such skimpy articles. But when we arrived in Brisbane all the girls were wearing even shorter skirts, which somehow miraculously covered their pants, and which had all the blokes going raving mad.

Being a Scandinavian in conventional Australia in 1971 meant everyone thought you believed in what was then called 'free love'. Few Australians could distinguish between ultra-conservative Norway and its sexually avant-garde neighbour, Sweden. It seemed natural to move back home with my parents, Fred and Olive, on return to Australia, and so, when Miss Norway arrived, Olive showed her into a separate bedroom, saying to me: 'There's to be none of that Scandinavian business under my roof.' No matter where we went, there was just no getting away from this cliché. One lunchtime in town, Miss Norway and I skipped across Edward Street to the Down Under Cafe for lunch, where she ordered pumpkin and ginger soup. The second time she put her spoon into the soup, out it came with a thick six-centimetre screw sitting lengthwise in it. We both laughed out loud in disbelief. I called for the manageress and held up the offending screw-laden spoon.

'You're lucky it wasn't a chisel with the state of the kitchen out there,' she said, looking down at us through Nana Mouskouri glasses. I knew I was back in Australia now.

In the tearoom at Prouds that afternoon the ladies gathered to discuss what important things they'd been up to lately, other than selling cuckoo clocks. Miss Norway always said little because she didn't engage in '*sladder and vaey*' (gossip and nonsense). All of the Prouds sales ladies wore stockings, long dark skirts and white blouses with large cuffs. And pearls. They were older ladies, beautifully presented— as befitting their job—and incredibly proper. At afternoon tea, one of these ladies asked Miss Norway how she was enjoying her day.

'Very good. I had a screw for lunch,' Miss Norway replied.

Ladies blushed. Ladies looked away. Miss Norway assumed they didn't realise the importance of what she had picked up in her spoon. 'It was a big one,' she said, holding her fingers several centimetres apart. The Prouds tearoom emptied. Those Scandinavians!

Jim Egoroff was disgusted that Miss Norway's comments had been so badly, as he put it, misconscrewed. 'I'll sue the pants off a kangaroo!' Jim exclaimed when he heard. 'What do they think this is, the rat race?'

Miss Norway had a knack of suddenly bringing things to a head: like when a boy at primary school in Norway announced he had kicked her ginger cat. Miss Norway surprised him, and everyone else at the school, by instantly leaping through the air from the ledge she was standing on and landing on him like a starving lion. One day, after several months in Australia, she suddenly stared into my eyes and announced: 'You will never move out of your parents' house.'

By this time I'd left the *Sunday Australian* and was now Queensland bureau chief of the *Oz* (David Jack having been promoted to Melbourne). I still moonlighted on the weekends as Len Nyster, and there hadn't been any time to go looking for a house. But a few days later I saw a photo of a lovely old timber Queensland house at 155

Central Avenue, Indooroopilly, which was coming up for auction: set up on two-metre-high wooden stumps, with wide verandahs and a large backyard. It looked cool—and you need a cool house in Brisbane because when summer strikes the cutlery can get hot to touch sitting in the kitchen drawer. Miss Norway wanted a pussycat and I wanted a dog: a boxer dog like Droopy, the one the Lunn family had owned when I was a boy. We drove past the house and Miss Norway immediately exclaimed how beautiful it was. When she had first arrived in Brisbane she thought all the houses were blocks of flats because they were so large compared with those in Europe. This house had front and side verandahs with dowelling railings below lattice panels and lattice front doors. It was on a flat quarter of an acre with some huge trees, and was just one and a half streets from the railway station. The area below the house was enclosed by black timber battens and was high enough for me to walk around. The house had VJ tongue-and-groove walls and four huge timber folding doors between the lounge and dining room. The lavatory, as with so many Queensland houses, post-dunnies, was outside the back door off the landing. Although it was less than ten kilometres from the city centre there was no sewerage, only a septic tank. The only worry, for me, was that the house was for sale by auction: I knew only too well how difficult that could be.

Earlier that year I had gone to a car auction at Albion to buy a second-hand Toyota Crown with four-on-the-floor. The auctioneer, Alex Overett, raced around auctioning cars until he came to my silver one, whereupon he announced that the price had to be paid by bank cheque on the fall of the hammer, the car did not backfire, and (this he added triumphantly) 'The battery is US.' Well, an American battery was fine by me. As I'd learnt in Vietnam, when it came to machinery the Americans were way out in front of everyone else. People, of course, were a different matter.

Moments later the car was mine. I climbed proudly inside, but it was as dead as a doornail. 'We told you the battery was US,' said one of the auctioneers. 'You know: up to shit.'

The ANZ Bank inspected the house but wouldn't lend me the money. It wasn't worth $15000, the bank manager said. But, I argued, the land alone, which had been zoned by the council for six apartments, was worth that much. 'Ah yes,' he said, 'the land is worth $15000. But the house-and-land is only worth $11000.' After I said I'd try another bank he rang back saying 'Twist a Holden dealer's arm,' which television ads were urging car buyers to do at that time.

I bought the house for $14700 in August 1971. As luck would have it, the auctioneer was Alex Overett again, and I enjoyed outbidding three builders who only wanted to demolish another original and distinctive Queensland house. Not that I stopped them: they just waited another decade until after I had moved on. Then they knocked it down and built *eight* apartments!

Miss Norway and I were extremely pleased with the purchase until the auctioneer began to auction the contents, whereupon a woman neighbour yelled out: 'You should give the furniture to this poor lad— he paid too much for the house.' We were given a kitten and named her Mini Mouse. Then we got a boxer pup and Miss Norway named him Bazza.

That first year in the new house we had almost no furniture and only a single iron bed. But we had a few parties at which our hi-fi rocked the house on its stumps as everyone danced to *Simple Simon Says*, *The Adventures of Barry McKenzie*, *Proud Mary*, and *The Ballad of John and Yoko*. But best of all, Miss Norway had a great Percy Sledge record and his soul sound echoed off the walls of our timber Brisbane home, turning it into a giant speaker-box, as Percy sang deep from within as we danced: *When a man loves a woman*; *Cover Me* and *Take Time to Know Her*. The hardest part was always the next morning, trying to convince a young, leather-jacketed local ABC reporter, Kerry O'Brien, that the sun was up and the party was over.

One morning, Miss Norway and I locked our house at Indooroopilly securely, with Bazza left on guard, and went off to the city to work. When we came home that evening, to our surprise, there was a brand new Astor refrigerator sitting in our kitchen all plugged in and working beautifully. How it got in there we hadn't a clue.

Let's just say it was something Jim knew we had both wished for.

3 A heart in the right place

One Saturday early in 1972, for the first time, Rupert's *Australian* sold more than 150 000 copies. 'Keep this up and soon we'll all be drinking champagne out of our navels,' said a telex message from the Editor, Owen Thomson, to all State bureau chiefs.

It wasn't the sort of irreverent message I'd expected to receive, but Owen Thomson—a sort of Larrikin Editor—was a man who spoke with a broad, almost deliberately down-market Australian accent, as if laughing at society from his position of strength as the Editor of a national newspaper. He always pronounced my name 'You', something that hadn't happened since I was at primary school.

Once the paper started making money, Owen said, it would have its own foreign correspondents, just like the *New York Times* and the *Times* of London. And Rupert had a cunning plan to increase sales even beyond 150 000.

Hearing from Owen Thomson personally was extremely rare, so I was surprised to hear his gravel voice on the phone in May 1972: 'You. You. Is that you, You?' Owen had lots of bright young men from Sydney to deal with the likes of me in the branch office a thousand kilometres away; deputy editors, assistant editors, associate editors, pictorial editors, news editors, features editors, magazine editors, weekend editors, supplement editors, finance editors... Too many for my liking. Newspapers have lots of bosses, but only one Editor: the man who runs the place. Since Owen Thomson was that man, I assumed something was seriously wrong. I couldn't tell from his tone because I hardly knew him. I'd been in his office in Sydney only the once. We were interrupted by the news editor, George Williams, who said a female reporter had just turned up asking for a job. Should he send her away or what?

'Has she got good legs?' drawled this Owen Thomson through widely spaced narrow teeth.

'Yes. In fact she has, Owen. Very good,' said George.

'Well what are you doing just standing there, George? Put her on,' said Owen.

I wondered if he had said it just for my benefit or because he really meant it.

This time, on the phone from Sydney, Owen Thomson was more businesslike. He told me to say nothing to no one, but to hire as many local reporters and sub-editors as I could get my hands on: and to get ready to bring out a daily twenty-page Queensland edition of the *Australian* to wrap around the national paper.

Rupert's printing presses in Brisbane were being used to full capacity only once a week for his successful *Sunday Sun,* formerly the *Sunday Truth.* (The name was changed because the old *Truth* had a scandalous reputation. Church-going Brisbane families would criticise others by saying: 'They wouldn't know it was Sunday unless the *Truth* came out!') To make more use of his *Sunday Sun* presses on the other six nights, Rupert had decided to print a tabloid edition of Queensland news to wrap neatly around the folded broadsheet edition of his national newspaper. The idea was to give Queensland readers an added reason to buy the paper. There was a better chance in Brisbane because Monday to Saturday there was only one local morning paper in a rapidly growing market, whereas in Sydney and Melbourne the *Australian* was up against two local morning papers. As it was,

Queensland news was occasionally stripped-in for the Queensland print run: something I objected to because it seemed to negate Rupert's whole idea of producing a national newspaper. 'Can you send me up a national newspaper to read?' I used to say to the Sydney office when this happened, which didn't exactly make me their pin-up boy. But a totally separate Queensland edition—with the intact full national newspaper inside—seemed ideal. Perfect, in fact. Two papers for the price of one.

Owen had earlier that day hired Harry Davis, the sports editor of the *Courier-Mail,* as editor of the wrap-around. To my surprise, Owen asked if I minded. I was in fact glad. I'd worked for the talented Harry when I was a cadet. Owen said I would be news editor and pictorial editor of the wrap-around as well as bureau chief for the national edition, which would still require the Queensland stories of national interest. So, suddenly, I had to be both foreign correspondent and xenophobic Queenslander. Owen then broke the headline news that he was coming up the next day.

Larrikin Editor was even more gap-toothed than I'd remembered. He was a bit too lean, 40-odd with receding blond wavy hair that stuck out—dare I say—a bit madly at the sides. We got the lift from our office down into Penneys and walked through the store out onto Queen Street where (before the Mall was built) the footpaths were so crowded with locals every lunchtime that you could scarcely make progress.

'G'day Len,' said a solicitor as he brushed past with one of those folded manila files tied with pink ribbon under his right arm. I ignored him, as I did every time I was called Len. I could see he was a Ballymore Rugby type from the leather patches on his sports jacket, the wool tie and his plaited, dark tan leather belt held together by two semicircular chrome loops. Churchie old boy, for sure.

'You. You. That bloke called you Len, You,' said Owen.

'Nah, I don't think so. Must have been mistaken.' We continued on through the daily Queen Street crush and eventually reached Bradley Garrett's Bistro downstairs in the Brisbane Arcade. Over lunch Owen fixed me with his pale blue eyes and started laughing, involuntarily showing his prominent teeth. 'You, four different people today have called you Len. Now, I'm your Editor, your big boss, You. Who are you, You? Are you You, or are you Len—or are you both of you, You? Do you know, You?'

I'd tried very hard to keep Len Nyster incognito by not talking to anyone at the sports events I covered. But interest in Rugby and athletics was so intense in Brisbane back in 1972 that people had started to ask at Lang Park (where the runners raced on a grass track) or at Ballymore: 'Which one's Len Nyster?' I could see Len being pointed out by officials, by runners, by referees, by fans, by footballers and by spectators. Such is the power of the press.

I explained to Rupert's Editor, and friend, that I needed the dough, so, yes, I was in fact the said Len Nyster. 'Unfortunately, Owen, as it turns out, everyone knows Len Nyster but no one knows me.'

'Well, Lenny Lunn,' Owen said, 'you'll never become known writing under another name.'

That night Miss Norway and I drove Owen to our Indooroopilly home in my Toyota Crown for dinner. Owen still gave orders, even as a passenger in the back seat, and it wasn't long before he and Miss Norway clashed, as I knew they would.

A fearsome Murdoch Editor and a fearless Viking.

'Oh-win, you are a backside driver,' Miss Norway said, causing Owen's fair hair to stick out even further at the sides. So much so that Miss Norway whispered that he looked, for all the world, like a Scandinavian troll: a cave-dwelling, frightening, supernatural being. I couldn't have agreed more.

When Owen walked in the front door he looked around and said: 'No wonder people want to live in Brisbane.' It wasn't just the natural beauty of the high-ceilinged Queensland house. Miss Norway had set about window-dressing the old house. Instead of one central naked lightbulb, Queensland-style, small lamps and candles were everywhere: a dozen lamps in the lounge room alone. She had painted the kitchen cupboards and shelves in unusual colours: dark blue, deep green, rich red. She had cut heart and flower shapes out of coloured sticky-backed vinyl and stuck them onto the now royal-blue fibro sink backboard. When we were still living at Fred and Olive's, she had painted the lounge room, making a feature wall with orange wallpaper. Miss Norway didn't think we were colourful enough in Brisbane: often accusing Jim Egoroff and myself of being 'blue and brown men'. But Jim still stuck up for her, saying, 'I'll tell you what, Lunn, she can really wrap a present.'

It has to be said Miss Norway was a beautiful blonde, and when she took off her black wool poncho to reveal her *hverdags dragt*—a suede top with long leather fringes hanging down over short yellow velvet shorts—Owen seemed distracted. It occurred to me that with those legs—made even longer by high, fire-engine-red wooden clogs—Miss Norway could get a job as a reporter on any newspaper in Sydney anytime she wanted (though the era of the ubiquitous model-turned-reporter in Australia was still two decades away).

She was a bit of a trick, Miss Norway. When I asked her during a trip to Norway to teach me to swear, she had me saying, every time I slipped on ice, 'Hadda whoda hadda spizer,' or something remotely resembling that. It gave me great satisfaction, until, alerted by strange looks, I found out I was saying 'five pieces of mullet'. Nothing much fazed her either. Once, when walking on a French beach with her girlfriend, they encountered a flasher. Miss Norway turned casually to her friend who was carrying a sewing basket and said: 'Pass the scissors'.

Miss Norway's decorative touch hadn't missed anywhere in the house. She had even stuck a red vinyl heart just above the waterline inside the toilet bowl. Owen Thomson looked bemused when he re-entered the house from the outside landing. 'Ya dunny's certainly got the feminine touch, Miss,' he said. 'I can see your heart's in the right place.'

'Your glory is slipping, Oh-win,' answered Miss Norway. 'That has nothing with it to do. Use your fantasy. The heart is for men, not women. It's for you to aim at so you might not splash your boots.'

Quickly tucking his black Florsheims well under our silky oak dining table, Owen warned that many important executives would be coming to Brisbane once the new wrap-around edition of the *Australian* was under way. 'There'll be executives from Sydney, editors from London, financial advisers from New York...perhaps even Rupert himself,' Owen said.

'We don't mind, Oh-win,' replied Miss Norway. 'So long as they don't bother us.'

For dessert, Miss Norway asked Owen if he would 'like some whipping'. Owen seemed very eager, and I'm sure I detected some disappointment when Miss Norway returned from the fridge and poured Pauls whipping cream over his steamed pears.

Miss Norway wasn't feeling herself that night because Mini Mouse, the cat, was very sick with fur balls in its stomach: something cats get from licking, and then swallowing, their fur. But this wasn't the sort of information you volunteered to the Editor of a national newspaper: at least not over roast leg of lamb and four veg.

Noticing her frown, Owen Thomson said: 'Cheer up, Miss. It might never happen.' It was only then that Miss Norway revealed her desperate problem.

'I tried to tell the ladies at Prouds what is wrong Oh-win,' Miss Norway said. 'But they could not be interested.'

Looking up at my Editor with her big baby blues, she said: 'It's a very, very sad thing, Oh-win. My cat has hairy balls.'

4 Pig of the week

A week after that dinner at home, Owen Thomson rang from Sydney with the news that Rupert had just purchased the Sydney *Daily Telegraph* and *Sunday Telegraph* and all their staff from Frank Packer.

Every time I started to climb up Rupert's ladder he extended the rungs much further. Now there were a few hundred more bright young Sydney men in front of me.

Owen said to cease hiring reporters and sub-editors for the new Brisbane wrap-around: 'Packer was over-staffed to buggery. Rupert's got a plague of reporters here now.' Owen had asked each of the Editors of Rupert's Sydney-based papers (now three Sunday papers and three dailies in the one city) to examine their rosters and choose three journalists each to send north to Brisbane, asking for 'people who will fit in to Queensland'. Hazel O'Rourke arranged their accommodation at the Park Royal Hotel in Alice Street opposite the Botanic Gardens (but with no daily newspapers supplied, as yet: 'I'll see what I think of this wrap-around first'). According to Owen, the *Daily Telegraph*, Sydney's only morning tabloid, had surprisingly always been anti-worker. He said Rupert thought that if it became more sympathetic to ordinary workers it would sell a lot more copies.

I had already hired a couple of local reporters, including Terry Ryan, one of the best reporters on Rupert's *Sunday Sun,* causing an *Australian* advertising manager to burst into my office screaming and shouting. He said I had to rescind the offer to Terry Ryan or lose my job. News Ltd papers were not allowed to poach staff from each other: it was a company rule. His tirade didn't worry me in the slightest. Back in 1972 I was 31 and flak-proof. And the one thing instilled in me as a journalist around the world was that advertising had no say in editorial. None whatsoever. Under any circumstances. Otherwise the newspaper lost all credibility: the one thing a paper needed to maintain reader confidence. And I stuck to this view, even though some advertising people said, 'Your stories are printed on the back of our ads.' So, for the first time in my career, I swore at a colleague and told him to get out of my office. Terry Ryan stayed: and my first sworn enemy in an office was born. It had taken just over a year at News Ltd.

What made my appointment of Terry Ryan even worse was that the journalists at the highly successful *Sunday Sun*—especially its Editor, Ron Richards—were upset that Rupert had decided that the *Australian* rather than their paper would be getting a new daily Queensland tabloid. A daily paper was what *they* had worked towards and wanted, and, because of the success of the *Sunday Sun*, seemed to deserve.

Two weeks later, the hand-picked eighteen journos arrived from Sydney looking like a reluctant orphanage tour group. There was former Queensland middleweight boxing champion Nigel Dique; Australian welterweight champion Tommy Burns's youngest son, Tony Murphy; and a former member of the Sydney Push—the wharfie, roof painter and member of the Castro militia that had defeated President Kennedy's CIA-backed Cuban exiles at the Bay of Pigs, Harry Reade. As I looked down the list, I was starting to get an idea of what Sydney people thought of Queensland. No wonder one Sydney editor told me: 'I'd love to live in Queensland, but I'm no good at street fighting.'

When Harry Reade arrived in the office to start work he wore a giant brown woollen sports coat that was, even so, way too small for his lumbering physique. He had something in his swollen, leather-backed right hand: a rope that led all the way down to a small fox terrier called 'Dog'. Harry tied Dog to his desk. I went to tell him he couldn't bring Dog into the office, but he stepped forward with all the confidence of Fidel Castro himself. Looking down on me, his eyes different colours, Harry enveloped my hand in his hairy paw, frowned, and then staggered backwards in pretend amazement—hands stretched out in the 'stop' position, fingers spread-eagled like a ham actor—and said, 'Shit. Shit…you're the youngest boss I've ever had.'

No wonder the CIA lost. Nigel Dique, who I knew from my Brisbane cadet days, pulled me aside. 'Don't say a thing about Dog,' he advised in his slow, quiet, relaxing voice while monitoring my eyes carefully and constantly with his hypnotic gaze, as only a middleweight champion could. 'Harry's got a huge parrot back in his room at the hotel. And the parrot answers back.'

Nigel was right. There was enough noise in the office as it was.

Luckily, Owen Thomson had also sent up Charlie Wright, a great reporter. Coincidentally, Charlie could fight like a man who had spent his childhood in State schools out west in the frontier mining town of Mt Isa and up in the tropical north of Townsville. Years later, Charlie offered to take on one of Australia's Test cricket fast bowlers when the bowler tried to put the frighteners on him for snooping around. But, seeing something in Charlie's eyes that Charlie could never quite disguise, the bowler wisely decided to stick to cricket. That was before Charlie briefly became a Rajneeshi and then wrote a book about them: *Oranges and Lemmings*.

Charlie Wright had been my stringer (a local correspondent who writes for money-per-line-published) in Townsville, from whence he managed to come up with national stories almost every day. He and the Mt Isa stringer, David Hooper, were as good, or better, than any journalist I had worked with at Reuters in London and I often wondered if anyone had noticed that more good stories came out of

41

Mt Isa and Townsville in 1971 than anywhere else in Australia. Once, after a man was taken by a five-metre crocodile, and a woman was rescued after days lost in Gulf mangroves, George Williams rang from Sydney and said: 'Are they making them up?' But all Charlie and David were doing was proving what I had slowly deduced: a story, any story, is only as good as the person writing it.

Charlie had decided to leave Townsville for Sydney after he went out onto his front landing during Cyclone Althea, Christmas Eve 1971, and something went past his head. It was the heavy cast-iron lid of his incinerator. Then he saw the house next door explode. Charlie carried wardrobes around his own house trying to plug holes. I took his copy over the phone and telexed it to Sydney, where it was splashed across the top of page one. Then Sydney told me to get up to Townsville and cover the devastation.

'But we've got Charlie Wright on the spot,' I said.

'Don't be silly. We can't have some bloody country bumpkin local reporter covering such a big story,' the Sydney news editor replied.

Getting to Townsville for the cyclone story wasn't easy. Photographer David May (better known as Comrade May) and I had ten dollars between us and all the banks were shut for Christmas. There were no ATMs back then, and no credit cards either (but neither did banks charge 'cash handling' fees or force their customers to queue out on the footpath). So I typed out a letter 'To Whom It May Concern' authorising David May and me to charge for all travel and expenses to Townsville, and signed it 'Owen Thomson, Editor, the *Australian*'. The letter worked everywhere we went: even to Magnetic Island to write how Sister Steptoe and daughter dragged a bleeding man out of the cyclonic winds into a brick toilet block—the only building left standing—and stitched up his wounds on the lavatory floor. Meanwhile Charlie Wright was seething at not being trusted to continue covering the cyclone for the *Oz*. But he got his revenge... Within six months of moving down to Sydney, Charlie himself was News Editor of the *Australian*.

A few days before publication of the first edition of the Queensland wrap-around, Wednesday, 5 July 1972, Owen Thomson announced that he would come to Brisbane for the first historic week. When I asked if this was really necessary, Owen's answer left no room for doubt: the wrap-around was Rupert's idea, and so it had to succeed. If it did, it would ensure the future of the *Oz*, the national paper Rupert himself had founded, and it would be a flea in the ear of the Brisbane *Courier-Mail,* the paper Rupert's family felt had been snitched from them when his father, Sir Keith, died in 1952 while Rupert was still a student at Oxford.

As Chief Executive of the Herald and Weekly Times, Sir Keith had expanded the company and made it rich and profitable. At a personal level, in 1933 he created the *Courier-Mail* by purchasing control of the *Courier* and then arranging for it to merge with the *Daily Mail*. This made Brisbane the centre of the Murdoch estate and in his will—according to one biography—Sir Keith said he desired that the *Courier-Mail* should provide his only son Rupert the opportunity to spend a useful, altruistic and full life in newspapers and broadcasting. Sir Keith's untimely death saw the Herald and Weekly Times end up owning the *Courier-Mail*, and the Murdoch family instead owning the weakest paper in the Herald group, the afternoon *News* in Adelaide.

Owen booked into the Park Royal Hotel for a week with the rest of the Sydney orphans. He had brought his secretary with him: beautiful, statuesque, known as 'Pussy'. So now we had all the ingredients for a successful newspaper; a Pussy, a parrot, a dog, a middleweight title, a veteran of the Bay of Pigs, and a drinking problem.

Harry Davis and I had been sharing my bureau chief's office, and now Owen moved in as well. The sub-editors took over my old back room and the two sports desks, their elbows touching. Some of the reporters had no place to sit and no typewriters. One corner was taken up by the telex machine operator, who sent stories noisily to Sydney, and the copy girl, who ran messages and did the tide times. We were so busy that I stood up all day as reporters, photographers and sub-editors queued to see me. Some wanted to know what a story bridge was? It was the name of the bridge, the Story Bridge. Others didn't know how to pronounce or spell Mt Coot-tha, Mt Gravatt, or Indooroopilly; or even where they were. In between, Owen briefed Harry Davis and me on what Rupert expected of the new wrap-around newspaper.

From what he said, Owen was a close friend of Rupert's.

There was to be a centre double-page spread of Brisbane pictures every day. Owen wanted 'pretty girls' sprinkled through the pages. Stories were not to be continued on another page, 'Rupert said'. If some famous person were arriving in town—like Ralph Nader, who was due on day one of publication—it was my job to learn all about them and tell the reporter what sort of questions should be asked. Political and economic stories were to be the province of the national edition. Local government; crime; lesser political stories; consumer; and light, bright Brisbane pieces with pictures were for the wrap-around.

Each morning Owen spoke to Rupert on the phone in my office for some time, telling him how preparations were going. Owen would actually name staff, rather than merely list the stories they were preparing. I was surprised that Rupert was interested in the names of the reporters covering the stories but that was before I got to know Rupert better and learned he had a phenomenal memory. I couldn't help but notice that Owen was totally relaxed with Rupert, as if he were talking to his best mate rather than his employer. So I believed Owen when he said he got around Sydney with Rupert, having a drink and some fun after work. Actually, it didn't surprise me that a rich, Oxford-educated, elite newspaper owner like Rupert had befriended a deliberate Sydney ocker larrikin like Owen: not when I got around with such an unlikely mate as Jim Egoroff. I imagined, as I listened to them on the phone, that Owen and Rupert might have a similar relationship to that of Jim and myself: the outlandish, off-the-wall, forthcoming, aggressive-to-all Caliban; and the mercurial, abstemious Prospero who is magical enough to tame and enjoy such qualities.

It's amazing what real mates will cop from each other without blinking: things that would be a deadly insult from someone else. I guess it's what a best mate is all about; and conversely, when a friend is silent about things important to you, then that is the greatest criticism. Jim certainly never clammed up when I'd done something to annoy him. He hated it whenever I couldn't remember some school-days incident that had become very important to him now that he was the wrong side of 30.

'What do you think it is Lunn—a bush Christmas?' he would say. 'I couldn't expect a wheezing, sneezing, slimy bathtub like yourself to remember. There, I feel better now I said that, mate. But I wish to hell you were a normal person. Let's go eat some short soup before I get annoyed again with you.'

After seven years away overseas it was great to be able to say absolutely whatever you liked to a childhood Australian friend. As I would say to Jim: 'You don't know anything about it, Jim. You wouldn't know, mate. You just haven't got a clue.'

I wondered if Rupert, like me, had found a friend with whom he could discuss things in that straightforward way. It would be a great shame if someone like Rupert surrounded himself with 'yes' men and no one he respected could ever tell him exactly what they thought. If absolutely everyone had to be nice to you at all times, you'd get completely the wrong idea of the world. We need earthy beings like Owen Thomson and Jim Egoroff to hand out reality like it's a vaccination; to stop you kidding yourself. 'Wipe that semi-glutinous compound from your nose, Lunn,' Jim had said, passing me a paper napkin, the first time he came to dinner to meet Miss Norway. Then he insisted I get rid of the napkin '...now that it is permeated, saturated, impregnated.' I told Jim that Miss Norway and I would have to leave in half an hour. Instead of being insulted he replied sincerely, 'That's all right; I'll be fed up with both of you by then.'

But despite all his bravado, Jim sometimes badly needed his mates around, as we all do. The day after that particular dinner Jim rang me at the office sounding sore and sorry, and I immediately suspended all work to go and see him when he said, 'Lunn, I'm out here on my Pat Maloney.'

Rupert and Owen, being newspaper executives, seemed to talk mostly about work: especially the *Courier-Mail* and what they perceived to be its faults. They would laugh together on the phone every time Owen said that we had them worried; particularly when he reported that the Herald and Weekly Times was so anxious about the new wrap-around that they had flown up no less than twenty of their top journos from Melbourne to ready the *Courier-Mail* for our onslaught.

On his second day in Brisbane, Owen told Rupert that Kerry O'Brien had reported on Brisbane ABC's *This Day Tonight* (this was, of course, back in the days when Queensland had its own nightly ABC current affairs program to help keep everyone honest) that the streets of Brisbane would be 'running with printer's ink'. They both enjoyed that one very much.

Rupert seemed very interested in Brisbane. Unusually so, because generally our city has always been considered a branch office back-water. Less than two months earlier, Rupert had been in Brisbane prior to the May 1972 Queensland election and, as bureau chief, I was invited to a function he put on at the Crest Hotel for *Sunday Sun* executives—management, editorial, circulation, accounts, production, distribution and advertising. The *Sunday Sun* was a very popular weekly tabloid covering action stories and scandal—and doing it particularly well—and thus uninterested in the day-to-day details of State politics.

It was embarrassing that day at the Crest Hotel when a dozen *Sunday Sun* executives, and me, stood in a semi-circle eating king prawns and oysters while Rupert asked questions about the upcoming election. Would Joh Bjelke-Petersen win again? Would Clem Jones help Labor to power? Could Sir Gordon Chalk take over from the unpopular Premier, since the Liberals got a much higher percentage of the votes? And if not, why not? Each time Rupert asked such a question everyone in the semi-circle looked down at his shoes.

I wasn't the political roundsman for the *Australian*, but I had occasionally written a thousand-word feature story on the election. So I started to answer all the questions: and Rupert soon started to direct them at me. Accompanying Rupert was another of those short-haired Sydney News Ltd executives, originally from Adelaide, in a too-tight suit. He nodded as Rupert told us that Australia had the one commodity the world would always need: food. I took it as a signal to grab another prawn and headed for the buffet table. Before I'd finished peeling, the short-haired, tight-suited executive came up to me: 'Rupert says he wants you to write a full run-down on each of the seventy-two Queensland seats. Rupert says he wants thumbnail sketches of all the candidates, their parties, their factions, the issues, who is likely to win, and by how much.'

'For the *Oz*?' I said.

'No. For him. Just for him.'

'Why?'

'Because Rupert says. Because he's interested, see.'

So Rupert needed to know even more about Queensland politics than he could read in his newspapers. He was even more interesting than I thought.

Owen Thomson said we had to produce a 'dummy-run' wrap-around newspaper on the day before launch day, to iron out any unforeseen difficulties. 'A full dress rehearsal,' he called it.

It was a real pain, as you can imagine, working for an edition of a newspaper that no one else would ever see: so it was hard for everyone to get motivated. Deadlines for the wrap-around were to be incredibly early for a morning paper. All stories, except those for the front page, were to be written by 4.30 p.m. The stories were then to be subbed (headlines written, stories cut to fit, mistakes fixed) and taken by copy boy in a taxi to the Valley to be set in type and made up into pages. I told Owen I thought it was ridiculous to produce a morning paper by 5.00 p.m., as we were bound to miss late stories.

'Look, You, Rupert has proven it's a fallacy that a newspaper has to be produced at midnight,' Owen said. 'Rupert says almost all of it can be done in office hours.'

In action for the dummy edition, I called in an A-grade reporter sent up from Sydney, explained the absolute deadline and allocated him three stories. He reassured me with a big smile, a handshake and a thumbs up. It was good to have such reliable, experienced staff. Late that night he phoned from a pub saying he had a 'great story; a wonderful, wonderful story'. I told him he was too late. 'Not for this story, matey,' he said. He was drunk. I asked what had happened to the three stories I had assigned. 'Forget them, matey. This is a great, great story, matey…'

A photographer came back with an unusual photo of a Scandinavian couple standing outside our lovely City Hall, the man with a beautiful baby in an unusual contraption strapped to his back. The baby was great, the City Hall was the perfect icon, and the contraption was brand new. But best of all, here was a man carrying a baby, something none of us had ever seen before. This was a real man-bites-dog picture. Owen loved it.

'You,' he said, 'well done. We couldn't have a better picture than that for page one of our dummy edition.'

Why was Owen congratulating me? I hadn't taken the picture.

Worried by Rupert's intrusion into their State, the board of Queensland Newspapers had invited Owen to dinner at Brisbane's Gateway Hotel that night. Owen was excited: 'They've heard what Rupert's done to the other papers in London. They want to pump me, You. They want me to spill my guts. But I'll go along anyway, You. I'll keep my trap shut and watch the bastards squirm.'

Owen was dressed that day in mustard-coloured, chunky corduroy trousers and a green-and-white paisley shirt with no tie. He was not a healthy specimen and said he had once had TB, so I was surprised when he lit his cigarettes down at the *Sunday Sun* by sucking deeply on them while touching the tobacco tip to the molten lead pots of the ancient linotype machines.

As the last early copy left by taxi for the Valley, Owen slowly nodded off in his chair on the other side of my desk. Perhaps he was bored by the dummy run? A cheeky young photographer came in and took a photo of Owen with a flash, which I didn't think was a very good idea, but Owen didn't awake. As the appointed time for the meeting with the Queensland Newspapers board came closer, Harry Davis poked Owen in the ribs a couple of times, but still nothing happened.

Then, right on time, Owen woke up, wiped the sleep from his eyes and headed for the exit on the other side of the full reporters' room where everyone was desperately getting ready for the morrow morn. At the doorway, Owen suddenly stopped, turned, and addressed his staff, who all knew he was off to dinner in mustard pants with the be-suited enemy, the traditional rulers of information in our town.

'Now they'll see what they're up against,' Owen said, Henry V like, and threw his head back laughing as he disappeared towards the lift.

Slowly the tale filtered back to our office.

Shortly after the mandatory prawn cocktail, Owen had fallen asleep again, after observing that Queensland Newspapers' version of keeping things at arm's length was 'keeping all business at arm's length from everyone else'. Deciding that Owen really had passed out—and wasn't just listening in—the board members rang an ambulance. Just as it arrived with siren screaming, Owen's secretary, Pussy, who had been alerted to Owen's condition, burst into the restaurant armed with a syringe. Without a word she injected him in the stomach, putting most of the board members (but not all, apparently) off their Steak Diane. Owen recovered so fast that he leapt up off the ambulance stretcher as he was being carried away and told the stunned ambulance officers to stop interfering with the freedom of the press.

According to the reports that filtered back to us, one suspicious Queensland Newspapers man muttered: 'Is this another Murdoch negotiating ploy?'

Owen couldn't have been too ill because he beat me into the office next morning to bring out the first real edition of the wrap-around. My job was to allocate stories and rounds: Liz Johnston, Brisbane's best news reporter, to interview Heather Ryan about her upcoming marriage to Australia's first Aboriginal senator, Neville Bonner; Nigel Dique to police rounds because his straight boxer's stare would worry bent coppers enough to make them talk; a New Zealander to City Hall because he might find its workings a surprise; Terry Ryan to government because it was the most important round; Harry Reade to new safety rules for boats, since he'd been there for the Bay of Pigs invasion; Charlie Wright, to add a bit of reality to the seventh Brisbane Film Festival. Courts, education, fashion...plus a column I had commissioned from journalist Sallyanne Atkinson, not because I had once been in love with her, but because she knew so many people in Brisbane and could write. (Fifteen years later the entire city voted her in as Lord Mayor.)

Harry Davis gave himself the job of writing a sports column called 'Listen Sport'. The real reason Harry had taken the risk that went with changing jobs (besides the fact that, according to him, Rupert had promised him a job for life) was that the *Courier-Mail* had dropped Harry's popular long-running Listen Sport column after Harry had dared suggest that horse-racing in Queensland wasn't exactly straight. This had offended lots of important people, and the *Courier-Mail*'s Editor, John Atherton, had insisted Harry appear before the racing stewards to apologise. Now an exuberant Harry—like myself, I suppose—was about to have his revenge on Atherton via the more radical Rupert. Harry began his first column for the first edition of the new wrap-around paper: 'As I was saying before I was so rudely interrupted, racing is a funny game...'

At 10.30 that first morning, as I was allocating stories to reporters, a surprisingly alert Owen Thomson turned and said: 'You. You. Pictorial editor! What's your front-page picture for tomorrow, You?'

Now I knew why I hadn't liked being congratulated for the baby picture that had been used for the dummy run the day before. I had no idea. How could I possibly know until all the photographers were back and their film processed?

'Too early to know, Owen,' I said tentatively.

'You,' said Owen bending his head forward. 'It's a fallacy to think you sit and wait for a front-page picture to come to you. You've got to know what picture you want and go out and get it. And I don't want any pictures of people on the phone…every bloody photographer's got a phone in the corner of their lens. Now, You, what's our front-page picture for tomorrow?' Not being able to see into the future, I looked to the past: to that morning's dummy run front page.

'Well, we've got that great picture of the couple outside City Hall with the bloke carrying the baby.'

'But we ran that this morning, You,' said Owen, frowning deeply.

'Yes, I know that. And you know that. And Harry Davis knows that. But no one else but us saw it,' I explained, shifting in my seat.

'That was yesterday's front-page picture, You. If you were gonna stay on the fucking farm, you should've stayed on the fucking farm. This is a newspaper, You. We need *today's* front-page picture.'

We stared at each other across my desk. I was weighing up whether or not to quit. At that moment, in walked one of the photographers— like all photographers, oblivious to everything except his photo. He was just back from the Gold Coast and dropped a large black-and-white picture on the desk. It was of an unshaven, long-haired ACTU boss, Bob Hawke, laughing and splashing around in the frothing Surfers Paradise beach break with a beautiful buxom woman in a tiny bikini.

'THE SEA HAWKE!' said Harry Davis in capital letters.

'Page one!' said Owen Thomson. 'Good work, You. You're learning very fast, You. We'll double your Christmas bonus.' (This was a favourite saying of Owen's, since News Ltd—unlike most companies back then—did not pay a Christmas bonus.)

Nigel Dique came back at three with an exclusive. A 23-year-old RAAF servicewoman had been missing for four days and police believed she had been abducted. Nigel even had her picture. This story became the page one lead for the wrap-around.

Next day I listened as Owen quietly told Rupert how the first edition fared. Owen gloated that we had scooped the *Courier-Mail* and all the TV stations, who must have been very embarrassed at missing a week-old abduction story. But when Owen got off the phone he didn't seem quite as buoyant as he'd been before the Rupert call.

'Rupert says, You, that it's the first time in his life, anywhere in the world, that he's seen two morning newspapers in the same city with two totally different sets of stories.'

'That's good,' I said, delighted.

'No. No it isn't good, You,' said Owen slowly. 'In this business— like in the motorcar manufacturing business—you never want to be too alone. It can make you seem peripheral. Like you're not competing, just being different. Rupert was very pleased we had exclusive stories, but he was annoyed that they had stories that we didn't have. Rupert says, You, that he'd told you once to never be without the story. Rupert loved the front page, though. Absolutely loved the Sea Hawke.'

I asked Owen how we could be absolutely sure that Rupert's criticism was valid.

'He's right because he owns the paper, and he's right because *he knows*,' Owen replied.

That night we all headed back to the Park Royal for a celebratory drink in Owen's suite. Pussy picked up the room phone and a few minutes later a waiter wheeled in a drinks trolley loaded top to bottom with every alcoholic drink you could think of. One of the reporters was so happy with our work that he rang Sydney from the party and told the acting Editor of the *Australian*: 'We want a better paper to wrap around.' Which wasn't very wise.

Over the next few days there were some problems with the staff working in such close proximity. One overseas reporter who had never heard of boxer Tommy Burns charged across the room at Tony Murphy...and ended up on his back. Someone brought Harry Reade to tears by leaving a message for him to ring a number urgently: it turned out to be dial-a-prayer. Why it affected him so badly I don't know. A businessman rang to say he was suing us for libel. I began to apologise, but Owen took the phone and shouted: 'We think it's in the public interest…if the public are interested. We'll see you in the Privy Council in London in five years and 25000 dollars time,' and hung up. We never heard from that caller again. 'You,' said Owen, 'if you have to ring up or write a letter to complain then you're a powerless punter.'

A few days later a reader rang to complain about a story just as my mate with all the great stories in the pub finally returned for the night. He answered the call. 'We'll sack that reporter,' he told the caller. 'I know he's a man with five little innocent children under six, but if he's going to make mistakes then out on the street he goes.' The reader begged him to forget about it.

By Sunday night an epidemic of July flu meant a cadet reporter had risen to chief sub-editor for the night. Seeing the opportunity, the fourth-year cadet announced to Harry Davis that if he didn't get his grading immediately he would resign. Harry told Owen we would have to grade him—anyway, he deserved it. 'He should have a big "S" on the front of his shirt,' Harry Davis said. It was Harry's ultimate praise to compare someone to Superman.

'Yes,' said Owen, 'cadet chief subs are hard to come by… But, bugger it. Let him go.'

Last time I saw the cadet he was serving in a drive-in bottle shop.

There was more bad news before Owen left town at the end of a very long week. I told Owen that the journalists union, of which you had to be a member to be on staff, had a list of complaints about lack of space, people not signing the time book, unpaid overtime… Owen interrupted. 'You, I've always found it's best to ignore the journalists union.' Owen said Rupert was annoyed by our front-page picture of a very old man with a walking stick: we weren't aiming for an audience of retirees. Owen also wanted to know why I didn't wear a watch when time was of the essence. 'I'm too busy catching up to keep looking at the time,' I said. Then he produced a huge drinks bill from the Park Royal. 'You,' Owen said. 'Look at this! Eight hundred dollars! There's too much drinking going on at the Park Royal. We can't afford this. You, you've got to put a stop to this.'

I was so glad Owen's week was finally up.

To fill an inside Monday morning page, because Sunday is a slow news day, we started Dog of the Week, featuring a photo of a cute homeless dog looking to be adopted. Unlike every other paper in Australia, we couldn't just fill up our pages with overseas stories. Australian papers increasingly do this these days, the reason being that overseas stories and features already exist and therefore cost much less than paying an Australian employee to write a local story from scratch.

With Owen gone and the Brisbane Ekka coming up, Comrade May came in with a great picture of a cute pig. 'Pig of the Week?' he said to Harry. So we ran with it, when we probably should have stuck to a dog. But somehow the pig seemed to suit the time.

A few weeks later, just when I realised I'd forgotten to get someone to take a Dog of the Week picture, Comrade May produced an absolutely delightful picture of a piglet. Son of Pig of the Week— why not?

Rupert had moved halfway around the globe to reside in England, where his London papers were now among the biggest and most financially successful in world history. Thus London had replaced Australia as the centre of Rupert's empire as surely as Sydney had replaced Adelaide in the '60s. Meanwhile, back in the land of the *Oz*, I should have seen the omen in 'Son of Pig of the Week', for I was soon to be demoted by a new Brisbane editor especially sent up from Sydney by Owen Thomson to straighten us out.

5 The last tango in Nanango

Several months later, in 1973, Owen demoted Harry Davis from editor of the wrap-around to sports editor, saying Harry had been too soft on his staff. In his defence, I told Owen that Harry worked long hours: six days a week from nine in the morning until eleven at night. The success of the wrap-around had become his life's ambition.

'You,' said Owen slowly, as if trying to explain something to a schoolboy, 'this isn't a fucking competition to see how many hours you can spend in the office.'

In what sounded distinctly like a threat, Owen said he was sending up a sub-editor from Sydney to replace Harry. 'He hasn't got your local knowledge, You, and he hasn't got Harry's editing background. But he's good, and he's tough.' I could have added, if I'd been game as Ned Kelly (which I wasn't), that the Sydney sub-editor was also getting the job for another reason—the reason most people get important jobs in Australia. He was getting the job because he lived in Sydney. Once again, I lamented, I would have to teach yet another Sydney journalist how to pronounce the names of ordinary places like Numinbah, Tiaro, Toowong, Coombabah and Goomeri.

Mr Tough Editor, it turned out, wasn't much older than my 32 years. The first thing he said on arrival in the office on the second floor of the *Sunday Sun* building in the Valley (where we had since moved) was that he always knew what was going on because he had once worked in intelligence in Africa, where he had learned, among other things, how to steam open envelopes. At his first daily news conference, when I said we had a good picture of a University of Queensland medical student standing next to a skeleton, Tough Editor took one look at the picture and said: 'What a strange idea you have of pictures.' I soon noticed that he never, ever, used my name—any name. To him I was anonymous.

The following Sunday, we had a sixteen-page wrap-around paper to produce and Tough Editor had rostered on seven sub-editors and just three reporters. At 4.00 p.m. he stood over my desk, generating so much heat that I felt he was about to steam *me* open.

'We're not going to fill this paper up,' he fumed.

'I know,' I said through the vapour. 'Not enough reporters and too many subs.'

'You're the news editor. What are you gonna do to get us out of this mess you've created?'

Without answering, I started writing a two-page feature on Queensland's Fraser Island, which was in the news because sand-mining leases had been granted for most of the unique, beautiful places on this, the biggest sand island in the world. In Australia, I had learnt since my return, a thing of beauty is a joy until we decide to do something with it.

I knew a lot about Fraser Island because in 1972 I'd had a week's holiday there with my school friend Rod, the cigarette smoker, who was now, a year later, dying of cancer in the Royal Brisbane Hospital. I was visiting him after work every day. Rod, poor Rod, had become addicted for death as a primary schoolboy. There'd already been a couple of years of cutting, irradiating and injecting with killer chemicals. Now Rod was nothing like the man he'd once been: the handsome young man with slicked-back dark hair and slightly bulging sky blue eyes. Rod, the part-time cattle property owner, was now the antithesis of the Marlboro Man: his body swollen with fluid to near twice its size; his face as round as a melon; weeping cold sores obscuring his upper lip; dark purple cysts all over his gums; a barely shuffling gait; a blob of blood protruding upwards from a bottom eyelid, which I couldn't bring myself to tell him about (Rod had long since stopped looking in mirrors).

Rod, aged 33, going, going, almost gone forever to cigarette heaven. Rod who had cried when we put him on a train to the bush to do his country service; Rod, the Hervey Bay High teacher whose students got so many 'A' passes in maths back in those days of public examinations when a country school could beat the Bell curve; Rod, who married a grazier's daughter just as my mother Olive had told him he would; Rod, dying too quickly since I'd met him, aged 13.

Rod, crying and dying. Yet still Australia allowed smoking in offices, and tobacco companies advertised cigarettes without limitation: in magazines, on TV, in our newspapers. Pretty girls handed them out at shopping centres and even the Blood Bank gave cigarettes to donors. They were glamorised by gorgeous ads, deodorised by an indifferent media, glorified for the suckers and sanctified by government taxes. How much for twenty thousand Australians a year? Every year. Every year. Every year…

Rod put tough editors into perspective back in 1973.

To illustrate the Fraser Island story I pulled out a picture of Miss Norway and Rod's wife, Helen, in their bikinis, standing on a headland overlooking part of the Fraser Island surf beach. This picture and article not only filled two empty news pages, but had the added benefit of giving one of the sub-editors something to do.

Next day, Tough Editor removed me as news editor of the wrap-around and sold my office Falcon. But I didn't mind. I knew I could go anywhere in the world and get a job. Miss Norway wanted to travel. I wasn't accustomed to working for people I didn't like. 'Have you got anywhere for me to sit?' I said.

Ambitious executives can sense when an employee doesn't need the job, or when they desperately do, and they react accordingly. I guess it's what takes them to the top. It's their job in a nutshell, really, to know how much you need the money or how much you need the position—with half the staff usually scared of being sacked and the other half desperate to be promoted. When reporters complained to me that they should be on a higher grading I would reply: 'Well, resign, and you'll find out what you're worth.'

After some hesitation, Tough Editor presented me with a desk right outside the door of his corner office. I didn't mind, because I was now sitting near my old mate from London days, the Abraham-Lincoln-bearded Adrian McGregor, who was working for us a few days a week as a casual while writing a novel. Adrian had taken six months leave from the *Sunday Australian* in Sydney to drive around Australia with his wife, Pam, and two pretty, freckle-faced daughters, Lesley and Laura, on a working holiday. But he'd only got as far as north Queensland when, while cutting cane, he heard the news that the *Sunday Oz* had been closed. So the McGregors had headed back south in Adrian's Yank-tank 1950s Chrysler, lived in my house while I was on Fraser Island, and enjoyed Brisbane so much they'd decided to stay.

You could tell that Adrian had escaped a lot of pressure by moving up to Brisbane. He motored into the Valley on a 100cc motorbike with a radio in his helmet: something he'd installed himself, speakers and all—he'd beaten Sony to the punch. Working as a casual sub-editor, Adrian wandered around the office in tight flared jeans and a T-shirt. His footware was either sandals, with the soles made out of recycled tyres, or clogs. (Until then, I'd thought I was the only bloke in Brisbane with Scandinavian clogs.) Tough Editor never pulled Adrian up for his casual clothing and I couldn't understand—still can't—how Adrian could manage Editors so well, when I couldn't. Tough Editor was a real softy as far as Adrian was concerned—as were loads of other Editors to come. In the end I decided it was because Adrian was the only person I'd ever known who couldn't be manipulated by praise or criticism, or implied responsibility for others. When friends of mine asked him: 'Don't you want to make something of

yourself?'—a purely Australian form of criticism—Adrian just smiled.
I admired this ability in him because I always worried people might
think badly of me. So much so that I bought a book on how to be
assertive—but someone pinched it.

I needed that book a few years later when Adrian asked me to
tow his Yank-tank to a dump at Ashgrove because, he said, it would
no longer go. Every rubbish dump I'd ever been to was down in a
valley, but this one was on top of a hill and, by the time we made it
to the top, I knew my car would never be the same again. We took
the handbrake off and rolled the Chrysler down the slope into the
combined rubbish of 100 000 people. Next day, Adrian's Chrysler was
gone: someone had driven it away.

Adrian and I teamed up because we had a few important things
in common. We both had a big brother watching our every move:
Craig McGregor in Sydney and Jack Lunn in Brisbane, both journalists. We agreed it added pressure, since we both had the same little
brother attitude—we didn't see ourselves as out there forging a path
to the top. We were looking after our own little world under the
house. We'd both tried Rugby League, Rugby Union, tennis, ping
pong and athletics...and weren't champions at any of them.

When Owen Thomson arrived for his 1973 visit from Sydney, he
had to walk right past me to see Tough Editor. While Adrian would
have made the first move and would have fronted him, I didn't even
bother to look up: no longer did I have to deal with the national
Editor, or want to. Observing that I had the attitude of the Vietcong—
'They don't care they die,' as my friend Dinh said in Vietnam—Owen
invited me out for a drink where he said he wanted me to understand that things were much tougher than before, and would get
worse. Gough Whitlam had upset the Americans by speaking and
acting independently of their interests. He had recognised the Chinese
Communists. He had overseen the withdrawal of our troops from
supporting the US in Vietnam. Our exports to the US and its field of
interest were falling rapidly. We were losing international trade

support. Inflation was taking off and would get worse. Unemployment was about to reach levels not seen since the 1930s.

'You,' Owen said, 'we've got to stop being so anti the Vietnam War, and everything else. The climate isn't right. We're just not getting any advertising from the big companies. They say we're anti-American.' And he named some huge corporations, multinationals who, Owen said, were refusing to advertise in our paper. 'If we're gonna survive, You, the paper's got to stop being so academic, stop dragging everything down, and fit in more.'

I didn't know what to say. It didn't sound at all like the aggressive Owen Thomson I knew: already the fourth Editor of the *Oz* in the nine years since Rupert had launched it. Before, Owen had been opinionated, certain, and very anti-establishment. Now he was talking about the importance of getting advertisements for luxury cars and whitegoods. 'Gee,' I said—probably betraying my Brisbane naivety and my Reuters, London background all at once—'that sounds a bit weak to me, Owen.'

'We live to fight another day, You,' Owen answered, suddenly cheering up. 'The bloody paper can't go on losing money forever or they'll convince Rupert to close us down.'

I reminded Owen that this was a threat he had made once before, when journalists were preparing to strike.

'It's not a threat, You. Nationally, we're down to twelve-page papers some days. Any less and it wouldn't be a newspaper, it'd be a bloody leaflet. The directors don't see the point: the bastards think the six million we lost last year would be better spent expanding News Ltd elsewhere and making profits. It's hard to argue against that from a company point of view because, by law in Australia, the only responsibility directors have is to the fucking shareholders. Rupert's the only one on the board who still thinks we have a future.' Owen added that the precedent had been set when the company shut down the *Sunday Australian*, the paper on which I had started.

Well, I was leaving anyway. Particularly now I had watched Rod die. I'd probably try my luck in Sydney again. After all, once you'd worked in London, and Jakarta, and Hong Kong, Sydney was only a small city. I said I definitely wouldn't stay under the new tough regime. To my surprise, Owen said he wanted me to be happy.

Owen had always advised that the easiest way to get rid of a reporter was not to sack them but to 'give them jobs they hate'— saying it was the best bit of management advice he'd ever learned. 'Get them to do things they can't stand and they won't be around for very long.' The corollary to this was that in order to keep someone you wanted, you had to give them a job they liked.

A few days later, a memo arrived from Owen announcing that I was now looking after all the requirements of the national edition in Brisbane. 'He is, in fact, the Brisbane representative of the national edition. If you have anything you require would you go directly to him.' I was our foreign correspondent once again. Tough Editor and myself had been separated. His national responsibilities had passed back to me.

I tried not to compete on news stories with the reporters on our wrap-around, but it was inevitable—especially on a national story like the Whiskey Au Go Go nightclub firebombing in the Valley. While the bureau covered the overnight fire and the fifteen deaths, I was instructed by Sydney to find 'a beautiful young blonde' who had escaped the blaze. By nightfall I had tracked down just such an 18-year-old, who lived in a small Queensland timber house in inner-north Brisbane with her parents and younger siblings. The photographer and I had several cups of tea with her family while she related the amazing tale of her escape. All questions were answered, but no matter how we came at it and for how long, the family didn't want her photo taken for the paper. No reason. They just didn't want it. After eight hours searching I had found her, I had the interview, but without a photo of this gorgeous girl who had escaped the thick blackness of the noxious burning plastic tablecloths, it wasn't the national story it could be.

As we left, the photographer pulled me aside and asked if I wanted him to blast off a pic as we got into the car. Oblivious to the threat, the lovely blonde 18-year-old followed us out, barefoot and in her pink brunch coat, to wave goodbye to the little yellow office Renault. I can still see her today. She made a great front-page picture standing there in a street-light halo outside the small Queensland house—smiling, waving, in the pink, beautifully alive, her happy family standing on the front timber stairs behind her. The photographer could take his snap and we'd drive away and knock off the wrap-around and every other paper.

I was terribly tempted: never underestimate a journalist's love for his story. But, when it came to it, I couldn't do it to her.

Let's go. Let go. Go.

Not only did I sometimes have to compete with the reporters in my office, but once I was asked to compete with our Canberra political writer when, in 1973, the Labor Party held its national conference at Surfers Paradise on the Gold Coast: its first full meeting in government for an entire generation. Thus the best political reporter in Australia, Alan Ramsey, was up from Canberra for our paper. He's still the only reporter I've ever met who has editors frightened of him—even Owen Thomson.

Owen rang me.

'You? You, get down to Surfers,' Owen said. 'We've got early deadlines and Ramsey won't write the bloody story till he thinks he knows everything that's happened. We're holding page one for him, but we need plenty of early copy to fill the inside pages. He won't accept that he needs help.'

'What if he tells me to bugger off?' After all, if Owen Thomson was scared of Ramsey why not me?

'Whatever you do, don't upset Ramsey. We need him. Try to avoid him, You, if you can,' Owen said. 'Just put your head down and write.'

At the Chevron Hotel rows of bored reporters listened as Labor officials droned on and on. The chairman, Bob Hawke, sat up on a stage at a desk with a gavel and said at one point: 'If the Honourable, the Prime Minister, would please shut up.' It surprised me to hear the leader of our country spoken to like that, but Hawke and Gough and everyone else in the party just laughed.

I grabbed an empty seat. Ramsey was not to be seen. I knew him from his picture in the paper: grim-lipped; big-nosed; thick haired; silent; staring eyes like an owl, all the power in the claws not the beak. In an industry that cuts and edits and paraphrases, Ramsey still stands out today because he expands a story, giving the full quote, the remembered detail, the necessary nuance. Unlike some Australian newspaper columnists, Ramsey exhibits an unconcealed respect for his readers.

Covering the speeches at such a political conference was like the 'five o'clock follies' in Saigon—the daily afternoon press conference put on by the US military. So I assumed Ramsey was wearing his helmet and flak jacket somewhere in the sandy Surfers Paradise trenches looking for the real story. I was looking forward to meeting him because I knew that Ramsey had also reported the Vietnam War. 'He was there,' as we who were there say.

Very little of such political conferences is actually reported. It's a bit like reporting court cases where evidence and argument continue for six or seven hours and you have to write six or seven paragraphs summing up both sides fairly—not to mention the hundreds of other court cases that are not covered, since newspapers usually have only one court reporter. Delegates at such national conferences speak and debate morning, afternoon and evening: it's the recreation of the political person. Arguing is their golf, their tennis. Maybe one-hundredth of one per cent of what is said is actually reported, and even less gets into the paper. Mostly, therefore, the speakers mouth platitudes. So what a shock for everyone when—in the midst of the public relations drone— Education Minister Kim Beazley (Snr) stood and shouted, pointing angrily at a fellow cabinet minister, 'He's gone behind my back!'

The room full of happy ALP comrades went quiet. The only sound was of reporters switching on tape recorders and uncapping pens. This was the first public split in the new government. Friends in power were fighting. After a generation of waiting for power, the Labor Party was arguing over it.

Beazley, red-faced, said his authority had been diminished. He accused his colleague of 'gross indecency'. Government members hurried to each other's side. It seemed everyone was whispering into an ear as the party strove to limit the damage. In a subsequent vote Whitlam sided with Beazley, Whitlam's friend Bill Hayden with the other minister.

The true believers had divided into the true and the false.

As I walked outside, Alan Ramsey—like Bob Hawke, smaller than I'd expected—silently swooped. He was clutching a thick notebook under his wing, which bulged with information newly provided by conference sources, most of which no longer mattered.

No doubt Ramsey could have caught up with the Beazley story in a dozen different ways, but he walked straight up, as if he knew me and knew I was in Surfers all along, and asked if I'd witnessed the outburst. Then he invited me back to his room at the Chevron. As we walked through the Pink Pussycat Bar, Hawke was sitting on a stool having a drink, the centre of attention.

When he telephoned Owen Thomson, Ramsey mentioned that I was in his room and we were working on the story. Mission accomplished. Next morning, as well as Ramsey's front-page splash, there were two full inside pages on the conference by-lined: 'From Alan Ramsey and our team in Surfers Paradise'. Not only was I now on our team: I *was* our team.

Occasionally it was my job to follow up for the national edition a good story broken in the Queensland wrap-around: like the story that debutantes had been withdrawn from the upcoming Nanango Ball because they were to be presented to an Aborigine, the new Liberal Party senator, Neville Bonner.

I was dispatched for the three-hour drive in the overworked yellow Renault, with Sydney photographer Neil Duncan, to do a national picture story. The debs, we ascertained when we arrived at sunset, were practising their curtsies in the local timber Tara's Hall behind three curved stained glass windows in green, marmalade and raspberry. But a couple of huge farmers with folded tanned forearms, angered by the *Australian* story, blocked the door. There was no way past. Local councillors denied Senator Bonner was the reason some girls had been withdrawn. The girls were simply too young, they said.

Mindful of the Marlon Brando film *The Last Tango in Paris*, which was making its own headlines at the time, I phoned through a 'Last Tango in Nanango' story from a public telephone booth and Neil and I drove helter-skelter back to Brisbane with his pictures.

Next day an irate Owen Thomson rang to complain that we hadn't got a picture of a row of pretty young Nanango girls curtseying to no one in their expensive ball gowns. Even when I explained that three irate farmers had blocked our way, that no one in town wanted to talk to us, and that the girls wouldn't have been dressed in their ball gowns anyway, Owen said we should have booked into a Nanango motel and not come back until we had the picture.

My reply was: 'Owen, we couldn't capture the girls, dress them in ball gowns, tie them up and then take their picture.' But I knew this was considered no excuse on a newspaper.

Not that it mattered in the end, because the one thing that was certain on the *Oz* was change. By 1974 the powerful Owen Thomson had joined the ever-lengthening list of former Editors: I heard a year or so later someone saw Owen vacuuming the floor in a jeans shop in Bondi.

The Editors of the *Oz*, to the day of writing, have all been male. Sometimes they have had slightly different titles—including Editor-in-Chief, and, once, Publisher—but in my seventeen years there I witnessed a long succession of men who ran the place editorially and who were, in effect, my Editor. They were dispensable: promoted, or demoted, or ousted, or they left. One even came back through the revolving door for a second stint. Clearly, the paper was Rupert's baby and he was changing the nappies.

By 1974 the wrap-around, too, had disappeared to become just a few extra broadsheet pages inside. And Tough Editor had left—gone off, it was said, to grow fruit.

While our office was contracting monthly, Rupert's optimism remained intact. He was busy expanding onto a third continent: buying newspapers in Texas, of all places, and, aged 43, starting his own hugely successful US national weekly paper the *Star*. Suddenly there were a lot of bright young men from America above me too. Though, in my own small way, I was flying high above the world too. In 1974, aged 33, I won the national Walkley Award for the best feature writing in Australia for a series of six articles on the Brisbane flood which had inundated ten thousand homes. So I was very proud, especially since no one in Queensland had ever won the Walkley for newspaper feature writing. For three days I did nothing but accept congratulatory phone calls from colleagues: including most of the staff of the opposition *Courier-Mail*, perhaps because I'd done my cadetship there and they knew I was an unlikely winner.

National journalism awards tended, at the time, to go almost exclusively to Australia's two dominant newspaper conglomerates— Sydney's Fairfax family papers and Melbourne's Herald and Weekly Times—who claimed of their smaller, younger rival that Murdoch's papers were not into quality journalism and, therefore, not into winning awards. But after my Walkley win, Rupert himself wrote to me at my far-flung outpost from News International, 30 Bouverie St, Fleet St, London EC4Y. The letter, signed with a fountain pen, read: 'Please accept my warmest congratulations on your winning this year's Walkley Award for your distinguished reporting on the January Brisbane floods.'

It wasn't the act of a man uninterested in quality.

6 Fatman and Robin

There was one Rupert boss I really got on well with: the Editor of Brisbane's *Sunday Sun*, Ron Richards. Ron was a diminutive, schoolboyish man with a thick head of black hair which made him look much younger than his mid-40s. He and his rugged, rounded news editor, Ken Blanch, gave Queenslanders a real—if only once a week—alternative to the *Courier-Mail*'s Melbourne-owned view of the world. The *Sunday Sun* 'kept 'em honest'.

Thus Ken Blanch and Ron Richards were known by reporters in this hot city as 'Fatman and Robin'.

I admired Ron—not just because he had made himself the best newspaperman in Brisbane after learning his trade in the small Queensland town of Warwick, but because he employed and protected several Brisbane journalists who had tremendous social problems. Many organisations would have sacked them. Alcoholism was a major difficulty for journalists back then, perhaps because providing drinks was the cheapest form of public relations for politicians and corporations, and because being a reporter very often entails waiting for the right time to strike your subject. Once I waited outside a room for six hours to get an interview with the ALP State Secretary Bart Lourigan; another time three hours to catch Joh Bjelke-Petersen.

One of Ron's reporters spent so much time in the Empire Hotel next door to the *Sunday Sun* building that eventually he moved in and lived there above the bar. Most spent hours there each day. Ken Edwards in *Time Magazine* said, very truly, that in the 1970s the bouncers at the Empire Hotel were employed to throw the journalists back in. Brian Bolton, known to all as 'the Eagle', was only an occasional heavy drinker, but on those occasions he would become incredibly abusive—his language and insults worsening in direct proportion to the importance of the executive who had displeased him. With large, bulging blue eyes, he had a raptorial tendency to hover close by while preying on police, politicians, bosses and even fellow reporters. The Eagle broke some scoop police stories in his time— including predicting a firebombing the week before the Whiskey Au Go Go burned. Brian once said he made a living 'taking the egg-beater to stories'—but he used his Mixmaster on colleagues.

I remember being on the receiving end of one of the Eagle's legendary serves when we were alone in the lift. In a tirade of almost all four-letter words, he told me what a hopeless, ugly, deformed, self-important bastard and useless wowser I was. But it was nowhere near as bad as the whipping he sometimes gave Ron. Each time, though, Ron ignored the barbs and simply said, 'Don't be like that, Eagle.'

One day I asked Ron why he copped such abuse from a staff member.

'When Cyclone Althea hit Townsville, the Eagle was phoning through his copy and I was taking the story down myself,' Ron replied. 'After a while, I said the phone line was bad: could he ring back on another phone? But the Eagle said he couldn't. No way. It turned out that he was in the only public phone box in Townsville that was still working—and it had been blown over by the cyclone. It was only then that the Eagle said 'Gimme a break, Robin. I had to crawl in here to test this bloody Superman box and I'm lying upside down inside and it's full of mud and it stinks.'

Ron Richards had started out on the *Sunday Sun* as a police roundsman in the 1950s and he loved journalists who put the job before personal comfort. It was why he personally drove young journalists home after the Queensland police had drunk them under the table.

Ron knew a lot about the discomforts of journalism. An angry woman had once tipped a full chamber pot over his head when she didn't want to be interviewed about an upcoming election. Another time, desperate to get a story, Ron went out fishing with a drunk Queensland copper on Moreton Bay. A few kilometres from shore, when Ron would not stop probing for information, the Queensland policeman went for his .45 and shot a hole in the dinghy. With Ron baling furiously they just made it to shore. Ron even followed a Queensland murder suspect to Europe, and leapt on a bus and sat next to him to get the only interview.

For Ron, everything was subordinated to the story and getting the newspaper out at minimum cost for Rupert. When I mentioned to Ron casually one day that, in London, newspapers paid double time on Saturdays he threatened to kill me if I ever said this aloud again.

At one time the *Australian*'s Brisbane bureau was in an old building out the back of the *Sunday Sun*. The Managing Director of News Ltd, Ken Cowley, was coming to town to oversee the introduction of 'the new technology' (i.e. computers), so Ron put three of his reporters over in our dingy office to hide them from the national boss. It was crowded in there for several weeks as these three outcasts squeezed in among us between stacks of old newspapers, a score of wastepaper baskets and the long shelves of leather-bound volumes containing the *Australian* since its inception: something only the Brisbane office had done. But, even so, yet a fourth *Sunday Sun* reporter—high on some-thing—came into editorial giggling uncontrollably and pointing at people. Ron, a foot shorter, marched up, turned the reporter around, shoved him out the door, down the stairs, and into a taxi.

Whenever there was an election on, Ron swung me in to cover the counting of votes on the Saturday night for his *Sunday Sun*, along with Fatman Ken Blanch. The Fatman and Robin team loved election nights as they represented another skirmish in the brilliant pair's weekly battle against the all-powerful *Courier-Mail* and *Sunday Mail*.

Thus Ron and I were in constant contact because, in the mid-1970s, there were lots of divisive, early, angry elections—both State and federal. Australia had elected its first Labor prime minister for a generation and conservatives couldn't understand—or stand—it. Fatman, Robin and I had a lot of fun covering these many election nights and—we believed—killed the *Sunday Mail*'s coverage.

This didn't help my standing on the *Australian*, which didn't want me writing under my own name for another paper—even though it too was a Rupert operation. 'Tell the *Sunday Sun* we want a pseudonym for you or no deal,' said the memo from Sydney from my latest *Oz* Editor, Mr Quiet Editor, in June 1975. But there was no way I was resurrecting Len Nyster; people thought he was up himself.

Unsure of what to do, I waited for change: knowing, after four years on the *Oz,* that it would surely come. And it did. Quiet Editor was gone before the next election was called six months later, so I continued to work with Fatman and Robin.

I wanted to work with Ron, not just because he was good company, but because it meant that on the Sunday morning I could arrive at work for the *Australian* knowing all about the election result and therefore what stories to chase. And Ron said he used me on elections because he liked my opinionated, predictive way of writing politics: though this style greatly annoyed some Brisbane journalists of the old school, which believed reporters should not inject their own opinions.

On an election night—because the *Sunday Sun* presses had to start printing by 7.00 p.m. in order to get enough copies run off for distribution around this giant State—I was always willing to predict results very early on, sometimes before even one vote had been counted.

On a Saturday morning, while people were voting in a federal election, I would write a story for Sunday's paper on how the Senate election looked like panning out. Very few Senate votes were counted on the Saturday night back in the 1970s, and the result would not be officially announced for a week, but if you knew how the system worked you could give readers almost all the Senate winners before voting had started. This put the *Sunday Sun* way ahead of the *Sunday*

Mail just for starters. The ability to add up has always been a weakness in journalism around the world, and few political writers back then seemed to understand that Australian Senate seats are won on quotas in each State. A Senate quota is arrived at by taking the number of seats being contested and adding one, then dividing that number into a hundred. (Perhaps the same person who thought up GST invented the system.) For example, if it was a half-Senate election, and five seats were therefore being contested back then, a quota was one hundred divided by six: nearly 16.7 per cent. When a party's number one Senate candidate reaches a quota, the excess votes cascade down the ticket to the next candidate. Thus it was safe in the extreme back then to say that the first two people on Labor's ticket had won Senate seats (because the ALP would easily get 33.4 per cent of the vote, or two quotas), and that the third Labor candidate would miss out, since there was no way Labor could muster more than fifty per cent of the vote in Queensland at that time.

Not all elections were this easy to call.

When Prime Minister Gough Whitlam was forced to a mid-term election in 1974, Ron Richards wrote three front page headlines—using type so large that it had to be specially etched—for possible use on the Saturday night for his tabloid paper: SUPER GOUGH; CLIFF-HANGER; and COALITION VICTORY. Ron started the *Sunday Sun* print run with CLIFF-HANGER. Actually, he always started with 'cliff-hanger' because our presses began rolling before one vote had been counted in order to get more than 400000 papers printed and distributed by early Sunday. (Counting in federal elections started at 8.00 p.m. in those days.) Meanwhile, because of our isolation in Brisbane, Ken Blanch and I wrote our stories by watching TV broadcasts from the Canberra tally-room.

By 10.00 p.m. both channels' experts were saying Labor had won, so Ron ran with our copy down the internal black steel stairs to the composing room, stopped the presses while he pulled out CLIFF-HANGER and slipped in the new front-page lead, SUPER GOUGH, then pressed the button to start the giant presses rolling again. On election nights, Ron ran every sheet of copy paper down the steel stairs himself. He just didn't trust anyone else.

Upstairs, we knew the change had been made when the building once more began to tremble. Then Fatman and I typed even more furiously as results in important seats, and then some close seats, poured in.

An hour later, just as we started to relax over coffee, a TV expert blurted out as he saw the latest figures in the Canberra tally-room: 'Hold on! Hold On A Moment! The government's in trouble! The Whitlam government's in trouble!'

Ken Blanch and I examined the new figures on the screen and I quickly typed a new lead. We watched as Ron's hands hesitated for a moment over COALITION VICTORY, before reaching once again for CLIFF-HANGER, and he again raced downstairs and stopped the giant presses which were shaking the white building. Another fifty thousand papers might be wrong, but the next fifty thousand could well be right. Anyway, libraries only keep one edition of a newspaper.

By midnight, counting had finished for the day and no expert or politician would say who had won government: there were too many seats in doubt. Ron turned, frowning, to me. I'd been surprised when he'd recently introduced me at his beef-and-burgundy club lunch as 'the State's leading political expert', since I'd never been the political writer on the *Oz*, just the bloke who wrote politics at election times to help out because we were a political newspaper.

'What do you think?' Ron asked gravely, as he surveyed his three huge headlines while nervously running one hand backwards over his lush head of dark hair and playing with his sock with the other, his right ankle resting on his left knee—a familiar nervous pose for Ron.

'Well, if you ask me, Ron, I'd say Gough's won for sure. Too many close seats need to go the other way. But he's definitely not "Super Gough" anymore.'

Ron waved his hand across his three headlines again, as if blessing each one of them. Once more he hesitated over COALITION VICTORY, as if not wanting to waste the one headline that had so far remained uninked. Then, suddenly, he grabbed a piece of copy paper to again change the news. This time, he set a brand new front-page headline but in smaller, standard, less confident type: ALP IN CLOSE VICTORY.

Usually Fatman, Robin and I met for a drink and talked about our election coverage the following week, but I hadn't heard from my old mate Ron for three weeks when I ran into him on the internal steel stairwell. 'Hey, we were right about the election result, Ron,' I said cheerfully. 'The *Sunday Sun* was the only newspaper in Australia that came out and said that Gough had won.'

'Yeah, but it took two weeks to find out,' Ron replied as he brushed brusquely past. At the top of the stairs, he turned and gave his boyish grin, which meant he was wrong to get annoyed and I was forgiven. People might think editors love to be right, but in my experience they'd generally much rather have the same story as everyone else: even if it's wrong.

At the end of 1975, Gough Whitlam—even though he had twice won nationwide elections in three years—was dismissed by the Queen of England's representative in Australia, the unelected Governor-General. This meant that Whitlam now had to face his third election in three years: presumably on the unheard of Westminster democratic principle of 'three times proves it'. This time Rupert's *Australian*— which had in 1972 championed Gough (breaking the nation's tradition of unwavering newspaper support for conservative leaders), and in 1974 had remained neutral—sensed the shift in public sentiment and turned against Whitlam under the new editorial boss, Bruce Rothwell, Mr Flamboyant Editor.

I'd only ever met Flamboyant Editor the once: I'd won a second national Walkley Award for best feature writing in 1975, and spent a day answering calls of congratulations, one of which included a job offer from the opposition *National Times*. Flamboyant Editor called me down to Sydney to discuss my resignation, and I was surprised to be greeted by an Editor-in-Chief who dressed like an executive:

tailored three-piece blue suit, gold cufflinks, silk tie and a red hand-kerchief protruding from his chest like a tongue. Waving his arms around and continually throwing his tie over his shoulder as if it were in the road, he immediately offered me a pay rise, a new title and 'an executive role'—so I gave in to the man in the better suit. Once that was settled, he startled me by saying: 'Shirts. Shirts. Everyone wears shirts. Give me a page three lead on shirts.' Like Ron Richards, Flamboyant Editor was a very good personal friend of Rupert's—or so he told me.

Many journalists had been attracted to the *Australian* over the previous eleven years because of Rupert's youthful political fresh air, so the 1975 anti-Gough turnaround incensed many editorial staff. In Sydney there was a strike over claims of political censorship (the journos didn't bother to tell us in Brisbane). Some, like the dazzling features editor, Nic Nagle, resigned because of this change of heart. He sent me a note when he left in 1975: 'You probably know all about the new Cultural Revolution by now and about my refusal to be in it.' (I didn't know.) He thanked me for 'all the good work you did over the years' and added ominously: 'Don't let the bastards grind you down.'

What could he mean?

Whitlam's defeat in an emotion-charged election left a lot of residual resentment—nay, hatred—between management and jour-nalists at the *Australian* in Sydney, and I was to walk unwittingly into the middle of it all from Brisbane.

Three months after the election, March 1976, Adrian McGregor and I were walking up Brunswick Street, the Valley after our usual pizza marguerita at Giardinetto's when we were stopped by Ron Richards. Ron said his 20-year-old son had just been forced to resign from the *Australian's* Brisbane bureau by our brand new Brisbane editor—the sixth local editor in my five years and the third sent up from Sydney. Ron was irate because his son had only recently been poached from the *Courier-Mail*, and the *Courier-Mail* would not take him back for at least two years because he had resigned to go to an opposition paper. So Ron's son would now have to leave town to get a job.

Ron told us that his son had been forced out purely to make room for another journalist the new Brisbane editor wanted. Adrian suggested that Ron hire his son himself, or protest to his good friend Rupert. (The pair were on the phone at all hours of the night, and, like a few other untouchable staff that Rupert loved, Ron Richards was to be kept on for life while many other editors around the world were not so lucky.) Ron replied it would be nepotism; he couldn't abuse his position.

Adrian was furious at the injustice of getting rid of a good young writer. It was one of the things I liked about Adrian: that he could get so upset about injustice—and bad football tactics. Even though Adrian depended on daily goodwill for his three days casual work, we called a meeting of bureau staff who agreed it was a black act and that we should protest to Sydney. Adrian finished his shift and hopped on his motorbike in his clogs, while I was told to drive three hours down into New South Wales to do a story.

The next day, 24 March 1976, Flamboyant Editor phoned me from Sydney and said I was the 'ringleader' causing trouble in the bureau. I replied that there were no ringleaders; everyone was as one on this issue. But he surprised me by saying that *another* staff meeting had been held after Adrian and I left, where it had been explained that I was just creating aggravation for the new Brisbane editor. The vote had then changed, Flamboyant Editor claimed. I said I very much doubted this was true.

'If you feel so strongly, then why don't you put your job on the line?' Bruce replied, with surprising aggression.

'I put my job on the line every day, Bruce,' I replied. (I had in mind not just the writing of difficult articles, but the time I was ordered up to Parliament House by a previous Brisbane editor to replace the political roundsman. When I told the roundsman the news he burst into tears...so I returned immediately to the office where I was promptly sacked. I was then reinstated when Quiet Editor flew to Brisbane to sort it out the next day.) So Flamboyant Editor didn't know it, but he was dealing with an employee who was ready to go at any time. 'I can see my brown leather jacket hanging on the wall over there, Bruce,' I threatened. 'I'm going over to put it on and then I'm leaving.'

Not knowing of the Cultural Revolution that had taken place in Sydney, and not yet having seen *Don's Party*, I thought Flamboyant Editor would back off. But he replied, 'Good!' and hung up.

Within eighteen months of receiving Rupert's letter of congratulation, I had lost my job. When I got home that afternoon, I wrote to the *Oz* 'as a courtesy, not a complaint', putting on paper what had happened in 'the shoddy sacking of poor young Richards'. And I added that the paper had recently: 'taken on a *Women's Weekly*–type role. Stories on royalty, fruit flies and Bobo Faulkner dominate the feature pages…while political features are cut to the bone'. I finished: 'The *Australian* keeps stabbing itself in the stomach here: men have been sacked on four separate occasions in my five years here; good men for no reason; often better men than their replacements. This has made the *Australian* a pariah among newspapermen in Brisbane.'

To my surprise, Flamboyant Editor's understudy with the title of Editor, Mr Steady Editor, rang to thank me for all my work over the last five years.

Things were bad. Unemployment had leapt from two per cent when I'd started on the *Australian* to five per cent, which was unprecedented in my lifetime. No wonder Whitlam had lost. So, while Rupert expanded across the US, arriving in New York by the time he was 45, back home in Australia I shrank, shrivelled really, all the way back to the kitchen of my house in Indooroopilly, to be left home alone, aged 35.

Sorry to say, the beautiful Miss Norway too had decided she'd had enough of me. After a few months she left.

And it wasn't long afterwards that Bazza, my faithful boxer dog, also pulled out, and moved in with Joan Jackson and her daughters up the road.

Even my dog was looking for some good company.

7 How the war ended

Whenever I felt too depressed about losing Miss Norway I'd take a cold shower and refuse to let myself get out from under the water until I'd promised to get on with life.

That winter of 1976 I had a hell of a lot of cold showers.

Adrian McGregor was now divorced and on his own, so we had lunch often and talked of the good times we'd had like the time Sydney Rugby Union champions Randwick came up to Brisbane for the first time to play the local champs, Brothers. I asked Adrian who he thought would win and, as an old boy of Randwick Boys High, he replied: 'Oh, the Galloping Greens! They'll be far too fast.' But I had learnt from Len Nyster that Brothers had some of the fastest men who'd ever played, including Jeff and Paul McLean. With Brothers leading 25–0 at half-time, I saw Adrian and tapped him on the shoulder: 'You're right, Adrian. Randwick are far too fast.' After that we went to lots of Ballymore and Lang Park matches together and we both barracked for Queensland.

We watched Jeff Thomson bowl his first overs for Queensland at the Gabba—the fastest anyone there had ever seen. (Queensland had bought Thommo from New South Wales because they realised they were never going to win the Sheffield Shield playing against him.)

At the gala opening of *Jesus Christ Superstar* we both wasted all night chatting up two chorus girls who turned out, at 4.00 a.m. not to be interested. There was a well-known ad at the time for Arpege perfume: 'Promise her anything but give her Arpege.' Adrian blew it when he told the girls he believed in the old saying: 'Promise her Arpege but give her anything'.

I enjoyed talking to Adrian because we had a similar attitude on many things, including no great desire to live our lives solely as employees who drank to keep mind and soul together. We teamed up as competition doubles tennis partners with a great understanding on court, and I admired his lightning forehand volley, his knowledge of words and his ability to always use correct medical terminology. Knowing I was living alone, unemployed, and moping around, Adrian went to the trouble of dropping around every Monday night with a girlfriend to watch the great English TV series *When the Boat Comes In* with all those lovely English characters Jack, Dolly, Jessie and Mrs Seaton.

Adrian had a theory on everything and there was much to learn from him—especially about women. His golden rule, which I'd never heard anywhere else but later learned to appreciate, was: 'A man ignores PMT at his peril.' But even Adrian couldn't help me when I was trying to chat up a beautiful Sydney reporter over tea at the Wentworth Hotel. I happened to mention that the following week I was flying to Roma to write about an oilfield. I meant the small, pretty country town in western Queensland, but she had much bigger aspirations: 'Ohhh Roma, Roma, Roma,' she said. 'Arrivederci Roma… bring me back some leather shoes.'

When Adrian's Red Hill home burned down to its stumps, he came to stay at my place while it was rebuilt. So I got to know his familiar pose with one leg stuck out stiffly in front while bending to look into the fridge hoping there might be a snack—any snack—inside; and I suffered his typing with the back door open and my blow heater on;

and I lived through that night in mid-winter when he took his girl-friend and all the blankets into the spare room and I almost froze.

But most of the time I was home alone.

There was, however, one tiny little extra piece of good news pene-trating the unfathomable gloom: my old Russian school mate, Jim Egoroff, was back in town from an extended stint overseas, or 'OS', to use the language of the time: a time when words like 'shibboleth', 'diabolical' and 'eyeball' were as common as 'absolutely', 'whatever' and 'hopefully' are today. I'm talking a generation ago here, back in the days of hotpants and terry-towelling hats, when the Australian dollar was worth half as much again as the mighty greenback; when you could buy a newspaper on every street corner from a little cabinet by leaving money in a tin box. I mean back before public phones became payphones; before they took the doors off phone boxes; and before broccoli, zucchini and fennel appeared on dinner plates. A time when no one ever imagined for a moment that one day Australians would buy water in bottles, lock churches, or put small white crosses at the site of car accidents to remember dead loved ones.

Jim Egoroff was, as I'd learned many times at primary and secondary school, a good man to turn to in a time of crisis. He'd saved me eight years earlier when I'd come home from Vietnam in March 1968 and sobbed inexplicably at the kitchen table in front of the whole family while telling them about being caught up in the middle of the Tet Offensive. Back then an Australian man wasn't supposed to cry in front of people: even when it really hurt. Real men were supposed to be sorrow proof. Gulps of air choking, chest heaving, body shaking, tears running, brain racing…when Jim arrived at the front door.

'G'day, Lunn, you Bastard Boy! How have you been going these couple of last years?'

I told him that so much had happened in Vietnam, I could write a book.

'Then you could do it,' said Jim. 'I will of have had of been your left-hand man.'

As often happened—even after eighteen years as friends—Jim

took me literally. I had said 'I could write a book'—the sort of thing Australians used to say all the time about matters that preoccupied their lives. This didn't mean I knew *how* to write a book, or that anyone would want to sell it in shops. It was just an old saying. So I told Jim that it was unfortunate that I didn't have all the office equipment needed to produce a manuscript during my eight-week Reuters holiday.

Next morning, Jim pulled up in a ute loaded down with two typist's desks, a wide-carriage typewriter, reams of A4 paper, a desk lamp, a thick bundle of carbon paper, biros, bottles of white-out, scissors, a bottle of red ink, rulers, paperclips, and his own boxed maroon fountain pen and propelling pencil set. 'There you are, Lunn,' said Jim. 'I know that if you force a fool to get down and pray he will most likely have of had knocked a hole in his head, but I am hoping you will give us some inlight into the Vietnam situation.'

Jim had helped save me back then, and now in another desperate situation in 1976, Jim turned up once again in the nick of time. I told him how Miss Norway's parents had sent me a pepper shaker (but no salt shaker) for my 30th birthday and I hadn't realised the significance at the time: that this was a gift Norwegians give to a man who reaches 30 without marrying. I told him how Miss Norway had complained that my life revolved around 'work, politics and sport'.

'Jim, this house now seems as large and as empty and as cold as our old freezer factory—except that now I'm the white, lifeless exhibit left alone inside.'

I told him I'd walked out on my job, leaving Rupert's empire to all the bright young men in Sydney, London and New York. And, while I was in the mood to break all the rules about unloading problems on a mate, I dropped my guard and revealed something I'd only told Adrian: that I'd developed a completely illogical fear of flying since the Vietnam War, which had made my life as a reporter difficult; that I now believed all fireworks were gunfire, even when I could see the colours in the sky.

After quitting the *Australian* I'd almost got a job with Australian

Associated Press (AAP), the newspaper-owned agency that distributed the best of overseas stories to our media. An executive had flown up to take me to lunch at Allegro and said they had a job for me because of my Reuters experience.

'That's great news,' I said, chuffed to be remembered.

'Yes, but we first need just a two-line letter from you asking for a job.'

'But you've offered me a job so why should I have to apply?' I said, mystified.

'Because we can't be seen to be poaching Rupert's staff.'

I refused to write the letter, thinking AAP would cave in, but I never heard from them again. I told Jim that the job market for journalists like me was much tighter than I had ever imagined, or read.

Jim was immediately very positive about my situation: which was what I loved most about him. He took absolutely no interest in politics or corporations, so he saw almost everything that happened in the world as good news.

'That is bloody fantastic, Lunn,' Jim said of my grim situation, 'because what I have of discovered these couple of last days is that Brisbane is only a fish and chip shop.' Jim said we should go to America. 'We could bombard atoms of Boron with protons! But you don't know the difference between fusion and fission. It's not funny you Bastard Boy. Boron has only five protons but six atoms...'

I interrupted, saying I was 35 years old now and I was looking for a job to pay the mortgage.

'Let me not interrupt myself,' said Jim, who was the sort of man who could never slow down long enough to watch television. 'That's what I'm saying, Lunn! Lord and behold, all power is transferable. If you had of had some intelligence you would know that money is energy, boy!'

'But, but Jim,' I said...

'Don't but my arse,' Jim said, misquoting Shakespeare. 'If you don't listen I will bloody well work over you. I can't believe you are so dumb, no offence meant, mate. I am no professor of chicken soup, but fusion is a great example of man's ingenuity to man.'

At least Jim had me laughing.

A month later he dropped around one morning at dawn to say he was leaving for London to build his own electric car in opposition to General Motors. Whereas I had no idea where my life was floating. I'd never imagined that I would end up out of work in my mid-30s, living on my own, my only asset the eight-year-old fading, unpublished Vietnam manuscript which had been rejected by publishers in Australia and the US. I'd always thought by 35 I'd have a wife and six kids and be a published author.

Jim said I should return to the *Australian*, but I said I wasn't going back there cap in hand.

'What the bloody hell,' said Jim. 'You will only outsmart yourself, Lunn. Quit while you're behind.' Jim put a huge arm on my shoulder: 'The Vietnam War is over, mate.'

The very next day another new Editor of the *Oz*, this one with the title of Publisher, Mark Day, flew up to Brisbane to ask if I'd please come back after five months of exile—saying over dinner that during 1976 circulation had inexplicably fallen to 'disastrous levels'. Mark was Mr Best Editor, and he offered me an office and a new title: assistant editor (national). I gratefully accepted, but the title didn't mean anything in the end. While I enjoyed working for Best Editor because he was sensible and knew a good story when he saw one, within eighteen months he had left to run *Penthouse* magazine.

Then, two years later, Rupert sold his successful national bi-weekly newspaper, *Melbourne Truth,* to Mark Day and Rupert's old mate Owen Thomson. Perhaps, as some said, Rupert no longer wanted to own this tabloid mixture of scandal, topless models, investigative journalism, and answers to sex problems. But it was a generous gesture. It seemed that Owen Thomson, like me, was back in favour.

8 Dining with the Murdochs

Rupert seems keen on January for buying newspapers, as if he sees every new year as another opportunity. Thus, in January 1977 Rupert bought the *New York Post* from a proprietor who was only prepared to sell to someone who, like Rupert, had started a quality non-establishment paper, like the *Australian*.

So our paper had paid, at long last, its first dividend.

All metropolitan newspaper owners and bosses join the class who judge, as they bestow adoration or ridicule on locals in every field: actors, playwrights, politicians, judges, athletes, businessmen, bankers. This gives a newspaper its immense power because every human has a need to be thought considerable at home. Thus the *New York Post*, as a daily newspaper in the most important city in the most important country in the world, enabled Rupert to join the most elite and smallest group in the world: the-class-who-judge-the-class-who-judge.

Meanwhile, back at the ranch in Indooroopilly, I set out to review the most powerful person in my home town, the Premier of Queensland. As I started chapter one of an unauthorised biography, *JOH: The Life and Political Adventures of Johannes Bjelke-Petersen*, I hoped this might lead one day to the publication of my Vietnam book which was still blushing unseen in a bottom drawer, ten years after Jim Egoroff had supplied the means of production. Publishers believed Australians did not want to read about the Vietnam War as it might upset them, and that Americans would not want to read a foreigner's view.

However, three different publishers came to try to sign me up for a book on Joh Bjelke-Petersen because he was such an unlikely political winner whose manoeuvres—with just over three per cent of the national vote—had removed the first federal Labor government for a generation in 1975. Bjelke-Petersen owed his Premiership to two things: the heavy weighting given to bush votes in a system known locally as the 'Bjelkemander'; and the support of his coalition Liberal Party, which was prepared to play a minor role even though, for the first decade of Joh's reign, they easily out-polled Bjelke-Petersen's Country/National Party.

Upon signing up with University of Queensland Press to write the book, one of the other publishers, a huge man, came banging on my front lattice door with the handle of a thick walking stick, shouting: 'I know you're in there. Come out.' But this Sydney publisher had missed out because he had insisted on a book authorised by the Premier, whereas UQP just wanted a book: subject, of course, to their lawyers looking at it. I was aided in this task by brilliant young editor Craig Munro who taught me how to put a book together. We sat in our singlets at UQP in the summer heat going through my manuscript.

Even writing a book about a politician is seen as a political act, especially if you try to present an unbiased account. Thus I began the book by saying it was written for people thirty years hence (2008). I wanted to capture not just the Premier but also the people around him: like press secretary Allen Callaghan, with whom I had worked at the ABC on my return from overseas in 1971.

The best way to describe Callaghan is to say he would never be seen dead wearing a leather jacket. Or coloured trousers. Callaghan hurried everywhere with the gait of a train driver and looked like a London cartoonist's propaganda drawing of an IRA hard man: a big man casting a large shadow, tight clothing, demonic black hair, long dark sideburns. Except that Callaghan always had a cheery look and wasn't carrying a dangerous weapon: except his wit. If Callaghan liked you, he called you 'monsieur'. A railway fanatic, he took Australian politics to a new level with his quick mind and ability to write quips, speeches and replies for the once imprecise and verbose farmer-Premier. They poured out as fast as Callaghan could type. He pioneered the political use of talk-back radio in Australia in 1973 and was famous for his 'Callaghan principles', which included: 4CA Cairns (make sure you look after even the most remote radio station); the Brisbane *Telegraph* (any well-written government announcement put out at exactly 8.00 a.m. would have a good chance of making the front page lead of the first edition of the afternoon paper); and Death, Disaster and Diatribe (the only news around on a Sunday, making it a good time to issue announcements).

These days he'd be called a spin doctor, but Callaghan was much more than that. Realising his boss was news, Callaghan made it hard for journalists to get to the Premier: thus making his product more valuable. He also brought aggression to the traditionally sycophantic art of public relations. 'Speak. It's your ten cents,' he would say when answering his phone, before he even knew who it was. Or: 'We deny everything.' Callaghan knew instinctively when a reporter looking for an interview would want to know about the gerrymander: 'The gerry-mander's in the basement with the crocodiles. We feed them at 3.00 p.m. if you would like to be there,' he would say before hanging up. As an ex-journalist himself, Callaghan knew that editors and owners want stories not excuses, and that the reporter would ring back rather than face a hostile editor who wanted the interview (and the circulation gain that might come with it).

Well do I remember the TV reporter who was sent to the Early Street Historical Village in Brisbane where Gough Whitlam, as Prime Minister, was to launch a book on a former Labor leader. Junie Morosi, a beautiful woman working for Whitlam's Treasurer, Jim Cairns, was headline news after the Treasurer had declared 'a kind of love' for her. The TV reporter confided—as a group of us waited for Whitlam to arrive—that his news editor had told him that if he didn't get Gough Whitlam to answer questions about Junie Morosi, not to bother coming back to the office. I had worked with this bloke on the *Australian* wrap-around when his job disappeared. Now he was desperate to hang on; so he was very nervous as we waited.

Everyone knew the Prime Minister would most likely brush us aside, say what he wanted to say to the audience, and leave. So easy. But this reporter leaped out in front of Whitlam as he got out of a government limo, shoved his microphone into Gough's face and asked about Junie Morosi. Surrounded by several aides, Gough, with large strides, brushed past, saying: 'I'm here to launch a book, inside.' To keep up, the TV reporter ran backwards in front of the Prime Minister along the twisting track through some bushes while trying to get in a second question. Just as he'd managed to block Whitlam's path, the reporter tripped on the root of a Moreton Bay fig tree and landed heavily flat on his back. Gough and staff stepped neatly around him and kept going. I never saw this bloke again after that, but I've often thought since that this was the real story. Not the Prime Minister. Not the book launch.

Despite my friendship with Allen Callaghan I was unable to get an interview with the Premier for my book. I had already travelled with him on assignment, but I wanted to ask Bjelke-Petersen about his childhood—to try to build up a picture of what had made him like he was. Finally, I rang the Premier at his home in Kingaroy. Every journalist in Brisbane could imitate the way Bjelke-Petersen answered the phone at home on the farm: 'Ha Ha Hallo. Ja Ja Joh Bjelke-Petersen speaking.'

He wanted to know who would get the royalties. I said that I would. The Premier was, as usual, very polite but—after a few more questions—said he wouldn't be in it 'because of your attitude from time to time generally'. Later, when the book came out, he told an interviewer that he hadn't cooperated because, while I had occasionally written a positive story, I would sometimes write negative stories about him. 'He goes around kicking me in the shins,' he said.

'Are you accusing Lunn of being impartial?' the quick-thinking 4ZZZ reporter, John Woods, asked.

'Yes I am,' said the Premier.

Joh had once said that he respected Max Jessop as a political writer because he was a life member of the ALP: 'At least I know where he stands.'

But I did get help from Joh's wife, Flo Bjelke-Petersen, who gave me the family photo albums despite the Premier's opposition. We met outside Indooroopilly State School where Flo handed them over from the boot of her Jaguar. When I asked her why she was helping me, Flo said: 'Because if you write the book people will read it.'

Luckily for me, at this time Joh Bjelke-Petersen was asked to appear on a new ABC TV show in which famous people sat in a chair before an audience and talked about their life, unprompted, for forty minutes. Not only did I make a transcript of that, but also the Premier practised for the show in his office, and the tapes of these long sessions came into my possession. Suddenly I had inside background on the Premier's childhood and youth: his early polio, his fist fights in the schoolyard at Taabinga State School.

By arrangement with Best Editor, the *Australian* agreed to employ me for just three days a week during 1977 so I could get the book written, and it was launched early in 1978 under a marquee in my backyard. In four days I did more than fifty media interviews. The *Australian* serialised the book every day for a week, using the previously unpublished pictures on the front page each day and picking out chapters like 'The Night of the Long Prawns' for extracts. UQP was hoping to sell five thousand in hardback, but quickly sold twenty thousand before the book went into paperback, even though the *Courier-Mail* and its sister afternoon paper, the Brisbane *Telegraph*, didn't review or mention this first book on Queensland's most hated–loved Premier—because I worked for Rupert. Some people thought the Premier was not a fit subject for a book. To which the reply could only be: 'Are there any other books you would like burned?'

Somehow, Joh ignored my book, and soon began to cooperate on the first of two authorised biographies on his life. The first, *Jigsaw* (1983)—in which the author optimistically addressed 'all my readers in whatever country'—postulated that the Bjelke-Petersen name may have been 'secretly bestowed by Scandinavian royalty for a service rendered'. 'While having always believed in God,' the author wrote, 'at no time have I felt so close to Him as when producing this manuscript.' This book said that Allen Callaghan—'when he generally became regarded as "the man responsible for the Premier's achievements as well as for his every move"...began riding on Joh's glory.' But *Jigsaw* escaped the media scrutiny mine had encountered, despite the fact that I especially brought parts of it to the attention of two Brisbane political writers. Of course, by 1983 Bjelke-Petersen had become a much more powerful figure than when my book came out in 1978.

Circumstances had led me to write a book on Joh. I'd much rather have written a biography on someone like, say, Australian reporter Steve Dunleavy who became the top reporter in Rupert's empire. Like Joh and Allen Callaghan, Rupert and Steve Dunleavy had an instant rapport and became another one of those highly successful, unexpected combinations.

I'd known and admired Steve in Hong Kong back in 1964–65 when he worked as a journalist by day and a nightclub bouncer in the Firecracker Bar by night. He was a great reporter and an excellent fist-fighter. So I knew that Steve was easy to like but frightening to hate. A former Bondi boy from Sydney, Steve Dunleavy always travelled on high-octane. There was nothing about him that said employee. Not as he strode so lightly up Nathan Road in Hong Kong, smiling, with that dimple in his chin, a gold ring on one finger, a long bodgie haircut swooped up and back and black, and wearing

The house at 155 Central Avenue Indooroopilly where Larrikin Editor came to dinner.

Newly arrived in black clogs and red mini-skirt, Miss Norway faces the floods and flatness of the Queensland bush, Bruce Highway, 1971.

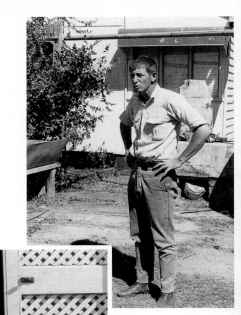

My mate Rod
the smoker who
died age 33.

Me and Bazza
left at home
alone.

Assignment: live as a millionaire on the Gold Coast for a weekend.

Cyclone Daisy, Maryborough, Queensland. The Eagle, Comrade May and Hugh Lunn make do in the dark.

Hugh Lunn and Max Jessop, before he was sacked in the 1982 purge.

JOURNALISM WITH BIG PAT

Queensland journalists Hugh Lunn (The Australian left, and Bob Johnston (Courier-Mail) right, with trade union man Pat Mackie on the Australian Government inspection tour of Fraser Island.

The intrepid journalists shared a tent with Mr Mackie, camping on the beach in the middle of winter for their stories.

They had to travel for hours to reach the only island telephone to file their stories and features. Most of the week was spent on the back of a giant six-wheel drive truck called Bigwheels.

They followed the inquiry to almost inaccessible parts of the giant island.

Lunn and Johnston walked through mangrove swamps, swam down a creek and trekked across open sand "blows" to inland lakes in their search for stories.

One of the hazards, they said, was the difficulty in absorbing all the knowledge that Pat Mackie had about conditions on the island.

To Pat's surprise, the government people knew just as much, so a cross-index of information was possible.

Lunn reports that the worst was the cold Pacific wind at night. One morning he was found wearing no less than nine shirts and jumpers and stuck in his sleeping bag.

Journalists fi

LONDON — Ten j dismissed over a wage picketing clash outside the newspaper office.

The court was told the leaving the premises by hurled eggs, soft drink them.—AAP-Reuter.

Newspaper clipping on Fraser with union man Pat Mackie and *Courier Mail* journalist Bob Johnston.

At Milton Centre, playing at charity day with Jumbo racquet in 1979.

Journalists all at sea covering PM Malcolm Fraser on a military exercise, 1979.

In jail for Amnesty International in Brisbane's King George Square, September 1980.

Interviewing Barry Humphries for the *Daily Sun* in 1982, on the eve of his Queensland tour. He admired my brown jacket. I didn't tell him my dog was named after him.

Queensland's 'anti-Joh' historian Doctor (later Professor) Ross Fitzgerald and Hugh Lunn sheltering from the 1980s political heat.

well-tailored suits and monogrammed shirts...moving, always, like the middle-weight champion of the world.

Even when he was standing still, you could imagine Dunleavy bobbing and weaving and jabbing straight lefts. He was so confident that in the nightclub (as I wrote in *Spies Like Us*) Steve had his daily 'going rate': the number of each nationality Steve reckoned an Australian like himself was worth in a fight. As I heard him volunteer one night to some sailors looking for trouble in the Firecracker Bar: 'The going rate tonight, gentlemen,' Steve said, fondling the knuckles of one hand with the palm of the other, 'is one Australian equals two Irishmen, any four Scotsmen and eight Poms.'

The Americans were easily sucked in: since Steve had deliberately left them out. 'Say, Dunleavy, you didn't say what the going rate for us Americans is?' one shouted above the live Filipino rock band.

'Oh Yanks?' said Steve. 'Yanks? Let me see. I'll tell you what, fellas. You Yanks...let me see...you Yanks, you can write your own ticket!'

After that, all the sailors shut up and enjoyed the band.

But in 1977 Steve Dunleavy wasn't yet famous enough to write a book about, though he was Rupert's brightest young man on the *New York Post*—and no doubt Rupert was pleased to have Steve chasing stories for him in New York, the toughest city in the world. Dunleavy was a Superman reporter who loved his work so much that in Sydney he had reputedly flattened the tyres of opposition reporters to get a beat on a story. Once it was the tyres on the news car his father (who worked for the opposition paper) was driving: though Steve explained that he didn't know it was his father driving the car at the time.

In Hong Kong in 1964 I was warned several times, as an unworldly 23-year-old, to be careful what I said to Steve, but I always found him very helpful and warm; and interesting, since his life revolved around newspaper stories and how to get them. Working for Rupert, Steve was to become in the 1990s 'one of the three or four most influential journalists in the US.' Several characters in novels and films reputedly have been based on Steve Dunleavy, including the Aussie tabloid TV host in Oliver Stone's *Natural Born Killers*.

Years later I got a very good idea of just how close Steve Dunleavy and Rupert Murdoch became from Rupert's son, Lachlan.

The story emerged like this.

There were nine of us at a dinner party in an apartment built between the stumps underneath an old Queensland colonial house in East Brisbane in 1995. It was the home of finance journalist Ali Cromie and her husband Gregor. Gregor's specialty was fish wrapped in foil and steamed in the dishwasher. This night Ali prepared a giant Great Barrier Reef coral trout. Lachlan was 23 years old at the time and was General Manager of Brisbane's *Courier-Mail*, which had finally returned to the Murdoch family. As I sat opposite Lachlan asking him to pass the mango sauce, it suddenly occurred to me that the last time the *Courier-Mail* had been owned by someone who actually lived in Brisbane...well it had never happened until now. Yet the paper so much influenced all our lives.

Now, at last, an owner was living our life. Among us. With us. Driving across the Story Bridge like the rest of us.

Even if it was only for a year or two.

Lachlan didn't act like an heir to Rupert's money and power: though, as I told him, he certainly looked like his father. 'People say I have his mannerisms,' he said matter-of-factly.

Lachlan arrived for the dinner exactly on time wearing pointy-toed riding boots, white denim jeans and a soft, black-and-white hound's-tooth cotton jacket. He was slimmer, more inquisitive, quieter and with a stronger physique than I had expected, no doubt the combined product of his hobbies at that time: rock climbing, shooting pool and—as he revealed that evening—making plaited bread. With his Rupert-like brown button eyes, Lachlan observed each person at the dinner as if assessing the coloured balls on a snooker table. He moved chairs in and out from the table for the women, served those around him with dexterity, and never openly disagreed. Like every Australian dinner party the conversation turned inevitably to US films. When someone said *Forrest Gump* was just more American propaganda, Lachlan asked: 'What do you mean by propaganda?' When I said I was disappointed in Clint Eastwood's *The Unforgiven*, Lachlan said he liked it because it showed that heroes were just as violent as bad guys.

For a 23-year-old, Lachlan knew a hell of a lot about the costs of producing newspapers and enjoyed talking about it. Like his father, he knew the detail; for example, exactly how long it took a roll of newsprint to run through the local presses. He knew the huge weekly increase in depreciation at the *Courier-Mail*'s giant new Murarrie printing plant, and he rightly still saw a great future for quality newspapers. He knew exactly the numbers of films made each year for Hollywood and for cable TV. Although born in England of Australian parents, in conversation Lachlan described himself as an American, saying his parents were American and they had let him make up his own mind about his nationality. Over fruit, I asked about my old acquaintance, Steve Dunleavy, and out came the story.

Rupert had invited Steve Dunleavy to celebrate Australia Day at a special dinner with the Murdoch family after work one 26 January night in New York (I found it interesting that Rupert, by this time an American citizen, still celebrated Australia Day). The waiter, Lachlan told us, was pouring the wine and, because Lachlan didn't want any 'as I was doing track work', he reached out and tipped his wine glass upside down on the starched white tablecloth.

'Steve immediately leaped up out of his chair,' Lachlan said quietly, so that we strained to hear. 'He whipped his jacket off and shaped up to fight me. I was just 17 years old and wondering what was going on, until Steve said, "You know what it means, Lachlan, this tipping your bloody glass upside down. You've just offered to fight anyone in the bar, and I'm bloody gratefully accepting your challenge. So get your coat off. We're going the knuckle." I was wondering if what he was saying was for real.' Lachlan said he looked to his father down the end of the table. Rupert nodded to acknowledge that what Steve was saying was correct.

Lachlan said he quickly righted his wine glass.

'I had to tell Steve I'd never heard of this strange Aussie ritual,' Lachlan said, laughing at himself. 'So Steve said he'd let me off this time. But just this once. Only then did I realise he was just kidding around.'

Which shows just how far friends can go with Rupert: well, anyway, how far reporters who always-get-the-story-no-matter-what can go. Lachlan said he used to see a lot of Steve, until Dunleavy left the *New York Post* to front Rupert's highly successful American *A Current Affair*, which he went on to host for years. Lachlan stuck up for Steve, saying those American films and books that were supposed to be based on Dunleavy were not necessarily so. He said that because Australian journalists pioneered tabloid TV in the United States, any fictional, rough-tough journo character was always made out to be Australian.

Not surprisingly, Dunleavy became a legend in News Corporation; such a larger-than-life figure that, back in his hometown of Sydney, other reporters and editors loved telling and hearing stories about him—just like they loved repeating stories about Rupert. Of course, Dunleavy stories didn't extend as far as Brisbane, which has always been isolated enough to have its own journalist heroes. Like the Eagle. Or the Count. Or the Frog. Brisbane didn't have Bea Miles or Mr Eternity; but we did have Tom Wallace and Rock'n'roll George.

And it isn't only journalists who love to tell stories about Steve and Rupert. On Mahogany Row, the top floor of News Ltd's Sydney headquarters, where all the Australian executives have their offices along a narrow carpeted corridor, outrageous Steve Dunleavy stories are a welcome splash of colour to enliven the view of the building across the road. One executive told me that Steve Dunleavy got very drunk one night in a New York bar, staggered back to the office and, although on a day off, flopped at his desk, where he became morose, tears running down his cheeks. A short while later, so the story went, Rupert made one of his 'terror from the sky' surprise visits for which he is famous. He only had to turn up once for everyone to believe he was coming every time a rumour went around: 'Rupert's in town! Pull all the stickers off the walls!'

No one ever seemed to know when Rupert was coming, or where he was going, or if he was still around, or when he was leaving, or even where he had been. No one dared ask. And it wasn't something you were going to find out by reading the papers or watching the news. In that respect, Rupert was very much like the Scarlet Pimpernel: is he in heaven or is he in hell?

Seeing his star reporter in some distress, so the story went, Rupert rushed to Dunleavy's side and, with a comforting hand on Steve's shoulder, turned to an editor and said, 'What's wrong with Steve? He looks terrible.'

Now, everyone in News Corporation knows that Rupert doesn't allow alcohol in his newspaper offices, so the editor hesitated before answering.

'Steve's crying,' said Rupert, kneeling.

'Yes,' lied the editor, thinking fast. 'His father died.' *Phew! Got out of that one.* Well, not quite.

'Good grief,' Rupert reportedly shouted. 'What is he doing here at his desk if his father has just died back in Australia? It's so typical of Steve! Are you completely and utterly heartless, man? Quickly: Get him on the next plane to Sydney so at least he makes the funeral.'

And so it was—or so it was said on Mahogany Row—that Steve woke up in a 747 looking down on the Sydney Harbour Bridge and wondering how come he felt like he was floating high above Sydney when he was sure as hell in a bar on 43rd Street.

It's a great story, and if by chance it is true it tells a lot about Rupert. As I was soon to discover myself, if you could do the job and Rupert noticed you he would admire and tell you.

Rupert certainly noticed my book about Joh.

After the book came out in 1978, Rupert's Managing Director in Australia, Ken May, wrote to say how very interesting he had found it. So, knowing Rupert's intense curiosity about Queensland politics,

I sent off a copy to New York inscribed: 'to Rupert'. A few months later, Rupert swept unexpectedly into the *Oz* bureau in Brisbane for a 'terror from the sky' with three or four top executives in tow.

By now I had a tiny cubicle with no door. Rupert marched straight in while Ron Richards and the other executives stood waiting outside: either because there was no room or because Rupert hadn't invited them. He asked how *Joh* had sold, the reaction to it, and how many reprints there had been. He seemed very friendly indeed.

'Are you writing any more books?' Rupert asked as a final question.

'Well, no,' I said, complimented that Rupert would think I had more than one book in me, and wondering whether to mention my ageing Vietnam manuscript in the bottom drawer. 'Not at the moment anyway,' I said, itching but not game enough to add 'Rupert' like I had written in the book I'd sent him.

'Good,' Rupert replied. 'Now you can do some work for us.'

I felt so hurt by his comment that, unable to come up with a coherent reply, I followed him out of the cubicle and blurted out that the *Australian* wasn't being printed properly in Brisbane: 'The type jumps around before your eyes. It's like seeing double.'

Rupert immediately went to the pile of daily *Australian*s we kept on a sloping, chest-high desk on the other side of the office and examined the pages carefully. I'd better be right. Without looking up he exclaimed: 'He's right!' and the posse of executives stiffened as if called to attention. Ron Richards ran his hand through his thick black hair, staring at me. Rupert swung around. 'Who's responsible for the etching of this paper?'

For some time I had complained to Ron about the quality of the printing of our paper, including creases in the pages printed in Queensland on the *Sunday Sun* presses. Also, readers complained that the ink came off on their hands. But all to no avail. Now I'd unwittingly got him into hot water. After Rupert's visit, I received a letter from Ron: 'Dear Hugh, your complaint on the fold in the *Australian* is quite justified, although I can assure you not a deliberate attempt to sabotage the gems that flow from your typewriter. Steps have been taken to minimise the chances of the faults recurring.'

Like Steve Dunleavy, I seemed to have a talent for starting fights.

9 The dreamboaters

New York journalist Tom Wolfe wrote in 1973 that the one thing never mentioned in books on journalism is that 'in every city, dreamboaters are competing for a tiny crown the rest of the world isn't even aware of: Best Feature Writer in Town.'

In the 1970s, Brisbane seemed to have more than its fair share of dreamboaters.

When I won a third Walkley Award for the best feature writing in Australia in 1979—for a series of articles about Vietnamese refugees—only a couple of people congratulated me, which I couldn't help contrasting with the hundreds who'd phoned the first time. My writing style had been parodied the previous year in an anonymous newspaper produced by some colleagues: 'A grizzled Marine aimed what was left of his face in MY direction... I smiled. I just lifted my weary head. I had just completed a five thousand word piece on ME.'

So I knew I'd become unpopular.

It seems bizarre now that some Brisbane journalists got so upset about my use of 'I' in stories written in the '70s, since so many have used the personal pronoun religiously ever since—including those who parodied me. But, way back then, the correct way to say 'I' in a story in Brisbane, if at all, was to say 'your scribe', or 'this reporter', or 'the free luncher', or 'the cautious commuter', or, most often, 'your correspondent'. Strangely enough, though, my critics didn't seem to mind a large number of English and American columnists at that time (like Michael Parkinson, Mike Royko, Peregrine Worsthorne, Henry Blofeld et al.) writing 'I' hundreds of times a week in Australian newspapers—even while taking money and space off local journalists, and writing about things that were not part of our lives. I guess, as long as the dreamboaters didn't know the writer—didn't see him strolling along Brunswick Street for a moussaka at JP's Cafe—then they didn't mind.

Tom Wolfe had warned that success as a feature writer would lead inevitably to bitterness, envy, resentment and, finally, parody. Wolfe said he read all the parodies of his own writing because: 'At the heart of every parody there is a little gold ball of tribute. Even hostile parodies admit from the start that the target has a distinct voice.'

And I could see that a distinct voice was exactly what a feature writer needed: so the readers could hear it. To me, it was the most natural thing in the world to add some of my own philosophy, thoughts and opinions to stories that had my name on top. In Saigon at the height of the Vietnam War, I often stood at the telex machines and read the outgoing stories of America's and Britain's top war correspondents. I noted that they invariably included what they themselves had seen, and what they concluded was really happening, rather than just quoting some lying general: it's what you have to do when the truths are lies.

Thus in 1979 I won the Walkley for feature writing by describing what shocked me when I arrived in Hong Kong:

It is a sight which no writer on mankind's future—neither Orwell nor Huxley—ever dared predict. Down at the Hong Kong wharves the big tin doors roll back to reveal five warehouses full of people. Gone are the cotton bales, the tobacco leaf, and the tea boxes from

the sprawling concrete floors—replaced by a new commodity, people.
The lofts, which once held soap, now overflow with humans.

In West Papua in 1969, if I had only quoted UN, Indonesian, Dutch
or even Australian officials in my stories for Reuters, no one would
have ever questioned the Act of Free Choice. Which would have
suited everyone, except of course the 800 000 Papuans who were left
alone to be swallowed by Indonesia. And it was no use looking to the
United States to condemn the takeover because it was sucking billions
of dollars out of Irian Jaya from the huge Freeport mine. These
Papuans are still fighting for their independence, with help from a
small band of Australians keeping the issue alive. One of these is
Bondi filmmaker Mark Worth, who interviewed me for a half-hour
documentary, *Act of No Choice,* shown on SBS in 1999: the thirtieth
anniversary of the takeover. The filmmaker, of course, wanted to
know what I saw, what I found, what I felt, what I thought; not what
governments had to say. But, back in the '70s, Brisbane was a city that
believed a journalist should be content merely to quote what a lot of
liars said.

Since opinion polls in a vastly decentralised place like Queensland
were so inaccurate in the '70s, local papers during an election would
basically write: Labor says they will win the election; the Liberals say
they will; and the Nationals say they will. Whereas I predicted who
I thought would win, and why. The *Australian* encouraged this by
sometimes putting my name in the posters that are put on the street
outside newagencies to advertise that day's paper: 'LUNN ON ALP'S
FUTURE' or 'HUGH LUNN: HOW QLD VOTING WORKS'.
Editors started ordering first-person stories: 'Go down the Gold Coast
and write what it's like to live in a building full of millionaires'; 'Write
a piece on what it's like living through the Brisbane blackouts'; 'Go
to all the other capital cities and write what a Queenslander thinks
of them'.

When the beautiful Fraser Island was going to be further sand-
mined—unless the 1978 Federal Investigative Commission into the

island's future found against it—I didn't hesitate to put myself into the story to help save the largest sand island in the world. I'd written several full-page anti-mining articles about Fraser Island over a number of years—one of which attracted a letter-to-the-Editor from Spike Milligan in London supporting the cause. There were some unpleasant consquences. A forester's wife shouted abuse at me during the Investigative Commission's tour, and sandminers addressed me as 'the Conservation Editor' which, back in the '70s, was considered the biggest put-down possible. But the *Oz* backed me all the way in this campaign. Best Editor had named Fraser Island advocate John Sinclair 1976 Australian of the Year, flying me back from a job in Adelaide to write the three-thousand-word article justifying his selection.

The Investigative Commission arrived on subtropical Fraser Island in mid-winter, with only the *Courier-Mail*'s Bob Johnston and the infamous (but sensible and intelligent) union advocate Pat Mackie, wearing his trademark red baseball cap, to cheer us up. The public was invited to attend, but because of the isolation, Pat was the sole member of the public to turn up. He had read my Fraser Island stories while working as a house painter in Sydney. The inquiry started on the island, with about thirty people including the two federal commissioners, four specialist assistants, two secretaries, plus conservation groups, foresters, sandminers, 'the public' and the press. Comrade Dave May took photos for the *Australian*. It was July and the sand looked dull, the water bleak, the sky grey. I worried that the two commissioners would think the island not worth saving for the world. So, to demonstrate how idyllic it truly was for ten months of the year, I stripped down to my underpants at beautiful Eli Creek (which was in a sandmining lease) in front of the commissioners and their assisting scientists. 'You've got to imagine it's a hundred degrees,' I told them, and dived into the freezing waters. I wanted to show them the thrill when the rush of deep fresh water—filtered through mountainous sandhills—carries you swimming downhill ('like Shane Gould!' I yelled) through twists and turns, to emerge eventually on the 150-kilometre white surf beach. Then, for a bit of further pressure on the

Commission, I wrote a story in the *Oz* about the swim. Thus, I was glad to read, years later, that Tom Wolfe thought feature writing had nothing to do with being objective or subjective: it was a matter of 'personality and style'…about avoiding a 'droning beige voice'.

The dreamboaters parodied this Fraser Island story too, and of course the pro-mining Bjelke-Petersen government didn't like it either. The Liberal (later National) Party member for Maryborough, Gilbert Allison, got up in Parliament and said the article was a:

> …wretched little piece by a so-called journalist named Hugh Lunn. I do not intend to waste much time on him. Apparently he stripped to his Y-fronts—whatever they are—to help stop mining on Fraser Island. From time to time I have read this gentleman's articles in the *Australian*, mostly with disgust…I would suggest to Mr Lunn that he hang up his Y-fronts and his pencil. He is not worth two bob.

Poison-pen letters typed on newspaper copy paper started to arrive regularly. More worrying, they were copied to the Editor of the *Australian*. One was addressed 'Poet Laureate, Sir, Mr President, Name-dropper Extraordinary, Master Journalist Lunn'! It said: 'You already know your giant-sized ego and blatant attempts at self-glorification in your stories and private life have made you the biggest joke on legs… Your old dad, who makes a living selling meat pies without meat, must be real proud of his offspring.'

I was in danger of becoming bad friends with everybody.

Diane Cilento—famous for her brilliant international film career and less so for being married to James Bond (Sean Connery) and being a novelist—returned to her home town to star onstage in *The Taming of the Shrew* in 1975 but I was unable to arrange an interview. Knowing that Diane had been raised in the Brisbane suburb of Annerley, I approached her at the theatre: 'Hi Diane, I'm Hugh Lunn from Annerley Junction.' She then chatted freely for my article.

Two years later, Diane was back in town but not talking: which is the quickest way to get the media interested. Told to get an interview, I drove around to Glen Road, Toowong, to her mother's house, which was two metres above the ground on stumps like most old Queensland homes. Dr Phyllis Cilento answered the door. No, Diane was not in—which was technically true. On the way out I peeked under the house, and there was blonde Diane leaning against a house stump in the shade admiring the Brisbane River.

I'd caught her out, but she was cool.

'Oh,' Diane said, 'it's the lovely Hugh Lunn. You fellows must have a sixth sense. I just got here.' I quoted this remark in the story, and was surprised at the derision from some colleagues.

There are dreamboaters in every town and city in the world. In London, the target was John Pilger—the Aussie in short sleeves I'd encountered at the London *Daily Mirror*. His distinguished writing merely caused English colleagues to coin the phrase 'to Pilger' which made it into the Oxford English Dictionary: until Pilger took action and it was removed.

I might have got away with my writing style if I hadn't long since stopped drinking in the Empire Hotel with everyone else. Adrian McGregor and I had started spending lunch hours in a snooker hall in Wickham Street and then, when the first computer game arrived, we'd stand on the footpath putting in twenty-cent pieces and playing computer ping-pong. Like me, Adrian didn't enjoy leaning on the bar in the pub and watching his money, mind and time go up in a cloud of smoke. He had done all that back in Sydney at the Journalists' Club where, he said, reporters would simply ignore the loudspeakers booming: 'Would all *Sunday Australian* staff please return to duty immediately.' Over lunch we talked of Rugby League and Rugby Union matches we had played. I loved the one Adrian told every few years about how he'd scored a try in a match at school and, when the referee disallowed it, he'd burst into tears. And the one where he broke another player's jaw.

We got around so much together that people used to mix us up: both when we played competition doubles and when we took evening journalism tutorials after work at Queensland University.

Adrian, since escaping Sydney, was more interested in fitness—

anaerobic and aerobic. His knowledge of physiology was a hell of a lot of help when we were selected for the University of Queensland's inter-varsity tennis team to compete at Sydney University. When neither of us could get out of bed after six sets of competition singles and doubles in one day, I groaned: 'I'm rooted Adrian. I'm stuffed. I can't possibly play another set.'

'Yeah,' said Adrian, 'you're suffering lactic acid build-up.'

This interest and knowledge led inevitably to Adrian's ground-breaking, record-making 1987 book *King Wally*, which proved to publishers that Rugby League fans do read books (something publishers hadn't believed until then). After that he was asked to write biographies of Greg Chappell and Cathy Freeman. Adrian really knew how to write a feature and I'll always remember how he segued from my mercurial tennis mate Ken Fletcher's flashy forehand to his gambling lifestyle: 'Fletcher lived his life much as he played his forehand...'

Once, a couple of dreamboaters came to see me, like a delegation, and said I should come down to the pub like everyone else: 'You can just drink Claytons if you like,' one said, as an apparent generous concession. I replied that I didn't enjoy the whole tiled pub scene, and the last time I'd been in the Empire, a dreamboater, like me in his mid-thirties, had come up and said: 'I can out-write you any day of the week, Lunny.'

In *Time* magazine more than a decade later—October 1992 to be precise—Ken Edwards profiled me as an author, saying that journalists in my office had once 'filed the letter "I" off Hugh Lunn's typewriter'. This never happened, but it's another wonderful apocryphal story. Edwards, a softly spoken former Brisbane journalist, worked in the *Sunday Sun* building back in the '70s. He mentioned the Valley's Empire Hotel, 'where the decor was nouveau hospital ward', saying journalists arrived there in shifts from next door 'to joke, flirt, brag and snipe'. He went on:

One favoured target, mostly in his absence, was Hugh Lunn... The complaint repeated until it came to sound like an extended version of his name: 'Who-the-hell-cares-what-Hugh-Lunn-thinks?' Lunn's supposed sin came down to one letter: 'I'. Lunn was using it in his stories, writing as though he actually had an opinion, as though he had been there during the interview. The bloody ego of the man.

It hadn't helped that at one stage in 1976 I had been given the management boardroom in the *Sunday Sun* building as my personal office. Our bureau had become more and more of a sweatshop as windows were shut off by the creation of individual executive offices along a windowed wall. There was no airconditioning, and no one would open the few windows left because of the noise from passing trucks off the Story Bridge. The poet Judith Wright came in to see me one stinking summer day when some of the windows were open. With her increasing deafness she couldn't hear me, and, with ears damaged from loud explosions in the Vietnam War, I couldn't hear her, so I never did find out what story she had to tell. On such summer days I sat and typed in singlet and bare feet because of the humidity, which Judith Wright didn't appear to notice.

Since no one else was interested in protesting, I wrote off a memo to Quiet Editor in Sydney quoting from Jacob Bronowski's *The Ascent of Man* about poor working conditions during the Industrial Revolution: 'It showed a heartless, mindless contempt for those who worked there. A squalid indifference for the health of the workers.' I pointed out that the Sydney office was airconditioned, as was our Melbourne office, over a thousand miles to the south. Quiet Editor took immediate action, but, instead of fixing the problem for everyone, I was moved into the airconditioned boardroom: the best office—with the only bar—in the building.

Ron Richards would visit, sit at the huge oval timber table with his right foot resting on his left knee; look around at the large windows, the bookshelves, the hat stand, the bar fridge, and shake his head: 'If it were up to me, you know I'd turf you out of here quick smart.' That was what I loved about Ron: the way he told me to my face what everyone else in the building was thinking. But Ron really wasn't too worried. Like me, he knew my tenure in this grand room couldn't last. I was cocooned there just long enough to annoy some of those who hadn't complained about their poor working conditions.

At the end of the '70s, a famous Melbourne-based journalist known to all as 'Crazy Horse' edited our *Weekend Magazine*. I often wondered about the nickname, until I met him. Crazy Horse looked, with his thick black hair and impressive large sculptured face, just like those actors who played the handsome 'Red Indian Chief' in Hollywood westerns in the 1950s. And he was outlandish. He was, after all, the Aussie who, when working for the London *Daily Mail* in 1959, was the first journalist to make phone contact with the Dalai Lama after his Holiness fled to India when China invaded Tibet. The entire *Daily Mail* newsroom fell silent as Crazy Horse yelled excitedly into the phone: 'The Dalai Lama? Is that the Dalai Lama?...Yes?...Well this is the *Dalai Mail*!'

One day, I confided to Crazy Horse—when he asked me to write a personal adventure story—that for the first time in my life some colleagues despised me, and that Brisbane dreamboaters were parodying my style. I wanted to know what the old war horse thought. Maybe, being so experienced, he would provide some mystical advice: like a medicine man.

Crazy Horse replied: 'You don't care do you?'

10 The parochialism of Sydney

Rupert wasn't getting things all his own way either. From mid-1972 until 1987, Rupert had great difficulty expanding in Australia, caught as he was between the giant Melbourne-based Herald and Weekly Times group and the super-rich Sydney Fairfax family. These two huge multimedia groups were able to close out Rupert because, between them, they controlled all of the richest and most influential daily newspapers in Australia. This was why Rupert, so hemmed-in here, had left to expand in England and the United States. Unlike me, Rupert was not one to sit and wait for things to change.

During the 1970s it was almost possible, within Australia, to feel sorry for Rupert Murdoch. He first attempted *Finance Week*, a money magazine that was two decades ahead of its time—appearing long before compulsory superannuation and privatisation of national institutions gave well-off Australians investment headaches. *Finance Week* soon folded and was never mentioned in polite circles again. Next, Rupert's ambitious and elegant *Sunday Australian*, which employed a dozen of Australia's best feature writers, folded after less than two years. Then, in 1974, his Brisbane *Oz* wrap-around disappeared after two years because it was no match for the traditional might of the Herald-controlled *Courier-Mail* in its home city.

Rupert tried a couple of times in the '70s to start a free colour magazine to be given away with his *Weekend Australian*. But, while these free magazines worked well in quality newspapers in England, they did not succeed in the *Oz* until Rupert's third or fourth try in 1988—twenty-four years after the *Australian* started. Of course, by then Rupert owned the *Times* and *Sunday Times* in London and could cheaply re-use features and material from the *Sunday Times* colour magazine: such as *Culture Vulture*, even though the culture we were getting was English or American.

Unfortunately, I was the person charged with writing the cover story for both the first and second failed Saturday *Oz* colour magazines.

Late in 1974, *Oz* features editor Nic Nagle rang and told me of Rupert's exciting plan. It was strictly hush-hush, to catch the Herald and Fairfax groups on the hop. Rupert, Nic said, wanted a five-thousand-word beautifully written article to kick-start his latest creation. It was to be 'written about something that deserves national focus; something dear to the heart of the nation; something Australians have all heard of, but know little about; something really big; something that will look spectacular in full colour'. Thus it was decided to do 'the effects of tourism on the Great Barrier Reef'—which fell to me because it was within Queensland's massive boundaries. In a panic, I pointed out that the Great Barrier Reef is much, much bigger than people in Sydney imagine: 'Two thousand kilometres long and at least 160 kilometres wide—twice the area of England, and almost all under water'. It would be difficult to get quickly from one island to another; I would have to return each time to the mainland and fly, or drive, to the next jump-off point.

I was being especially cagey this time, because sometime previously a Sydney editor, on receiving one of those crazy stories from over-seas—'Colonel Gaddafi's Libyan guerrillas are thought to be training on Australia's Great Barrier Reef'—had rung me very, very excited and said, 'Hugh! Ring up the Great Barrier Reef and find out what's going on!'

Nic Nagle, being much more sensible, understood the problem. 'Take as long as you like,' he said. 'But don't break the bank.'

I started at the southern end of the reef with a four-hour boat trip from Gladstone out to Heron Island, which is so different from the mainland that you feel you might well be on the Moon. I hired goggles and flippers and swam underwater out along a two-hundred-metre channel, which, I'd heard, had been dynamited through the coral to make it easy to bring in the tourist boats, thus changing the tide speed. Since it was undercover work, I slipped silently under the ocean and wrote that the channel was 'like a deep scar. Broken coral pieces lie like dog bones along the sandy bottom...one tiny staghorn coral, the only regrowth, struggles up through the sand'.

Five islands and sixteen hundred kilometres of mainland later, I finished with a stopover at Lizard Island, north-east of Cooktown— running over hills to the scientific station and then back across to the tourist resort to get some interviews before the plane departed, disturbing as I went dozens of two-metre-long lizards which scuttled off noisily into the scrub. I had chosen Lizard because it was here that Captain Cook climbed the island's mountain to see his way out of the barrier of reefs. This was also where lone woman Mrs Mary Watson perished with her baby, Ferrier, in 1881. A few years later, I went back to Lizard on another story, and followed in both Mrs Watson's and Captain Cook's footsteps, and near perished myself—I'll tell this story when I get to it, if I can fit it in.

After more than two weeks away, and after a week of writing my first cover story for a colour magazine, I typed my conclusion: that the colours of the Great Barrier Reef sure beat neon signs. Then I rang Nic to say that the deed was done. 'Oh! Didn't anyone tell you?' Nic said. 'The colour magazine was canned two weeks ago! Not enough advertisers were attracted to the concept.' Too used to news-papers, I accepted this without complaint, though I was very disappointed. Nic ran my story as a normal feature, but then the newly formed Australian Conservation Foundation bought the story from the *Oz* and republished it in their brand new colour magazine, *Habitat*. So it made a colour magazine after all.

About three years later, Rupert had another go at an *Oz* colour magazine. This time six weekly editions appeared before it folded. For the first edition, this time they chose the Gold Coast. Nic Nagle was long gone, and rather than one big article, the editor wanted seven smaller ones on different angles. After a week traipsing around as a stranger in paradise I still hadn't come up with a seventh story. So I decided to do a creative writing job: to go to the top of a high-rise apartment block and describe the Gold Coast from up there, since most people only ever see Australia's most famous beach city from down among the thongs. One of these massive buildings in Surfers Paradise was unusual in that it was round, so I went up there. It was called 'Focus', and from on top I described the view way out to sea, out over the hinterland, and up and down the golden strip of beaches and islands.

When the new colour magazine appeared, I was flabbergasted to read in my story that I was no longer writing from on top of the round Focus building, but from on top of a nearby rectangular block of brand new apartments! Inside the magazine was a double-page colour advertisement for the apartment block that I had supposedly been on. So I bolted around to advertising and accosted the acting manager.

'You changed my story,' I said angrily.

He smiled and nodded triumphantly, as if I were praising him. 'Well what's it matter which building you were on? The view's the same from them all,' he replied.

'But you changed my story to get that ad,' I said. 'That's not how newspapers work; advertisers can't change editorial.' He smiled at me as if he felt sorry for someone who was so naive. 'Not only that,' I said, pointing. 'Someone inserted a line into my story that said I could see Brisbane from on top! There's absolutely no way you can see

Brisbane from on top of a Gold Coast apartment block. Ever hear of Mt Cotton?'

The advertising man smiled again, as if he had the answer, and turned to an older, smaller salesman sitting next to a window. 'Tom [or whatever his name was], tell me, for six thousand dollars worth of advertising can you see Gold Coast apartment buildings out of that window?' Tom stood up and, for effect, shaded his eyes and squinted south towards the pub across the road, the Hacienda.

'Yes. Lots of tall skyscrapers,' said Tom. 'And wow! Look at those bikini girls on the beach at Surfers Paradise!'

If Rupert thought he had problems squeezed between two powerful old established conservative newspaper firms, then what about me, squeezed by a succession of Sydney editors, most of whom knew very little about the northern half of the country and weren't in a hurry to leave the pleasant foreshores of Sydney Harbour to find out. One Sydney editor, an Englishman, would proudly announce he was 'coming down to Brisbane': what map was he using?

Whenever a cyclone appeared on the horizon, the Sydney office went berserk. They invariably rang in a panic to say a cyclone was 'headed for' some major town. Perhaps because a cyclone has an eye and, back then, a woman's name, Sydney editors succumbed to anthropomorphism and thought cyclones knew where they were going. Anyone who knows anything about cyclones—and has seen the maps of their paths, which look like tangled string—knows that they don't 'head' for anywhere. Cyclones career wildly around like a blown-up balloon let loose, and therefore mostly miss the coast—while the resultant publicity ruins the summer for all tourist operators within a thousand kilometres. Also, cyclones largely lose their destructive wind power before reaching Brisbane because the ocean isn't warm enough this far south; floods and thunderstorms are the destructive forces that hit Brisbane—but try telling that to a Sydney editor.

In 1972 Cyclone Daisy was 'headed' for Bundaberg, about three hundred kilometres north of Brisbane, and was due to hit in three hours. An editor rang, very excited, to say I should get to Bundaberg and be there when the cyclone hit. 'We want a blow-by-blow description of what it's like to be in the eyes [*sic*] of one of these cyclones,' he said, adding with great fanfare that—as luck would have it—we could get to Bundaberg because an *Oz* photographer was up in Brisbane from Sydney and he OWNED A FOUR-WHEEL DRIVE! I didn't bother telling this bloke it was a bitumen highway all the way to Bundaberg. I just said we would leave immediately: but he should know that we would not get there for four hours.

'It's that far north then?'

'Yes.'

'Look, I'll tell you what. Charlie Wright's still in Townsville! [He was packing to leave.] Get him to drive down from there then.'

Townsville, of course, is more than three times further from Bundaberg than Brisbane is, so I checked with the airlines and was amazed to find a Fokker Friendship flight was about to leave for Bundaberg via Maryborough. No, it hadn't been cancelled. Why?

Photographer Comrade Dave May and I just made it to the airport in time for our second big cyclone in a year.

The winds were so fierce over Maryborough that the cane fields below were flat. Each time the pilot tried to land into the wind we rose like an eagle catching an updraught. So the pilot decided to land with the wind. But we approached so fast that he overshot. This was some Fokker. From my aisle seat I could see the pilot pointing left above his co-pilot, who was pointing over him to the right: for someone who'd lost his taste for flying it wasn't a good flight to be on. Meanwhile, our air hostess was strapped in a seat and bawling her eyes out. But the pilot, unfortunately now minus the peaked cap that inspires so much confidence in passengers, and with his white shirt unbuttoned to the waist, finally got us down. He ran into the terminal to the public phone, inserted some coins and started to heatedly argue with his head office in Sydney. No, he wasn't getting back in that Fokker. He didn't care if that Fokker was worth ten million dollars. No! But he did, and got that valuable aeroplane up and out of there and headed back to Brisbane, while we stayed because we'd accidentally found our cyclone.

David May, Eric Donnelly, the Eagle and I heard that Hervey Bay—thirty kilometres away on the coast—was bearing the brunt, so we headed there in a hire car.

We were really zooming along thinking how powerful that little car was. We passed a house with no verandah and then a parked car with a sheet of corrugated iron stuck through the roof like a dagger. Then a tree further up the highway twisted around and snapped off three metres up the trunk. Trees lined both sides of the highway to Hervey Bay and all were twisting viciously. There was no way through. We turned back, whereupon Comrade May realised why we had been zooming along on our way out: the wind was so strong that the front wheels were now lifting and steering was difficult. We found a motel and booked into a room with a radio, a TV and a phone: everything we needed to cover the story safely. Then a large pine tree fell over and we had nothing: just a couple of candles that Comrade May was smart enough to bring along. So we ended up making a two-hundred-metre dash on foot to the post office, past downed electricity lines, to send gram photos and phone stories.

Flamboyant Editor, the one who liked shirts, particularly loved cyclones. 'Cyclones. Cyclones. Everyone loves a cyclone. We want a full-page feature on cyclones,' he said in 1971. So I interviewed Brisbane Weather Bureau boss Arch Shields.

'Why do you want to write about cyclones?' Arch said. 'Why not write about the flood that's going to devastate this city one day?'

'Look, Mr Shields,' I said, 'you don't know much about newspapers do you? When the Editor wants cyclones, you must give him cyclones. That's why he's Editor.'

Little did I realise I was making a huge mistake and missing the real story. But my family had lived in or near Brisbane all their lives and we'd never heard of any giant floods. A few creeks, maybe. And always the Rocklea underpass. But that was it. Not ten thousand homes under the Brisbane River as was to happen in January 1974.

A few days later I rang Sydney to say I'd finished the three thousand words on cyclones just hours before the deadline. 'We've had a big storm in Sydney. Cars have been flooded!' said Flamboyant Editor. 'Can you stay away from the cyclone angle and give us more of an "east coast storms" angle. Storms, storms! Everyone's talking storms!'

As soon as the Brisbane flood hit in 1974, I went in search of Arch Shields to belatedly ask how he knew. Shields said Brisbane had had two much higher floods in 1893. 'That sort of event was certain to recur; the only question was when,' he said.

A public servant who was not afraid to speak out, Arch Shields opposed the closure of Somerset Dam to let the Brisbane floodwaters recede. 'If another cyclone comes down the coast and dumps its rain in the Brisbane catchment we will need to have the dam empty,' he warned. But the politicians decided to keep the dam full so that the Brisbane floodwaters receded more quickly—and they were highly praised for it.

'Full dams hold no water,' was all Arch Shields said of their decision.

A week later, while Somerset Dam was still full to overflowing, a giant cyclone wandered down the coast, but missed Brisbane. 'Two degrees west and we might have lost that dam,' Arch Shields said. 'The water would have spilled, say, five metres deep over the top of the dam and could have gouged out the sides. Dams are a problem for a river like the Brisbane because politicians want to keep them full so people can water their lawns.'

Nowadays, every time I read that there is good news because rain has filled Brisbane's dams, I remember what Arch Shields said. And I particularly remember his observation: 'From a hydrologist's point of view a lot of Brisbane people are living *in* the river not *on* the river.' His team knew from computer models just how big a flood Brisbane could theoretically get. But he refused to tell me. 'You'll frighten people,' he said.

The parochialism of Sydney had to be experienced to be believed.

'Please describe how the sandmining equipment dominates the land-scape on Fraser Island,' said a features editor's telex message. Didn't he realise that Fraser Island was 150 kilometres long and up to thirty kilometres wide with rain forests and mountainous sand dunes?

In 1973 I thought I was onto a really good story. The new Whitlam government had allocated a large amount of seed money to get Australians writing more books. I noticed that of the eighty-two government grants, only two had gone to people living in Queensland, which had one-sixth of the population. And these were the two least valuable.

'But where's the story there?' said the Sydney news editor, whose nickname was 'Rat'. 'You'd expect that wouldn't you?'

Well, Rat, no actually.

When I heard that graziers at Taroom—five hours drive north-west of Brisbane back then—were shooting their cattle because Australia's overseas beef market had collapsed in the mid-'70s under Whitlam, I suggested I drive out there with Comrade May in the ageing, yellow, four-cylinder office Renault 16TS and describe what was happening. Next day the Editor rang from Sydney to say he had heard at a Melbourne cocktail party that Brunette Downs, one of the biggest and richest cattle properties in the country, was also suffering. 'While you're so far west out at Taroom, slip over to Brunette Downs in the Northern Territory and check that out too.'

Slip over to Brunette Downs? Back then I would have needed a Land Rover and enough petrol, water and supplies to make a week's journey through western Queensland and deep into the Territory. It was like asking a reporter in London to slip over in an old car to Siberia in the middle of a winter freeze. After consulting a map, we drove back to Brisbane from Taroom and I caught a jet two hours to Mt Isa, jumped a small plane to Tennant Creek, then hired a single-engined aircraft to Brunette Downs where, at first, we couldn't land because of the kangaroos on the airstrip. The quickest way home from there was a flight to Katherine, then Darwin, and a four-hour Boeing jet to Brisbane. No doubt the Editor wondered why I was absent for so long.

When news broke that the Whitlam government had wasted three million dollars on a turtle-farming scheme in the Torres Strait, I was told to get up to the turtle farm and interview the Scotsman behind the scheme, a Dr Robert Bustard. In four years no turtles had been sold; no marketing scheme had been set up. Now Dr Bustard had been summoned to the national capital to explain what had happened to the money, but he had elected not to go; instead, he said, he was returning home to Scotland the next day.

There were a few minor problems to face. Dr Bustard's turtle headquarters were on Darnley Island, two hundred kilometres north-east of Thursday Island. I could get to Cairns that day (Cairns is further from Brisbane than is Melbourne), but there was no flight to Thursday Island until the next day, and by the time it got there Dr Bustard would have departed for Scotland.

'Well, catch a ferry then!' said an editor. He had no idea that Thursday Island was a little bit further away from Cairns than Manly was from Circular Quay—eight hundred kilometres further away in fact. Hobart was closer to Brisbane than Thursday Island, and much easier to get to. Of course, from Thursday Island I still had to get to Darnley Island and the turtle farm.

So, I stayed in Brisbane and read a book written by Dr Bustard to find out what sort of man the Australian government had given three million dollars: a man who'd promised that by 1980 he would be farming 150 000 green turtles in a twelve million dollar industry. I was thus able to reveal to Canberra that the man they had invested in was not only more than three thousand kilometres, or a week's travel, away from Canberra, he was the sort of person who particularly hated crabs. 'Those cold, characterless, automatons,' was how he described them in his book.

But, at the same time, Dr Bustard was also the sort of person who loved turtles, which he said were like pet cats: 'not responsive animals like dogs, but rather independently minded creatures'.

Perhaps that's why he couldn't farm them.

The Torres Strait is a little-known area of Australia that contains sixteen thousand square kilometres of sea and at least a dozen populated islands. Because Australia's border there extends right up to the mudflats of New Guinea, in the 1970s there were a couple of attempts by Australian governments to move the border south to halfway across Torres Strait. This led to political battles and constitutional arguments that continued for years because Queensland opposed moving the frontier south, saying that this was Queensland's sovereign border, something the federation of Australia had no right to move.

A party of journalists and public servants travelled through the Strait in a small wooden fishing boat with Premier Bjelke-Petersen on his 'border not change' tour. We watched as the islanders, who were very keen to stay part of Australia, hailed Joh as a hero. Gough Whitlam's government wanted to change the border as part of granting independence to Papua New Guinea in 1975. But Bjelke-Petersen was to win that fight with a line even the erudite Whitlam could not match. Joh told islander leaders: 'By Jove, I'm not going to get political, but you can't trust the ALP.'

After Whitlam failed to change the border, in 1976 the new Prime Minister, Malcolm Fraser, visited the Torres Strait islands—and this time we travelled around the islands in a large ship, the HMAS *Moreton*. Canberra may have had more money than the State government, but they knew less about this area than almost anyone in Queensland. Those travelling on this tour were urged, among other things, to 'bring a woollen jumper', something you would never, ever need in the Torres Strait.

Malcolm Fraser met with all the islander leaders—dispensing with his trousers to wrap a lava-lava around his waist—thinking he could change their view on the border by carefully explaining that what was proposed by Canberra was merely 'a line in the sand, a border on the sea bed' which they wouldn't even see. To which a local leader, George Mye, who was as tall as Fraser, stood and replied: 'But Prime Minister, we are afraid your border will rise up to the surface, and then up to the sky.'

It says much about Australia that the Australian government was never able to change Queensland's border with New Guinea even though, throughout the '70s, journalists and media advisers, public servants both State and federal, Papuans and islanders, and premiers and prime ministers all argued over this invisible sea border.

Rupert, of course, had long since realised that sovereign perimeters were a thing of the past; that borders no longer mattered in a frightening new world without frontiers, and without limits.

11 Was it a fair cow?

One of the problems with being a reporter is you never know where your next big story is coming from. Working for Rupert helped me overcome this tension because Best Editor, driving me around Sydney in his small yellow Japanese car, told me to stop fretting: 'Rupert doesn't employ highly paid journalists to write the big stories. He says that anyone can write the big stories. What we need are people who can write the ordinary stories.'

The more I thought about this, the truer I could see it was. Anyone could write about a jumbo crash, because the story would write itself: 'Four hundred people are dead and ten missing after a 747 jumbo jet plunged in a fiery ball into a nearby forest on take-off from such-and-such airport last night.' Thus I spent most of my years on the *Australian* following Rupert's dictum—trying to find the ordinary Queensland stories and make them interesting for the nation.

I had learnt a lot about writing stories while working for Reuters: write what you see rather than what you are told; don't touch a cliché with a ten-foot pole; always try to capture the nature of the event. And state the circumstances under which a statement is made: Was it in answer to an unexpected question in a doorway? Was it a prepared statement read out by someone's lawyer at a press conference? Was the tennis match played on a fast grass surface or on slow clay? And, because I looked mostly for the stories others weren't writing, I tried not to rely on the score of set-up announcements put out every day by pressure groups, politicians and companies seeking—and mostly getting—publicity: it's one reason why every TV channel has the same twenty stories on the six o'clock news each night.

In 1971 a University of Queensland philosophy lecturer warned that overpopulation 'roughly adds up to a disaster of a major kind'. When I heard that he had six children himself, I went to see the bearded academic, 43-year-old Dr Peter Wertheim, at his Chapel Hill house hidden among lots of trees and bushes on a large block of land. He had just finished dinner with his children, aged six to 13. While the kids did the washing- and wiping-up, Dr Wertheim explained that he hadn't thought about the problem of overpopulation when he and his wife were having their family. 'Of course we have the children now, and I can't describe the pleasure I get from them, but if I knew what I know now I doubt if we would have had anything like this number,' he said as the six kids swarmed around. It was only later that he had come across the problem of overpopulation 'by accident'. 'I'm astounded that it was possible for me to get an education in Australia without finding out the problems facing spaceship earth,' he said.

It was lucky that Peter Wertheim didn't find out about zero population growth earlier, because the pretty, dark-haired little girl wiping-up at the sink that night, Margaret, went on to become a rare human being: a scientist who could communicate worldwide. She hosts and writes the American PBS network's *Faith and Reason* in Los Angeles and wrote, among other things, *Pythagoras' Trousers*, a book which took science to the masses and made a much bigger splash in the *Australian* than my story on her father did back in 1971.

On Rupert's paper there was more than the usual amount of pressure to come up with interesting and different stories every day. Newspapers around the world have a news editor whose highly paid job it is to watch for, and allocate, stories. But, because the *Australian* covered an entire continent, State writers had to come up with their own story ideas. To a news editor, a story was just 'one quick phone call', but the left ear I'd burnt as a six-year-old got very sore every day while on the telephone looking for ordinary stories.

It was tough enough dealing with just one news editor, but once, early in the 1970s, a strange situation arose where the *Oz* had three news editors at once. It was one of those surreal times, like that time a few minutes before the official launch of the *Sunday Australian* when an editor addressed reporters: 'Rupert is coming to the launch, and he doesn't like people with beards or suede shoes.' The reporters looked around the newsroom at each other—at David Evans, at Chris Forsyth, at Adrian McGregor, at Arnold Earnshaw et al.—and it quickly dawned that every reporter in the room had a beard and suede shoes! As it turned out, Rupert didn't seem to mind.

When I realised that three different men in Sydney were claiming to be the news editor of the *Australian*, I said to one of them, the best over all the years, George Williams, 'But that's like having three Popes!'

'Yeah, well just remember that I'm the one who's infallible today,' George replied.

This sort of competition for promotion was called 'creative tension'. So, for a few mad weeks, I was phoned each day by each of the three news editors, each allocating his own stories, and each telling me to address all stories only to him. After George, the second news editor sent me a telex saying: 'I'm here from 7.00 a.m. until midnight every day of the week, so ring me at any time.' The third rang and said: 'It's your turn. What have you got for me?'

Not surprisingly, there was a faster turnover of news editors than of Editors. Mostly, the news editor was obsessed with the need for a long list of stories for the 11.00 a.m. news conference. He was expected to have the full list of stories for that day, even though it was rare for anything much to have happened by that time of morning. Conference was attended by all the section editors on the paper and conducted by the Editor. Personally, I thought this conference system—though used around the world—put everyone in a straightjacket for the rest of the day, whether they realised it or not. And it imposed the current Editor's will right down the line. To me, it's a system of bulk thought where everyone picks up the Editor's view on every issue, and he or she soon gets an idea of each section head's beliefs and opinions.

Every new Editor, and every new news editor, had a different idea of what made a story—and who could argue, since news is, like beauty, in the eye of the beholder. Change the Editor and you can bet that a story that would previously have made page one will rate one sentence on page nine. Few stories are big enough for everyone to agree that they are page one material.

But what if you get two such big stories on the same day?

When I first started on the *Sunday Australian*, one Saturday evening two really big stories (for the time) broke: Princess Anne fell off her horse, and an Australian biscuit millionairess went missing. Both of these stories combined the perfect elements for Australian editors: English royalty and horseflesh, food and money. After much angst, our first edition came out with Princess Anne on top of page one and the missing biscuit woman underneath. However, over at the opposition Sydney *Sun-Herald*, their first edition appeared with the millionairess on top and Princess Anne underneath. Both Editors saw each other's first edition, and both Editors then reversed the two stories for their home edition.

The one type of story I could be sure would always appeal to our paper's bulk thought was one involving a beautiful woman. In 1975 I got to interview Papuan separatist leader Josephine Abaijah just because she was exquisitely photogenic. Conference loved that one, but got even more excited when I found out that Bettina Arndt, the good-looking 24-year-old psychologist who advised people on their sex problems on radio and TV, had been banned from live broadcasts by the Australian Broadcasting Control Board. The *Oz* adored the photo of Bettina in a tiny mini-skirt.

Stories without beautiful women were much more difficult to pick. When I worked as a casual on the London *Mirror* in mid-1965 I was watching a late-night TV talk show about censorship on the stage. Suddenly, a playwright being interviewed said: 'Well, to some people, the word "fuck" should be censored, but…' He was interrupted by the host who tossed his clipboard away saying: 'Well thanks a lot. That's the end of my TV career.' I flipped over backwards across the bed I was sitting on—remember this was thirty-four years before that word was heard on Australian TV. No one had ever uttered such a word on television before, even in Swinging London, so I rang the *Mirror*'s night editor. But I was a 24-year-old Aussie casual, not even on staff, so he didn't think there was a story in it. Two days later 'THAT WORD ON TV!' was the front-page lead of every Fleet Street paper.

Another night I noticed that the BBC had accidentally edited out a rare English goal in a soccer international against Poland. Again I rang the *Mirror* news desk, and again the story was ignored until it became big news elsewhere the next day. Then, of course, it became headlines in the *Mirror* too.

By contrast, in 1974 I missed a major scoop on Senator Vince Gair's planned resignation to become Ambassador to Ireland to give Prime Minister Gough Whitlam the numbers in the Senate: a plan foiled by Premier Bjelke-Petersen, who issued the writs for the Senate election before Gair had time to actually resign. (Gair was deliberately kept busy eating his favourite tiger prawns while the election writs were drawn up and signed by the Queensland Governor. This meant the election had begun before Gair had vacated his seat, and Labor's chance to regain control of the Senate was lost.)

Not knowing that Whitlam had already secretly agreed to appoint Gair to Dublin, I rang the DLP senator on another matter at his Annerley Road home a few days before the story broke. 'Hugh Lunn here, Senator,' I said. 'From the *Australian* newspaper.'

'Ah no!' Senator Gair said. 'You mean Hughie Lunn from Mary Immaculate Convent.' Senator Gair's son, Paul, had been in my Mary Immaculate Rugby League First Thirteen in the early 1950s, and Gair—then Premier of Queensland—had driven us to footy matches.

So, now that he had remembered me so fondly, I was in a great position: and Gair wasn't letting me down. The conservative senator said of the Liberal's new national Opposition Leader, Billy Snedden—a leader Gair was automatically expected to support—'That Snedden, Hughie, he's such a bloody lightweight he wouldn't make footprints in a cushion.'

'Geez, Senator,' I said, as I carefully wrote that down—realising that it was a front-page story—and framed my next question, which was to be: 'Are you thinking of voting with Whitlam then?' But Gair stopped me in my tracks: 'You know better than to blaspheme, Lunn. You were taught better than that by the Josephite nuns and the Christian Brothers. Goodbye, sir,' and he hung up. It didn't seem to matter, until a few days later when the story broke of his secret deal with Whitlam.

News editor Chris Forsyth taught me a valuable lesson about how to write seemingly ordinary news stories. Police had found a skeleton in a house at Slade Point, near Mackay. It was of a 51-year-old man who had died without anyone missing him. Newspapers in Queensland merely recorded the finding, but Chris Forsyth realised the potential and told me to write six hundred words. I rang Forsyth back and explained that there was no plane to Mackay until the next day. 'Don't go to Mackay!' he said. 'Just sit down at a typewriter and write the story in twenty-five minutes.' And he hung up. Annoyed, I got a clock, put it on my desk and decided to teach him a valuable lesson by sending whatever I had written in twenty-five minutes. I began:

A man can die in his bed in Australia and not be missed.

Ron Mackay, 51, proved that this week when his skeleton was found in his bed two years and five months after he died. Yet his nearest neighbour was just thirty yards away.

His power had been cut off for more than two years because he hadn't paid the bill; neighbours complained about noise from the house next door to Ron Mackay; but they didn't worry about Ron.

Ron was silent.

To my surprise, I beat the clock and learned that some stories are 'writing jobs'—stories where all the effort goes into the form of words.

I also learned back then that the most difficult people to interview are those on big salaries with even bigger superannuation, or those with corporate sponsors. Such people avoid controversy. In 1976, Best Editor had the brilliant idea—since we were selling nationally to the more educated, the 'A–B profile' advertisers talk about—to send out a team of writers to do in-depth interviews with each of the vice-chancellors of our universities: to write a series of long articles about the thoughts of these brilliant people and their insights into the major issues affecting Australia. I drew the University of Queensland's Zelman Cowen but, despite two hours of questioning over lunch, I had difficulty coming up with enough newsworthy quotes for an article. The one really quotable thing Cowen said, from my point of view as a journalist, was: 'A man's right to swing his arm ends where another man's nose begins.' (This quote eventually came in handy when Cowen was named Australia's new Governor-General at 6.00 p.m. one Friday night.)

Frustrated that I couldn't write an interesting story, I rang Best Editor. 'Don't worry,' Mark Day said. 'We've canned the whole idea. They all tried, but none of our writers came back with anything new worth writing.'

Sometimes I tried too hard to make the ordinary into a big story. When Brisbane was planning an arts festival, I interviewed the dignified middle-aged woman in charge about her plans. She was what we called back then 'a lady'. At first she was reluctant to reveal details, but I pushed and pushed until she said: 'Well, I'd really like to project huge, colourful images onto the facades of landmark Brisbane buildings to light up and enliven the city so everyone can see that art is being celebrated.'

'What sort of images do you have in mind?'

'Well, you know Red Comb House in the city?' she asked. I nodded, since it stood out on the city skyline—a tall, round, concrete silo that poked up to the sky through surrounding buildings. 'Well I'd like to project a giant cock onto Red Comb House.'

I closed my notebook and staggered back down Queen Street to the Valley, knowing full well that I wouldn't be allowed to write this amazing story of radical pornographic art for our family newspaper. Only years later did it dawn on me what she meant. Red Comb House stored chicken feed and the tall concrete silo had a red neon rooster that pecked up and down on top.

I pushed too far another time when interviewing Germaine Greer in Brisbane about her great book *The Female Eunuch*. Trying to get something different from everyone else, I suggested to her that if it weren't for sex, Aussie men would probably prefer to live together because they would have unlimited chances to watch football on the TV, go off to the cricket and talk sport. 'What are you?' Germaine said with a withering look. 'Another bloody Australian jock?' It was so refreshing to meet a person involved in the arts who didn't feel the need to ingratiate herself with the media.

From my current perspective, now that I have been away from journalism for fourteen years, too often news stories are predictable. The latest model car is always a huge improvement on last year's model; 'profit-takers' sell shares and 'bargain-hunters' buy them; the price of real estate in Brisbane is always about to take off; coffee, red wine, chocolates or tea—depending on which commodity is making the announcement—are good for your health; sweeping changes will be made to clean up the building industry; shareholders who stand up for themselves at annual general meetings are 'agitators' or 'disgruntled' or 'dissident shareholders'. 'We'll all soon be shopping by computer' has been a good media standby over the years: I wrote my first version of this in 1979. 'The paperless office' is a good one that has never happened. And for some strange mathematical reason, a story that begins 'One in four people...' is guaranteed a run in a newspaper.

There are myriad less predictable stories that could be written: the modern use of eight different asterisk-like symbols to subtly alter offers made in advertisements; the home that hasn't sold—including interviews with the distraught owners; the fact that the biggest use being made of freedom of information laws is not by journalists but by debt collectors; or those beer ads on TV—which seem so strange to sober people—that are actually aimed at the low-income man 'who drinks 20 beers a night'. (See interview with advertising filmmaker Dick Marks, maker of big budget beer campaigns, in *Queensland Images in Film and Televison* edited by Jonathan Dawson and Bruce Molloy, UQP.)

Even our ABC still thinks it's news to show racing car drivers spraying each other with champagne, or tennis players kissing the Wimbledon trophy. We don't have an ABC to hear about 'the Middle East peace process' every hour on radio news bulletins which mostly sound like repeats from last week, or last month, or last year.

One ordinary different story I wrote in the *Australian* was just a single column that otherwise would never have made news. As I typed this story, I bore in mind the 1959 speech by Viscount Kilmuir, Lord Chancellor of England, in which he said: 'Justice is not a cloistered virtue: she must be allowed to suffer the scrutiny and respectful (even though outspoken) comments of ordinary men.' It told how three Aborigines were convicted in the District Court in Charleville, western Queensland, of killing a Hereford cow to steal meat from the carcass. One of these Aborigines was almost blind and supporting seven kids under eleven and had no previous convictions; one was supporting ten children and had not previously been convicted of a similar offence; and the third was an 18-year-old unemployed youth who had once stolen poultry worth twenty dollars. They had killed the cow for food, but each was sentenced to eighteen months in jail.

Not surprisingly, the case was taken to the Queensland Court of Criminal Appeal on the grounds that the sentence was excessive. But the three appeal judges agreed the jail term should stand, with Chief Justice Hanger adding: 'If there were any error in it at all, it was on the light side.'

I contrasted this with another case a few months later; it happened in another western Queensland town, Roma, and again was heard in the District Court, with a different judge. This time a man pleaded guilty to a charge of having stolen fourteen calves; this time the cows were sold for profit; this time it was a white property manager before the court. This time the sentence was half that for each of the three Aborigines: nine months in jail.

Which posed a question for all Australians: was it a fair cow?

12 'Don't say you don't know'

Crazy Horse sent me up the thousand kilometre long Sepik River in New Guinea in 1978. 'Somewhere on that giant river is a village where the only income is from prostitution because it's built over the water,' Crazy Horse said. 'Thus men arriving with clams get sex. Get yourself a bag of clams.'

A week later, I was six hundred kilometres upstream on the Sepik when I ran into a former assistant piano tuner from Melbourne, Jeff Liversidge, who had lived on the river for twelve years, at first as a crocodile hunter, before hunting was banned.

His wife, a local village girl, was expecting their sixth child when I was there. Jeff said he had seen something that made him turn his back on Australia forever. Was it the size and beauty of the Sepik— over a kilometre wide at some points? Was it the scores of tribes along the banks, each with their own special culture? 'No, it was the colour of the crocodile's eye,' said Jeff, as I scanned his tanned face, his thin moustache, his short greying hair, and his steel eyes. 'There's no other thing in nature like it. Like neon lights back in Australia? But then I haven't seen any of those for seventeen years.'

Always in bare feet, Jeff Liversidge took me into the jungle at night to see bird-eating spiders; to spirit houses; to see a 'glassman' (witchdoctor). All his isolated years on the Sepik showed when Jeff talked. Most of his sentences began: 'Before...' or 'I will be asking you to listen to a story, please...' He told how he once killed 135 crocodiles in one night before his dugout canoe sank in the middle of the river. He told frightening stories of jungle spirits, black magic, crocodile initiation ceremonies where young men are cut open without anaesthetic and marked on their backs like a crocodile: 'a beautiful ceremony' which Jeff himself was about to undergo to become the first 'white crocodile'. And about the Sanguma man who specialises in committing the perfect murder. Jeff gave several examples of how such murder was done—like scraping the tiny fine hairs from the leaves of wild sugarcane into a tube and blowing them into the nose of the victim while he sleeps.

Very late one night, Jeff took me and two Americans spear-fishing in a small flat-bottomed aluminium outboard driven by a Papuan mate. We went to an isolated lake off a tributary of the Sepik. It was in an area of a few hundred square kilometres where no one lived, and which Jeff called 'my land'. With his powerful light shining down into the very shallow water, Jeff and I balanced tippy-toe on the front of the boat, spears raised ready to strike any fish from above...but nothing.

'That's funny,' said Jeff. 'Three days ago this lake was teaming with fish. Don't tell me!' and he shone his torch slowly around the tiny lake in the dense darkness. Suddenly there it was, popping up from under some water lilies: a giant croc's eye. 'Seventeen footer,' Jeff said. He could tell from the size of the eye.

I wrote that night in my notebook:

The eye of the crocodile is the most colourful jewel I've seen. As the torch catches it in the dark of the river it glows red with a depth of fire that drags the gaze inwards, as through an arch, until it is the only thing in view, though it may be just a dot half a mile away: for the crocodile eye glows even beyond the apparent end of a torch beam. The glow is heightened in the overlay of another of the body's senses:

fear—the certain knowledge that the red glow is the sign of an under-water monster that few have seen and very, very few have killed. The sense of fear and the sense of beauty play on the mind as if you have just been born...The eye gets bigger and bigger until it turns: and then there are two.

The croc disappeared and we motored across in the dark for a closer look—spears raised—when suddenly the croc's head came back up out of the water from under our toes with a mouth like an open suitcase.

'Back 'im back. Back 'im back,' shouted Jeff to the Papuan on the outboard motor. I wondered why the famous crocodile hunter who had shot 135 of them in just one night from a sinking dugout canoe, no less, was in such a panic, until he said hoarsely: 'He's so big that if he stands up he'll tip us all in with him.'

Trying to back 'im back, the Papuan snuffed the motor and we silently and slowly glided straight ahead over the top. Then we stopped. There was silence. The American woman spoke for us all: 'What am I doing here?'

To get home to Brisbane, I sped down the middle of the Sepik in Jeff's boat with the Papuan driver at the back, heading for Angoram still looking for Crazy Horse's village of prostitution. Jeff had said we would reach there in daylight, but we were still hurtling along the twisting river at midnight when, of a sudden, an island appeared out of the dark a few metres in front of our boat. Part of the bank of the river must have broken away and floated out to the middle. Stung into action by my warning yell, the driver just managed to miss the room-sized island. A second later and we'd have been sharing it with the crocodiles.

I finally got to the village of prostitution by dugout canoe from Angoram: it was a couple of dozen huts on high, thin stilts above the water, but it was deserted. It turned out that the government—embarrassed by its existence—had moved the villagers to farmland a year previously.

When I got back to Australia, after two weeks away, I telexed to Sydney the four thousand words that I'd typed and retyped on my portable typewriter on the banks of the Sepik: all about Jeff Liversidge the piano-tuning White Crocodile and our adventures among the spiders and the Sepik witchdoctors. I was pretty pleased to have found such an amazing story of an Australian in such strange circumstances.

Crazy Horse rang a few days later: 'Yeah, yeah, all very interesting. But what about the village that lives off prostitution?'

My Sepik trip was a frightening experience, but nothing was as scary as the time in 1979 when Ron Richards rang my office to say:

'Rupert wants to see you downstairs. Now.'

It was bad enough when Rupert popped into our office unexpectedly, or when you met him along with a score of other employees. But when Rupert demanded to see YOU personally... well, I couldn't think of anything worse.

This was worse than the time I slid and waded hip-deep through miles of mangroves along the edge of the Endeavour River at Cooktown with nothing but Vaseline to protect me from the sharks and crocodiles that fed along the murky banks. At first I'd tried climbing from one mangrove to the other, but the slimy, sloping roots soon sent me crashing into the stagnant gloom of the estuary. After three tumbles I gave up and stayed in the water. The Vaseline was the only effective protection against the thousands of biting midges, which drowned when they landed in it.

It was worse than when I climbed a vertical ladder, in the dark, up the side of an Indooroopilly Bridge tower in leather-soled shoes. The man who lived in the bridge—who hadn't wanted to be interviewed—had invited me to join him on the top. I thought he was testing my love for the story, but once at the top, as we looked out across Brisbane, he said he still didn't want to be interviewed.

It was worse than one dark night in September 1977, which still makes me sweat a little. It was a Saturday night, and that morning in a *Weekend Australian Magazine* article, 'The Police Brotherhood', I had named four Queensland policemen as being perjurers and forgers.

Brisbane newspapers, perhaps understandably, had somehow over-looked this small section of the *Criminal Law Inquiry Report* which told how the four policemen—including an inspector and two sergeants—had 'conspired together to commit perjury and forgery' not knowing that their conversations were being taped by one brave honest copper:

> *Okay. Well now listen: we didn't go across the border that day—or did we?...We could brick him in but then the magistrate might think we're bloody lying...You don't want to write your best, because you must remember you are writing this out in the car...But we are not saying that, are we? Forget about them, right? You came up here—four of youse together. Is that the story? When we come back up we don't park there, we park here.*
>
> The Sergeant (talking about writing out warrants): *But you would have to have possession of your Bible down there that day?*
>
> Inspector: *I reckon I carry my Bible all the time, don't I?* (laughter).

The Criminal Law Inquiry noted that all four were later promoted. But then, this was ten years before the Fitzgerald Inquiry exposed widespread corruption in parts of the Queensland Police Force.

After this full-page story appeared nationally, my gung-ho attitude dissipated as fast as newspapers are printed—particularly after an Italian film producer, Hugo Moriarty, dropped over specially that morning to tell me how brave I was. It suddenly came to me that there was no one in society to protect *me* from the Queensland police. So I parked my car a couple of streets away to make it appear I wasn't at home. In the middle of the night there was a loud, demanding banging on the heavy timber front door. The crooked coppers had arrived and, like the bushranger Ben Hall, I was fast asleep. And we all know what happened to him. I got out of bed and crept down the hallway in the dark, my wooden Slazenger tennis racquet in hand, through the house and out onto the verandah behind them only to find Bazza, back home for a change, lying against the front door and whacking it as he scratched his fleas.

Being called down to see Rupert in the boardroom was even worse than when I was told: 'The next time the boss of Utah sees you, you'd better be prepared to duck!'

An American-owned coal mining company, Utah had as its slogan 'Utah's Backing Australia', but Utah wasn't backing the *Australian*. The Editor rang to say Utah wouldn't advertise with us. 'We owe them no favours,' he said. 'Write an article on the hundred million dollars they send back to America every year in profits.'

It's hard to make a dent in a corporation that can afford to use Aussie actor Rod Taylor to advertise its goodness on TV in a million-dollar campaign. So I decided to play their strength. At that time a popular Australian movie was *The Picture Show Man*, starring Rod Taylor and John Meillon. So I wrote an article comparing Taylor's role in the movie to the role Utah was playing in Australia—an American smart-alec outwitting an old-fashioned Australian at his own business; taking the Aussie's profits and, finally, the girl.

But what about—and here it is at long last—that infamous night that I got lost on Lizard Island? Was that worse than seeing Rupert? I doubt anyone in our Sydney office ever knew it happened, or would have been at all interested had I told them. Which is probably why I want to tell this story here.

A woman reporter in Sydney found out that—unbeknown to anybody on the mainland—marine scientists on Lizard Island had built a tiny platform on the edge of the outer Barrier Reef 250 kilometres north of Cairns and seventy-seven kilometres out to sea, using steel-tube scaffolding. They built it so that occasionally scientists could stay out on the reef overnight. Unfortunately for me, because the Sydney office decided they 'couldn't send a woman' I was told to sleep a night on this tropical platform out where the Pacific Ocean pounds the Barrier Reef. Not for me a bed in the Lizard Island Resort, where royalty and celebrities holiday: that was for travel writers. Instead, I was shown to a tent, 'the driftwood suite', at the scientific station on the other side of the island. From there I watched scientists walk down into the water to observe what the 'fishes' were up to, and emerge hours later. I had been told to bring my own food, but I didn't bring enough. The weather was so rough that, after a week of waiting, we still hadn't dared to set out for the isolated platform. I got an uneasy feeling when, under questioning, the scientists confessed that none of them had yet spent a night out on their four-month-old structure.

Everyone was pleasant to their non-marine visitor, but the scientists jealously guarded their precious food in the mess tent, as there were no shops on the island. After several days I found myself furtively pinching a slice of biologist's bread, some researcher's raisin toast, a PhD's biscuits, and I quickly learned what all our convict ancestors knew: that we're all thieves when hungry.

Bored, and wishing I was back home with my new girlfriend, I decided to climb the island mountain: the one Captain Cook had ascended two centuries earlier when trying to devise a path through the ribbon-like barrier of reefs in his damaged ship. I filled a beer bottle with drinking water and set off up the ill-defined track. Soon, I had nothing but admiration for Captain Cook's fitness—not only did he have no track to follow back then, but, according to his log, he climbed that mountain twice in twenty-four hours, once in daylight and again that night. After a couple of hours, I knew what Pope meant when he wrote 'hills mount on hills and alps on alps arise'. Every time I thought I could see the top up ahead, it turned out to be just another crest along the way. Eventually, my water long gone, I made it to a stone cairn on top and looked out to near the horizon at the occasionally broken line of reefs that form the great barrier to the Pacific Ocean. As I looked for where the platform was located (it was far too small to see from such a distance of, perhaps, twenty-seven kilometres), I felt like Captain Cook himself as he finally saw his way back home. A quick boat ride, a night on the platform, and back to Brissie, Brissie, Brissie. But, when that night I read Captain Cook's logbook account of what it was like out there, it came to me that it wasn't going to be easy: '... the sea broke very high, and I feared I should be charged with timorousness.'

On the way down the mountain I got lost. I kept coming to dead ends and sheer drops. The sun had set by the time I made it to the bottom. Exhausted and hungry, I lay down on the sand for a rest.

When I awoke it was dark. So I decided the best way back to the scientific station was via the airstrip. I set out past Mrs Watson's collapsing stone cottage with its air of facing death alone.

In 1881, while Mrs Watson's husband was away fishing, a party of Aboriginal men arrived in the night, killed one of her Chinese servants and stabbed the other, Ah Sam. After a four-day siege in the stone cottage, Mrs Watson fled with her seven-month-old baby, Ferrier, and the wounded Ah Sam. With no boat, they climbed into a small square iron tank and paddled out to sea. Mrs Watson kept a diary which told of their experiences and the five horrific days at sea before they all perished of thirst.

I walked along the airstrip to the end, then into the bush looking for the winding path that led to the scientific station. But all I found were spider-webs of spun steel and lots of giant lizards looking for a feed. So I headed straight for the coast. Knowing the island was only twelve kilometres around, I reasoned that if I turned right when I hit the beach, the scientific station could be no more than a six-kilometre stroll along the sand.

It was so lovely to arrive on that small white beach. It was quite a bright night out in the open. No shadows stalking. No spiders spinning. No lizards leaping. Opposite was a small, uninhabitable island that I could also see from the station. Now I was on the way.

At the end of the beach there was a small rocky outcrop blocking the way, as at most beaches, which I soon clambered over to another small beach, and then more rocks. Then the next pile was maybe ten metres high. The only way round was to return to the bush or enter the water. So I climbed up and over the rocks: but didn't see a large hole in the dark because it was covered by seaweed. The whole of my right leg disappeared into the hole and I emerged limping. Another few easy ones, then the next rock pile was so high that I only got around by clinging to grass and bushes on the cliff face above the rocks. Any slip was death. I was tempted to turn back, but couldn't face the two dangerous climbs all over again.

The worst thing was that the small island opposite never seemed to move, no matter how far I travelled.

After another climb at the end of the next beach my legs had turned to jelly. But I was surely getting close? At the next rocks I couldn't face another climb, and decided—in a weakened state—to do what I should never have considered: to enter the Barrier Reef waters at night when no one knew I was there. But I reasoned it wasn't far around the rocks. It was only six or seven metres, so I wasn't worried about sharks. Just that I couldn't see beneath the water.

Neck deep in the unlit ocean, I was pushed around by the water and cut on the rocks as I clung to them: not being much of a swimmer I didn't want to lose contact with the precious hardness of the land. For a moment I was in over my head. Then more rocks, and I emerged bleeding and shaking, Robinson-Crusoe-like, on a much longer white beach. And there it was up ahead in the distance: the scientific station. Every light was on and they were all out searching for me, riding their tractors through the bush and yelling. They said they thought I might still be up on the mountain. They never imagined I was in the water.

Because I knew the Sydney editors would think I was bludging on a tourist resort like a bloated travel writer, I sent a telegram explaining that I'd been held up for a week by bad weather. Then I begged to be taken to the platform. The scientists claimed the weather was still too bad, but I said it didn't seem that bad to me. I wanted to get the story and go home. So the next morning Barry Goldman, Hugh Sweatman and I made for the platform. The first wave, as we came around the corner of the island, was as high as a house on stumps: they'd been right about the weather. All the way to the outer reef in our speedboat I was hit in the face by buckets of water as we thumped each wave.

Now, one thing I can inform you is that the problem with having a fixed platform in the ocean is that the platform doesn't rise and fall with your boat. So, as our boat heaved and plunged on the two-metre swell, our job was to leap through the air and grab hold of some scaffolding on the platform, which was anchored into the coral by eight wire guys. It was no use trying to grab the platform while riding the front of the boat: I tried and nearly ripped my arm off as the boat dropped vertically beneath me. Finally, bruised but onboard, I clung desperately and timorously to the steel scaffolding as the Pacific winds ripped remorselessly through.

The three by four metre platform had no sides. But sleeping on it with the ocean waves passing just beneath would have been all right if: (a) Barry hadn't turned out the kerosene lamp, leaving us suspended in the dark, and (b) our boat had not been tied to the platform. With every wave the boat tugged at the scaffolding, all night, until it pulled one of the guy wires out of the coral at 2.00 a.m., leaving just the one wire holding the north-west corner. The boat shook the platform even more after that. I counted the waves that tugged at the boat—our only connection with the world—until dawn arrived. And I still had to face the prospect of leaping back into the bucking boat.

But this, even this, didn't hold as many terrors as Ron Richards' phone call did that day back in 1979.

A Statewide strike had put out the lights and Premier Joh Bjelke-Petersen was threatening to sack striking electricity workers. Ron said Rupert wanted to be briefed on what was going to happen. I explained on the phone to my old mate Ron that, while I knew a fair bit about politics, all I knew about the strike was what I'd read in the papers and heard on the radio. Our industrial roundsman, Max Jessop, and our political roundsman, Joe Begley, were in the city on the story at that very moment and would report back in a few hours.

'Rupert wants to know now. Rupert wants you to tell him,' said Ron, sounding troubled. 'This is Rupert Murdoch I've got down here. And he wants to see you. *Now*. So stop arguing the toss and get down to the boardroom.'

I tipped my typewriter over on its back, as reporters used to do back then to clear a space on the desk, put on a jacket, left a message in case my girlfriend rang back, straightened my tie, checked the mirror in the men's room, and made my way to the set of black steel stairs which led down from the third floor to the second, emerging directly opposite the boardroom.

The spectre of Rupert seemed to hang over everything at News Ltd. Advertising staff operated not on the Gregorian calendar, not on the financial year calendar, but on what they called 'Rupert's Calendar', which numbered the weeks one to fifty-two. Sometimes Rupert's year had fifty-three weeks. The look and body language of executives, Editors and section editors changed at the mention of his name. When Rupert hit town they became like a herd of wildebeest: first excited that they would be near him, then frightened that he wouldn't like what they had been doing, and, finally, they were drawn into a controlled, instinctive panic leading occasionally to their own destruction. Rupert's visit was a much, much bigger occasion for editors than if some other world figure, merely the Pope, say, came to appraise their work. The Pope might also have a large degree of infallibility, but he could only threaten their *next* life, not this one. The Queen might bestow an honour on an editor, but not dishonour. Whereas Rupert would not hesitate to describe a paper as dull and boring, which meant the Editor and his editors were dull and boring. Rupert would even notice the technical errors and the small mistakes—if the pictures were taken from too far away, the feature was too long, the headline didn't fit, the use of capital letters was incorrect, and the inevitable spelling mistakes—which was what made him frightening.

Thus editors became much more critical when Rupert was around.

In April 1980, Rupert's Ansett Airlines decided to try to break the Qantas monopoly on overseas flights. Rupert arrived for the one-off Townsville to Singapore flight and at a *Townsville Bulletin* dinner several hundred locals were thrilled that Rupert himself had come to their city to connect them with the world. Rupert told them their *Bulletin* was 'a great newspaper' and raised a nervous laugh when he said, 'I see the *Bulletin* calls itself "totally independent": I presume that means it is proud to have nothing to do with me!' (Within a decade Rupert owned it.)

The next day I interviewed Rupert and sent the story to Sydney. But it only got me into trouble with the Editor, who complained angrily that he'd wasted two hours trying to re-write my poorly written story.

And now, right now, as I reached the bottom of that terrible walk down the black steel stairs, to my surprise, Ron Richards was waiting. A newspaperman who found confident humour facing all sorts of difficult deadlines, Ron grabbed my elbow and looked up into my eyes as we walked the seven paces across the newsroom from the stairs to the boardroom entrance. Slowly and deliberately, as if spelling a word, he said, 'Don't say you don't know.'

A paperboy walked into the newsroom selling the afternoon Brisbane *Telegraph*. 'Gimme that,' I said aggressively, ripping one from underneath his arm. Slamming it on a desk I ran a finger quickly down the front-page splash on the power strike as if drawing a free-hand line.

I handed the paper back, and walked in.

Rupert and his merry men filled up my former office. News executives from Sydney and Adelaide were working at the long table checking figures, and files, and accounts. But I couldn't see them all for the man in front of me: Rupert, who had just stood up from a chair in the corner of the crowded room. Unlike the others, he wasn't reading anything or anywhere near a telephone; it was as if he were waiting for something to happen. Normally, Rupert was immaculate, but this time—on a hot Brisbane day—he appeared slightly ill at ease in a white shirt, tie and trousers: no jacket. As there was so little space in the room, Rupert asked me to sit down next to him in his tight corner, and, with all the other chairs taken, I found myself on a much lower chair than his: on his sinister side. It was a bit like being on your knees while the priest listened to your sins.

Rupert, exactly as Ron had predicted, asked what I thought would happen in the electricity strike. I looked across the room at Ron whose

friendly words of advice still rang in my ears: 'Don't...say...you...
don't...know!'

'Oh, they'll go back to work. It'll be all over sometime today,' I
said, with as much confidence as I could muster.

'What do you base this on?' asked Rupert quietly.

'On what ordinary people are saying about the blackouts...and
union sources...and, and my own knowledge of things Queensland,'
I said, smiling inappropriately.

I felt like I was lying in confession: a sacrilege.

'Well that's very strange,' said Rupert, causing me several ectopic
heartbeats. 'I've just walked back down here from the Premier's office
and he tells me that he's about to invoke a State of Emergency.'

Hmmm. Interesting.

'Yes,' I gulped. 'The unions realise that possibility.'

Rupert changed tack and talked about what he saw as the likeli-
hood of Bob Hawke becoming Prime Minister. Which was also news
to me, since Hawke wasn't even yet in Parliament. I gathered Rupert
wasn't particularly impressed with Hawke; not at all in fact. But he
believed Hawke would one day get the top job.

Rupert then said something I found strange indeed. He asked if I
thought Malcolm Fraser's coalition government could survive an election if home loan interest rates hit fourteen per cent.

'Hell no,' I said, feeling on very safe ground while commenting on
something that I knew could never happen. No one would put up
with paying interest rates that high. Well, said Rupert, that's what's
going to happen in the next few years. Here were Rupert and I
talking politics, when I should have been asking him where to invest
my savings now that I was 38 years old. If I'd only listened to him,
I'd never have ended up almost going broke paying interest after
investing with my solicitor in 1981.

We talked about Malcolm Fraser and about the in-fighting among
Labor factions, an aspect of the ALP that seemed to annoy Rupert.
As we talked, the suit of executives worked quietly away, mumbling
to each other, not listening at all. Rupert's concentration was total, and

he was never at all arrogant or aggressive, which was a charming thing about him. He just seemed to want a chat. He had, I noticed from close up, perfect pale skin, as if it had been dipped in something: the texture of new mango leaves. For a man who spent most of his life in aeroplanes, presumably in first class, he was obviously not eating airline food. Over the last eight years, Rupert had been getting thinner rather than fatter. It seemed that the more success he had, the less he self-indulged; the more powerful he got, the less he needed to reward himself. I guess Rupert got his reward from expanding the company. But I couldn't imagine how a female reporter friend saw him as 'the sexiest man I've ever seen'.

When we'd finished, we both stood up and Rupert said, 'I enjoy reading your stories wherever I am in the world.' Being a writer, I recorded the words in my mind. I wanted to ask him which stories, and what parts of which stories he liked best, and what parts of which sentences, and make a few suggestions as to the possibilities. But I thought better of it. Though I did know that a few of my stories had been published in one of his American papers. Anyway, the good news was that, after all this chat, he'd forgotten about the electricity strike.

As I turned to leave, Rupert tucked both thumbs into the top of his trousers and tugged them back into the line they must have lost on his long, hot walk from the other side of the city and said, slightly bemused, 'So, you think the electricity workers will go back to work today?'

'Well I certainly hope so, now that I've told you,' I said.

As luck would have it, the electricity workers went back to work later that night.

13 Marooned in Queensland

In November 1979, out of the blue, a Sydney head-hunter rang to ask if I would join Prime Minister Malcolm Fraser's staff to write his speeches.

I refused immediately, saying, 'But Fraser's a terrible public speaker.'

The headhunter was not put off. 'That's because his speeches have been written by a committee of three—which is why he's looking for just one writer. If they're bad, then there's a greater challenge for you.' I would be mad to knock back a free first-class trip to Canberra for an interview with the Prime Minister of Australia, she said. Well, although I didn't want the job, it was something I could tell the grand-kids. And I had to go to Canberra anyway, to collect a National Press Club award: 'Best Sports Feature of 1979' for '*The Battle of Ballymore*', about a Rugby Union match between Queensland and New South Wales.

Flying first class to Canberra to see the Prime Minister, I ended up sharing a double seat up front with my best contact in the ALP: Senator Ron McAuliffe. The Senator had attended the same school as me, St Joseph's College, Gregory Terrace, and he also ran the Queensland Rugby League. It tells you a lot about Queensland that the Labor Senator was not fazed by the Liberals' job offer, but he was agitated by my article on the Queensland Rugby Union team. 'Rugby Union is taking crowds away from us,' he said. 'They're playing like a club team.' I suggested he buy their star players, but McAuliffe revealed this had already been tried. 'The ARL (Australian Rugby League) sent up some of their scouts but they said none of those Queensland Union boys would be good enough to make it in our game.' Not even Mark Loane? 'Yeah, they said he might make a good winger.'

I knew McAuliffe fairly well because every year in May I made sure I wrote a preview for the *Australian* about the first Queensland–New South Wales League clash of the season at Lang Park. Posing for a picture, Ron would splay out the palms of his hands close to the front of his chest, as was his habit. I'd been going to these interstate games since I was a boy. Hadn't I seen the tears well up in the eyes of a row of old men behind me when Queensland scored a try in 1974? They had seen few Queensland tries since.

In those days, the local clubs constantly lost players who were enticed south to the rich Sydney clubs. Thus Queensland lost year after year to a New South Wales team containing Queensland stars: by my reckoning we had won just two of the last thirty-four matches.

For the next hour and a half we talked about Queensland's efforts to win an interstate series: how in 1973 they brought John Sattler up from Sydney to sort out the New South Wales forwards; held psychological tests to determine if Maroon players really believed they could defeat the Blues; organised in-depth studies by southern consultants; established a ways and means committee and a protection and procurement committee; even christened the Blues 'cockroaches'. Still, the Senator was reluctant to agree that the interstate matches had fallen into disrepute. I told him that in 1971 I had been one of ten thousand fans outside Lang Park who couldn't get in because the match was sold out. Some fans had got so excited when they heard the infamous Lang Park 'boo' signifying the arrival of the hated Blues, that they'd prised the gates open and a few hundred of us slid through just in time to see Wayne Bennett racing on the wing. But in 1979 I'd had a hundred metres of the outer to myself. If McAuliffe wanted to compete with Rugby Union then he simply had to take up the age-old idea of a 'State of Origin' match.

'Our organisation has discussed all that a dozen times,' McAuliffe said. 'I know that some of our boys have been over the top too often, but why should we reward players who desert our competition? Why should we present them with our precious maroon jersey? If we did, then what's to stop all the young stars like Wally Lewis and Mal Meninga and Gary Belcher also leaving for the south?' McAuliffe's voice softened as if he were about to tell a secret: 'And—while I know we would never contemplate it—what if we hold a State of Origin and we lose? We've been saying to our fans for decades that we'd thrash these southerners if only we had all our champions back. But where would we go from there if we still lost?' Anyway, he doubted Sydney clubs would release Queenslanders in the middle of their club season. 'And, just say they do: will men who have lived and played in Sydney for twelve or thirteen years, since they were 17, give their all against their Sydney clubmates? Give their all for our noble jersey?'

'There's no such thing as an ex-Queenslander Ron,' I countered. 'They're like Catholics, there's only ever lapsed Queenslanders.' Rugby League was dead in the water if he wouldn't do it.

As we got off the plane in Canberra, Senator McAuliffe said he was glad we'd had our 'little talk'. 'I'll tell you what,' he said, 'if we lose the first two matches badly next winter with our new young stars—and mind you I don't think we will—then I'll hold one of these Origin matches and I'll invite you to dinner in the boardroom before kick-off.'

At the Prime Minister's office in Canberra, the city where the entire population has been screened through the interview process, I felt surrounded by Malcolm Fraser and Liberal Party Director Tony Eggleton as Fraser poured coffee from a silver pot. As he talked, I was reminded of the time in September 1975 when Fraser had arrived like a hero in Brisbane as the Liberals' great hope to defeat Gough

Whitlam, the ogre who had already knocked off two Liberal leaders at two successive elections. More than five hundred Brisbane businesspeople had paid twenty dollars a head at Lennons Hotel to hear Fraser speak and I wrote a long descriptive piece for the *Australian* about this night of frights.

Queensland conservatives had heard much of this man, a big man with a bigger reputation standing a forehead above even Whitlam. But when Fraser stood up he couldn't stir the willing crowd who at first roared like at a footy final but slowly fell silent. With the lights reflecting in his glasses Fraser fell into a dreary monotone. A Queensland Liberal looked across the table at me and rolled his eyes like a man looking at his partner as their racehorse came last. Eventually, there was one embarrassingly lonely 'Hear, Hear!', causing Fraser to look up from his speech to remark: 'Well I'm glad there's somebody on side.'

When my story hadn't been published after a few days, I rang the features editor to find out what had happened. 'The last time I saw your story, Hugh, it was in the Editor's pocket and he was flying to Canberra.' I had an immediate vision of Flamboyant Editor—the one who was so keen on shirts—with a red tongue of handkerchief poking out of one pocket and a white tongue of telex paper sticking out of another.

I now wondered if this was the office where my story had ended up.

'But I've got a good job,' I said.

'I'm sure your boss wouldn't mind lending you to me for a few years,' Fraser replied.

'But I want to live in Queensland.'

'You can,' said the Prime Minister. 'We'll fly you down whenever you're needed here to write a speech.'

It could possibly lead to a permanent government job. It could lead to an overseas posting. Geneva?

But I couldn't bring myself to give up my maroon jersey.

The following June, 1980, my phone rang. Queensland had of

course lost the first two interstate matches and the voice of Senator McAuliffe said, 'The time has come for all loyal Queenslanders to gather at Lang Park.'

It was on!

That cold night, 8 July 1980, I sat next to Senator Ron McAuliffe at dinner, and later next to him again on a cushioned seat overlooking the halfway line in the grandstand during the match—which, of course, Queensland won. Lang Park was once again full, and McAuliffe, chatting to his dinner guests before the match, no longer held any doubts that Queenslanders living in Sydney might fail to perform when they pulled on maroon:

> Champions are like good horses: they rise to the occasion. Once they get out on the track and the saddle is put on the adrenalin will flow. Arthur Beetson and Rod Reddy are two immortals who haven't played for Queensland until tonight. They are two old warriors who have heard the bugle call. Patriotism is a great thing, you know. Deep down the real ambition of all our football players is to play for Queensland. And if somewhere along the line they are waylaid because of money—understandable in a working-class sport—the older you get the more you regret that you didn't play. When the kids say, 'Dad, why didn't you ever play for Queensland?' it doesn't impress them much if you start talking about southern money deals and big offers.

Later that year, in November 1980, I was offered another southern money deal myself—a big offer. The Editor of the Melbourne *Herald*, Pat Hinton, rang to offer me a job as the *Herald's* feature writer in Melbourne. 'It's an important position; you'll be sitting in the office next to mine.' I said no, but Hinton was smart. He said there must be something I wanted. Thinking it could never be done, I countered: 'Well, I'd want to be based in Brisbane, and I'd want an office with a window in the middle of the city overlooking Queen Street.' Within twenty-four hours Hinton rang back and said he had arranged for a

Brisbane office with a window overlooking Queen Street. So I resigned from the *Oz*.

Since I was leaving, I decided to let Rupert know what I thought about how the *Oz* was run—to explain why I was resigning after ten years. I wrote a single page to him in Sydney because I had no idea where he was in the world. Next morning I picked up my green direct-line phone and a voice said, 'It's Rupert Murdoch here.' But was it really? Journalists loved to ring each other and say for effect: 'It's Rupert here! You haven't written anything for a month.' More likely, it was a hoax call. Adrian McGregor had caught me out dangerously a few years before when he left on my desk a false telex message from Flamboyant Editor giving me a real bollocking. I was angrily dialling the Editor to resign when Adrian walked in, grinning.

'Oh yeah!' I said dismissively to the smart-alec 'Rupert Murdoch' on the other end of the line.

'I got your letter,' Rupert said quietly. 'I realise you're very determined to leave us, but I'd like you to come down to Sydney and talk about it.'

It was him.

'But I'm definitely leaving,' I said.

'OK. Fly down, stay as long as you like, wherever you like, at my expense. Look on it as a free trip, a fully paid holiday. There's no obligation. So come down.'

Seated on the red reception lounge chairs at the entrance to Mahogany Row on the top floor of Rupert's old chocolate factory building in Surry Hills, I waited nervously for a secretary to come and usher me in. After a while, I spied Mark Day walking purposefully up the corridor and out, without seeming to see me. What was he doing here? He'd left the paper two years earlier. Then up the corridor, strolling jauntily and smiling all the way, as if he were a man without a care in the world, came Rupert himself to greet me with an avuncular grin. He walked me to his office, past the small antique desk he often used when in town, and into the office of his Managing Director and close friend, Ken Cowley, whose square, clean jaw always put me in mind of Chesty Bond. This large office was totally free of any clutter: no files, no newspapers, no biros, no bits of paper, no books, no paperweights. So much so, that a visitor might have concluded that neither of these businessmen had anything to do.

Rupert sat back in shirtsleeves and chatted away about his paper. He was the exact opposite of standoffish, leaping out of his seat to show me the artwork for an upcoming double-page broadsheet advertisement for Ansett Airlines, which was half-owned by News Ltd—acquired the previous year when Rupert bought Channel 10 in Sydney (which later led to his getting Channel 10 in Melbourne).

I was surprised by the advertisement, which was trumpeting Ansett's new fleet of Boeing 737s and 727s, and was scheduled to go in the *Australian* and other broadsheet newspapers. The full left-hand page was a picture of a beautiful air hostess standing front-on in the aisle of a passenger jet with the short galley curtain clutched alluringly to her otherwise naked body as she faced two rows of male passengers. 'If the hostess was out of uniform would you know which airline you were flying with?' said the headline on the opposite page.

Rupert waited.

'It would be very controversial,' I said. Rupert agreed, but, even so, remained enthusiastic and amused by the ad, which appeared around Australia a few weeks later. A secretary interrupted us to say Lord so-and-so was on the phone from London. In my experience, people always put the telephone call ahead of the person who is standing or sitting in front of them. So I was surprised when Rupert turned and said offhandedly, 'Tell him I'll ring him back.' Rupert obviously had a policy of concentrating on the person at hand.

Rupert took his time before asking about my resignation. I said I felt the *Australian* had lost the excellent feature writers it had once had and I named names, including Phil Cornford, Janet Hawley, Rob Drewe, Ian Moffitt and my old mate Charlie Wright from Townsville. Charlie had been shunted off to Perth after he wrote a series of hilarious but biting TV reviews which upset the commercial stations. Once, the *Australian* had been forced to print a large 'Apology to TCN9

Sydney' in a black border like a funeral notice after a vicious but funny Charlie review which really socked it to Nine for their unhappy choice of yet another American TV program.

Breathing deep, I said the *Australian* badly needed five good feature writers, and was surprised when Rupert gazumped me. 'We need a dozen,' he said.

I complained about being isolated from all decision-making in Sydney, so Rupert suggested that I be included by phone in the two daily *Oz* conferences. But I said it would take up too much time sitting and listening to fourteen people talking in Sydney.

Fair enough, said Rupert.

My next complaint was that the latest Editor (Mr Reporter Editor) never talked to me. Rupert replied that this Editor was a great journalist, but that didn't mean he knew how to deal with people in isolated bureaus. Then Rupert turned away from me to Ken Cowley and I noticed that both men were so clean skinned that they must have shaved twice that morning. 'Ken,' Rupert said, 'I never knew Hugh was so unhappy.' Just then we were interrupted by a News Ltd executive who had recently retired, one of Rupert's old Adelaide days mob who started showing Rupert photos of his family. Rupert, to my surprise, amiably looked at all the photos one at a time.

Since I was still determined to leave, I took some risks. I pointed out that our paper had sacked a heap of good people in Brisbane in my ten years and each time they had replaced some with reporters who were not as good. Rupert replied that being subject to economic fluctuations was the vulnerable side of starting a national newspaper from scratch, squeezed as he was between the Herald and Fairfax groups, but, although the *Oz* was still losing significant amounts of money, this sort of thing would not be happening again.

'So what do you want to stay on?' Rupert said. 'You just name it and we'll put it in a contract and I promise you I'll sign it.'

'Oh, I don't want a contract,' I said. 'I'd feel too tied down.'

'A contract only protects you. It doesn't protect me,' said Rupert matter-of-factly. 'You can still walk out and there's absolutely nothing I can do about it. Well, what do you want to stay?'

He had put it on me: what did I want that would make me stay? I missed not working in the middle of the city like we used to in the Penneys Building. The Valley was such a down-market dump next to the Empire Hotel. I thought of what I'd told the *Herald*. 'I'd stay for an office with a window overlooking Queen Street with some proper office furniture,' I found myself saying.

Rupert agreed, and he threw in a pay rise as well.

Back in Brisbane, Ron Richards was annoyed when my Rupert requests were passed on down the line to him. 'You're a prickly bastard,' he said, shaking his head. 'An office with a window overlooking Queen Street? What a weird request to make to Rupert! You'd be away from everyone else in your bureau. How are you going to be in charge and know what everyone else is writing?'

I agreed there was logic in what Ron said.

'Why don't you let us build you a nice office with a clear-glass window in this building?' OK Ron, I said—and ended up being able to glimpse God's beautiful Story Bridge out of the top-floor window from my new high-backed chrome and black leather swivel chair behind an impressive new timber desk next to a two-tone blue four-drawer filing cabinet.

Things were really going well, though not everyone was impressed. The brand new Editor of the *Australian*, Mr Humorous Editor, when he saw the bill for my furniture, cut out a newspaper advertisement for a tiny student's desk for ninety-nine dollars and sent it up in the overnight bag with a letter saying: 'Ken Cowley has approved your exorbitant quote for superb new office furniture.' Editors, I could see, didn't like the fact that I'd dealt directly with Rupert.

The first new feature writer Rupert hired was Adrian McGregor from the *National Times* in Brisbane on a contract that made him Australia's highest paid feature writer. So Rupert really meant business.

Two months later, Rupert bought the *Times* of London. Suddenly, at one stroke, he had become one of the most powerful people in the world, making friends with Margaret Thatcher and Ronald Reagan. Whereas I was sitting in an expensive new chair in the same old job in the same old branch office in the same old Fortitude Valley in Brisbane's red light district.

Rupert was proving a hard man to keep up with.

14 Telling stories

Learning to write a newspaper feature story wasn't easy for me.

In Vietnam in 1967 when I was with an American company that captured a Vietcong base camp in the jungle I was surprised how organised the guerrillas were. They had thatched-roof huts with no walls and a dirt floor that was half a metre below ground level: like a permanent trench. One hut was a bicycle repair shop, another a classroom full of incredibly neat exercise books that contained children's drawings of American soldiers being bayoneted in the stomach.

Outside there was, as expected, a well, and the usual vertical holes in the ground leading down to tunnels. But there was also the unexpected: a volleyball court in a clearing under the triple-canopy jungle, plus an open-air ping-pong table.

As I stumbled around through this camp taking voluminous notes, I knew I was on to a great story. There was the table-tennis bat booby trap that almost got me, the claymore mine we stepped over, the tunnel that the American 'tunnel rat' soldier sensibly refused to enter. I was 25 and could instantly write a fifteen-sentence news story on any announcement; but this was different—where was the news? No one had been killed or wounded. No helicopters had been shot down.

There had been no escalation of the Vietnam War. I slaved over a typewriter for three days and nights writing a poor feature when all I had to do was to sit down and quickly type something I had seen that readers didn't already know: 'While the American military command believes the Vietcong are hiding in fear in the triple-canopy jungles of Vietnam, the guerrillas are actually out there beneath the rainforest trees playing volleyball and table tennis and going to school.' It was only by reading what Johnny Apple Jnr sent back to the *New York Times* through our office, and Tom Buckley or Bernie Weinraub or David Greenway of *Time,* that I came to realise that these famous US journalists had one thing in common: they wrote what they saw. You knew that they were there. Plus there was something else: they always told readers something new in the first paragraph.

So the next time I was on the spot in Vietnam I wrote: 'American Marines who said they were entering the UN's Demilitarised Zone that divides Vietnam "to show that the southern half of the DMZ is ours" came out today carrying their dead piled high on their tanks and saying they had been ambushed.'

It took me nearly ten years of journalism to work out how to write a feature story the reader would enjoy; not one that would fill the space. Now, thirty-four years and thousands of articles later, I know that writers like Janet Hawley, Frank Robson, Jane Cadzow, Valerie Lawson, Hedley Thomas, David Marr or Mike Colman would only have had to fly low in a helicopter over that Vietcong base camp to write a wonderful story: 'How the VC Live'.

The principles I learned in Vietnam stood me in good stead when I got back to Australia. I worked out that you must think of the reader with every sentence that you write. When I had to profile Joh Bjelke-Petersen, I rejected the usual newspaper repeat-everything-we-already-know intro—'Joh Bjelke-Petersen is an ultra right-wing, anti-intellectual Queensland politician famous for his low vote and bumbling speech and his wife's pumpkin scones'—and wrote, instead, that the Premier of Queensland was like he was because, when he

At work at the *Australian*'s Brisbane bureau with secretary Lee Watters.

Aboard
Joh's plane,
1970s.

Helen and me
the year
after we
got married.

Helen at work in the 'Women's News' section of the *Courier-Mail*, 1980.

Burning the midnight oil, 1982.

Adrian McGregor ready for battle on my tennis court, 1980.

THE AUSTRALIAN

NUMBER 3988   SATURDAY MAY 14 1977   15 CENTS* AIR FREIGHT EXTRA   Phone Brisbane

The inspiring story of how a baby with a shockingly disfigured face was remade—and given a chance at life

ROBERT HOGE, born in Brisbane four years ago with a massive tumor in the centre of his face, had a life of mental and physical anguish ahead of him.

Now doctors at Brisbane's Mater Hospital have completely rebuilt his face in a 12-hour operation likely to astound world interest.

The doctors pioneered techniques which offer new hope for parents of deformed children.

When Robert was born in 1972 he was so ugly that even his mother, Mrs Mary Hoge, of Manly, Brisbane, rejected him. "I didn't want to bring him home ... I thought he would be better in an institution," Mrs Hoge said this week.

"But I don't regret having felt like that. You have to have feelings and if I lie about that I am only fooling myself. I would have doubts about any woman who said they could accept something like this straight away."

But while Robert was ugly, he had no brain damage. After a month Mrs Hoge consulted her husband Vince and four children and they all said "bring him home."

That was in 1972. At that stage Robert faced a cholesterol future hidden from prying eyes — and certain psychological damage when he became old enough to realise he was horribly different. There was little hope that he would ever make it in normal life.

But a couple of Brisbane doctors

Triumph of love — and medicine

By HUGH LUNN

view the latest surgical techniques which enable doctors for the first time to carve up the skull and move the basic structures of the face.

They practised night and day on skulls to perfect the ability to remake Robert's face.

Then they added their own tooth

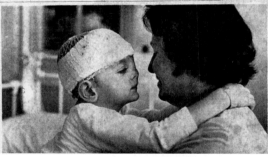

Little Robert Hoge after being remade in Brisbane's Mater Hospital with his mum, Mary. Page 1 clipping from the *Australian*, 1977.

Collecting a Walkley award from Mr Walkley (left), 1974.

Jim Egoroff in our Brisbane factory, getting organised to take on Kelvinator.

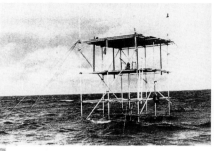

A sleepless night on the scientists' platform at the Great Barrier Reef, 1981.

The Ghost Who Walks deals with some roughnecks at the *Queenslanders* book launch, 1984.

Never trust a man in a black hat.

was 15, the inventive, bookish, older brother that he so much admired, Christian, died. And Joh thought all that study helped kill Christian.

When told to do a feature story on the collapse of cattle prices in the mid-'70s, I flew to Rockhampton, hired a car, drove up the highway for an hour or so, and turned left into a property—any property—to describe how the occupants lived. Pat Moran and his wife Geraldine had 'won' this piece of hot, dry land in a State government ballot and now lived in a large tin shed with two kids, lounge seats ripped out of an old Holden, two old timber wardrobes as a room divider, no stereo, no TV, no carpet, no light shades, no en suite. As I noted, it was as if Japan and Myers had been deliberately excluded from their lives. I accepted an invitation to stay the night and soon realised that only a tough man could survive here with his young family. Pat Moran was thin, but his fingers were swollen and his large forearms hung Popeye-like below slender shoulders. He'd recently been gored by a bull through the foot, and broken bones had left lumps in several places. But how could I quickly capture just how tough he was?

At tea that evening, the little daughter found a large redback spider on the biscuit tin lid and dropped it on the table in front of me. The cave-black nut-hard body with its drop of blood red seared itself on my brain as if my ancestors had passed down an important message of fear in my DNA. I reared back as the ugly monster rolled my way, but Pat Moran leaned across and stubbed the spider out with his gnarled forefinger as if stubbing out a cigarette—and never mentioned the incident. Not bad. But it wasn't until the next morning, when I yelled from in the shower was there any shampoo, that I found what I was watching and waiting for to start my story. Pat had long since ridden off into the scrub looking for wild bulls and Geraldine called through the tin wall: 'The Solvol soap. Pat washes his hair with the Solvol soap.' At that time in Australia, a bone safari suit had become a sign of rugged independence—but only if accompanied by a man's perfume called cologne and a shag hair-cut washed with Soft Frosting men's hair conditioner. Yet I had found a man who washed his hair with a dirty bloody great grey lump of sandpaper called Solvol soap.

After that, I always tried to tell the story through a person. And I soon learned that you have to watch them carefully, because they can't tell you what they're like: they don't know. They think their unusual circumstances are normal. Like Fraser Island anti-sand-mining campaigner John Sinclair, whose dining-room table, when I arrived, was deep in letters and donations from all over Australia—which he hadn't bothered to mention. We hopped in his 1960 pink and grey Holden to slip down to the paper shop in his hometown of Maryborough and, as we drove past a garage, I noticed a large sign out front: 'Sinclair Not Served Here.' John Sinclair hadn't thought to mention that either. It was only then that he told me his little scout troop had been booed when they marched into the ring at the annual Maryborough Show. It was the price he had paid for Fraser Island.

Of course, it is far easier to write the first thing that comes into your head, the thing that everybody already knows. Over the years I've seen hundreds of examples of such first paragraphs, almost all in Australian metropolitan dailies: 'Roads are vital because they connect one town with another...'; 'Children are our most important and valu-able hope for the future...'; 'Australia stops to watch the Melbourne Cup race on the first Tuesday in November every year...'; 'Coronation Drive leads to the leafy south-western suburbs of Brisbane...' (It would be bloody surprising if it didn't); 'The swimming pool is a place for apartment owners to meet and sun themselves and exercise...'; 'Phones make it possible to stay in contact with each other over long distances...'; 'Cartoons are well recognised for their ability to satirise and amuse on topical subjects, and are assured of wide appeal through their publication in the press' (You don't say).

From my experience, most editors don't want *the* story, they want *a* story; one that arrives on time and exactly fits the space pre-allotted. If you do that you are feted; if you demand time to get it right, or argue that a particular story is worth more space, then you are a prickly bastard. The brand new features editor (and there were even more of those than Editors or news editors) rang me at home at 10.00 p.m. one night and demanded a thousand words on the just-announced Queensland election by noon the next day. I said I couldn't possibly write the article by then: I hadn't written anything on politics for two years and I was in the middle of writing three thousand words about a weird, unexplained plane crash in western Queensland on a dark, moonless night. Two unmarked dead parrots had been found in the wreckage of Flight Kilo Tango Echo with the twelve dead men who had been turned into little more than paste.

'Hey, I'm not looking for a fight with anyone,' the new features editor said. 'Just give me the article by noon.' Some twenty years later I saw his photo in the paper. He looked nothing like I'd imagined: quite nice really. But back then, most editors were just a voice on the phone.

There are myriad ways to avoid writing an interesting newspaper feature story. Some people start with three, or four, or even six questions: 'But what sort of woman is she? And where does she come from? And how did she make all her money? And where is she going in the future?' That might be all right, up to a point, but usually it ensures that the writer is avoiding providing any of the answers. It is as if the writer loses sight of why they're writing the story in the first place. Or they write about poor Claire and then add: 'Claire is not her real name.' Many others begin: 'The *Oxford Dictionary* definition of...'; or 'Life wasn't meant to be easy'; or 'A Sydney taxi driver told me...'; or the ever-popular 'The Editor rang and told me to go and write an article on the following subject...' Still others start with a long quotation which is meaningless because the reader doesn't know who is saying this, or why, or under what circumstances. If the writer really wants to impress an Australian Editor, they will start with a scene from a Hollywood movie—any Hollywood movie—though most people won't have seen it.

Columnists often repeat the main story of the week for the first six paragraphs of their column, as if they think no one has been reading their paper.

Perhaps they're right.

Many people think a story is in-depth if it includes the subject's middle name—'Rodney George Laver,' 'Robert James Lee Hawke'. Or businessmen are described as 'mild-mannered and unassuming', as if they got to the top by being nice to all the people now beneath them. Toilets, bathrooms, phones, supermarkets and backyards are preceded by 'the humble'. Most incidents are just the tip of the iceberg and small towns are always a tight-knit community. In my day, all stories on Flo Bjelke-Petersen had to include a reference in the first paragraph to pumpkin scones: I failed to please one editor because I wouldn't do it. Brisbane, of course, is always 'a big country town'.

For TV, two clichés are always better than one—'The British government is bending over backwards to adopt a low profile in Hong Kong'—because the producer knows the audience has heard these phrases before.

The real story is not that easy to write.

One day I rolled up for work and was told the High Court was bringing down its decision on whether or not Canberra had the power to stop Tasmania from constructing a giant dam in a pristine wilderness area on the Franklin River. The entire case had been heard down south over many months, but, because the High Court happened to be making a rare visit to Brisbane, the decision was to be brought down here.

The giant courtroom was full. Up front, behind a long, elevated, polished timber bench, were seven carved, padded chairs with backs as high as an average person. I'd never seen our High Court, which is cloistered in the national capital in Canberra, and so I was surprised to find—when seven people dressed in black filed out and stood behind the chairs, and a hundred barristers and solicitors and reporters rose to their feet—that there were a couple of women. But, a minute later, seven men in black gowns with grey wigs over what was left of their grey hair emerged and sat on the ornate chairs as the first seven pulled the large chairs out for the judges. Then another man in black walked below the bench with a black cushion on his right hand, palm bent backwards over his right shoulder, and the judgment of each judge was placed on this cushion.

With pen poised, I prepared to write down the decision the entire nation was awaiting. The Chief Justice addressed the crowded court-room. 'To question 1a, No; to 1b, Perhaps; 1c, Yes; 2a, Maybe; 2b Of course; 3a...' (or some such). I hadn't even known that there was a list of questions: so how could I possibly write what the answers meant? The seven assistants then pulled out the tall chairs, and the judges left. As I phoned every lawyer I knew trying to find out what had transpired, it came to me that those who earn the most money do the same job over and over and over again, while those who must tackle something totally different every day earn much less.

The feature writer tackles a different subject every time.

Looking for something new when writing a feature on Brisbane's Story Bridge, I found it was by far the biggest bridge designed and built in Australia: designed by a local, Dr John Job Crew Bradfield of Sandgate. He had made it a web of steel because steel is a symbol of man's love for one another. Bradfield wrote of his bridge plans:

> Steel is man's masterpiece. Mythology tells us that we owe steel, the most potent factor in the building progress of the world, to the goddess of the Pole Star. This goddess, descending from the starry firmament, became enamoured of a mortal, Siderite, but he, loving none but his brother Sidere, repulsed her. In her wrath she transformed the devoted brothers into lode stone and iron... One force can draw it from the star above; iron, the symbol of fraternal love.

The interest for the writer is mostly in such small, unknown details. When Brisbane was hit by the flood of 1974 the writer's story was in the little 'For Sale' signs which quickly appeared on many mud-filled homes: 'FOR SALE River views at certain times'; 'FOR SALE Price: a dozen XXXX beer and a clean glass'; 'FOR SALE This house holds three million gallons of water'.

The feature writer's goal is to write stories that readers talk about: *Did you see the article saying ten elderly men with exactly the same farm background rule Queensland? Did you see that a Queensland committee found the only good thing about daylight saving would be 'the opportunity to enjoy tea without annoying insects'?* (Not that the insects would mind.) *Did you see where buck-toothed Queensland country singer Chad 'The Sheikh of Scrubby Creek' Morgan said he thought Sydney's Paul Hogan and Melbourne's Barry Humphries were just New Australians?*

Every year or so the Editor goes looking for someone to go on the 'last great cattle drive'. When my turn arrived I had no idea what to write six thousand words about. So I kept an eye on the head drover, Chris Herrmann. I picked on him when I noted that he stubbed out his cigarettes in the palm of his left hand, to prevent bushfires; carried all his possessions in a steel .303 cartridge box; and wore his hat to bed in his swag on the ground at night 'to keep the moonlight out'. In the morning, Chris Herrmann washed his face in the cattle trough with the cows (instead of in the dam with the ringers) 'because the water's warmer'. Everything had a ten-to-one chance of happening, and all distances were measured in chains. When we found a hole in the dingo fence west of Urandangie, he said: 'Ten to one it's been like that for forty years. The government spent millions, but the fence isn't worth two bob.' Then he looked up at the sky: 'Come on. The sun's still got ten chains to go.' The next day a plague of grasshoppers stopped the eight hundred head of Droughtmaster cattle: they wouldn't walk over the seething layer on the ground before them. 'I'll take the stock-whip to the bastards,' said Chris, and, like Moses parting the waters, led the cattle through. Every time he cracked the whip Chris yelled and the grasshoppers took off. They were so thick that every time I threw a stone through the air it hit one. Then a sawtooth-legged jumper got inside my shirt and another up my trouser leg. I yelled to Chris for help but he said, as I ran jumping through the bush like a brumby, 'Them? They're just along for the ride.'

One of the good things about being a writer on the *Australian* was that often I got to write the stories that I wanted to write, because Rupert was the first major Australian owner to give writers an expansive go. When I established that drunk drivers who killed in

Queensland were getting fined $500 to $750—little more than the punishment for the offence of drink-driving itself—and that most of their victims were young women, the *Australian* gave the stories full-page treatment. So many mothers wrote in that I wrote two more stories based on their sad letters, and, while the headline on my article was 'Death by Car', the mothers showed a much better appreciation of what was happening: they referred to the article as 'Murder by Car'. Patricia O'Neill, of Crow's Nest in New South Wales, formed an organisation to fight the problem nationwide. The power of Rupert's national paper soon became apparent. A few months after these articles were published, a driver who crashed his car while drunk, killing his young girlfriend, was given eighteen months in jail. Not only that, but the Court of Criminal Appeal in Brisbane later doubled the sentence to three years. Within eight years, the Queensland sentence for drink-driving causing death had been upped to a maximum ten years in jail.

Another time I was able to write a long article on a pet theory: 'Queensland—the different state'. I travelled all over the State doing interviews, and arrived in Ipswich on a forty degree day and stood in the street asking people what they thought made Queensland different from the rest of the country. After an hour, an old bloke said: 'Well if you've worked all over the world and you've been to China and to Vietnam and to Moscow and London...then why the hell are you standing on a hot street corner in Ipswich asking me?' I went home and wrote two stories: one on my interviews and the other my personal view. I showed them both to Adrian McGregor and he said, 'That bloke in Ipswich was right. Stick to your own theories, they're much more interesting.'

While some politicians derided my theory, a Sydney advertising agency rang to say my articles had inspired them to change their beer-advertising slogan in Queensland to 'OUR BEER': not something I felt proud of.

On the other hand, much of the time I had to write about things or people only my editors found of interest. And the more conservative our paper became as the 1980s rolled on, the worse the jobs became for me.

Ironically, as the business excesses of the '80s succeeded, the *Australian* seemed bent on wooing the corporate world that our paper had jousted with in the '70s. In a society in which the stock market can operate on rumour, our finance pages started lauding business and condemning the ordinary people who once had been our heroes. One finance columnist wrote that Australians were so happy on the dole that ginger growers in Queensland couldn't get enough workers to pick their crops. I was told to follow up his story.

Up around Yandina all the ginger farms turned out to be miles and miles up various dirt roads. You couldn't get to them unless you owned a car; you couldn't buy lunch; reasonable, cheap accommodation was hard to find nearby. In Sydney they probably thought there would be ferries, buses, trains—even monorails—stopping outside each ginger farm. I wrote the real story, the one they didn't want, and a bright young editor in Sydney rang to complain about my story and said that the pictures weren't good enough.

'I don't take the photos,' I said, making a new enemy.

I was sent to Perth to interview Rupert's Ansett Airlines partner, the boss of the worldwide transport company TNT, Sir Peter Abeles. According to the Editor, this was an 'exclusive interview situation': it was vital that we do an excellent job.

When I got on the plane in Brisbane, aged 44, I sat down next to a beautiful young woman reporter from the *Courier-Mail* whom I knew because, a couple of years before, she had been a copy-girl on Rupert's *Daily Sun*. She now wrote the stock market report in the *Courier*. To my surprise she too was going to Perth for an exclusive interview with Sir Peter.

More than twenty journalists gathered in Ansett's refurbished Gateway Hotel in Perth that evening for what was to be the launch of a new passenger aircraft by Sir Peter the next day. I felt set up. If I came away without this interview, I'd be in trouble. So I stuck it up Sir Peter's several PR men. The *Australian* had been lied to; this wasn't an interview, it was publicity for a plane. One of the PRs saw my invidious position and promised to see what he could do.

Late that evening he took me up to Sir Peter's hotel suite. The door was slightly ajar and the PR knocked tentatively as I prepared to meet one of Australia's most powerful men. As we walked into the suite, Sir Peter smiled happily from a lounge chair in the far corner, holding a glass in his left hand. Seated next to him was one of the other PR minders...and, laughing delightfully, seated in the other corner, was the beautiful young woman reporter from Brisbane, who held up a champagne glass and said: 'Many happy returns, Sir Peter. And what are you getting for your birthday?'

I got a drink but no interview.

Inside a hangar somewhere at Perth's sprawling airport the next day I listened as Sir Peter launched the new BAe-146-200 jet. Then he disappeared with various dignitaries and all I had was what he chose to say about the aircraft in front of every news organisation in the country. I watched the workers noisily stack up the hundreds of steel seats, and missed the bus back to the hotel. I began walking down a long, narrow, deserted bitumen road with no traffic. It had to lead somewhere. A chauffeur-driven limo pulled up. Sir Peter was sitting in the back and he offered me a lift to town. 'That's very nice of you, Sir Peter,' I said. 'Well, I am the biggest transport operator in the country. So I should be able to give you a lift,' he replied in his heavy Hungarian accent.

For the next twenty minutes, in airconditioned comfort, Sir Peter answered all my questions. I was saved for another week.

The *Australian* was very slowly metamorphosing into something I shouldn't have been working for. People like me, once popular, were increasingly seen as do-gooders: the worst thing you could say about a person now that greed was good and good was bad. Some former staff looked back longingly to the 1960s Editorship of Adrian Deamer who, they said, had trail-blazed the reporting of social issues, including Aboriginal rights. Since then, the subject of Aborigines had not been an issue on the *Australian*. For example, I had never been assigned to write on Aborigines, but came up with a few articles off my own bat, which the *Oz* happily ran in full. I made a futile attempt to understand the racist Queensland Aboriginal and Torres Strait Islander Act of Parliament, which proved incomprehensible. Another story concerned a secretly taped police conversation in which a sergeant said the only thing whites had done wrong by Aborigines was that: 'They didn't kill enough of the buggers.' He went on: 'Oh the good old days are gone with the blacks. You can't give them a bloody razzle-dazzle like you used to be able to.'

These articles prompted a white Queensland public servant to contact me late in 1981 to say that the government's own files on Aborigines showed how badly they had been treated in our lifetimes. He gave examples. Did I want some files, if he could smuggle them out?

'Don't use your own name when next you contact me,' I said. 'Let's give you a pseudonym, say…Chris Prince.'

One of my rules as bureau chief on the *Australian* was that I spoke to anyone who rang or came into our office: as long as they gave their name and said what they wanted. This meant I had to see and speak to many people. In Sydney there was an entire organisation for this purpose; in Brisbane there was me. A few months later my secretary, Lee Watters, came into my office and said, 'There's a Chris Prince on the phone but he won't say what he wants.'

'Look, Lee, you know the rule: if they won't say what it's about, then I won't talk to them.'

Lee left but came back: 'He insists that you know him; that it's very important. Chris Prince?'

'Never heard of him,' I said.

Lee, always an excellent judge, returned for another go. 'Something's going on. I think you should talk to him.'

I took the call, and next day picked up two files from an agreed spot.

These were just two files on Aboriginal lives from the fifty thousand files held in George Street. One was about the Protector of

Aborigines in a north Queensland town who in 1955 had, according to a confidential government report, raped three generations of women from an Aboriginal family: the married mother, her 15-year-old daughter and the 80-year-old grandmother. But, despite the mother signing her statutory declaration with a thumbprint, and police investigators writing, 'we have no doubt that the complaint of these Aboriginals is genuine and truthful,' a decision was taken in Brisbane *not* to bring the Protector to court.

The happenings in the other file were also in my lifetime. They were about an Aboriginal woman who fell in love with a young single white man she met on a train. Two months later the man wrote to the Native Affairs Minister in Brisbane asking to be allowed to marry her, saying: 'We are very devoted to each other.' More letters and government enquiries followed, including a police investigation into whether the man had any 'communist tendencies'. After a couple of years of pure racist bureaucracy the couple had a baby. 'The baby is very dark,' said the government records when they finally decided *not* to allow them to marry. At the end of the thick file, was a memo written seven years later by an officer of the State Heath Department. It read: 'Re. a man called... She wants to get in touch with him. She claims he desires to marry her.'

I tracked down the elderly Aboriginal woman to a small fibro house on the outskirts of Toowoomba, but when I mentioned the man and her love affair she became distressed. 'How do you know this. No one knows this.' I realised, too late, that I should not have been interfering in her life, no matter how telling the story. Thus I broke my own rule and wrote the article without her name and in a way in which she could not be recognised, even though it greatly weakened the story: those who didn't want to believe such things had ever happened in Australia could say it was made up. I even went as far as to tell the only deliberate lie I ever wrote. To protect the 'illegitimate' love baby, the little baby boy became a baby girl. Ron Richards hid the two damning files in his bat cave so they could not be repossessed from me to track down the civil servant.

After the stories appeared in the *Oz* in 1982, the elderly Aboriginal lady arrived one day in my office, all dressed up in gloves and hat. She was extremely pleased with the story, and suggested a movie be made starring her niece, who she said looked just like her at that age. A Griffith University student film unit did just that—organising the filming of the niece on an old train—and they interviewed the woman and me. But their work disappeared, they said, when someone at the university accidentally taped over the video.

Meanwhile, I had moved on to my next two features: also about the mistreatment of Aborigines. I wanted to make this a huge four-part series for maximum national impact. On 6 May 1981, Fred Bamboo, an Aborigine living on a mission in north Queensland, stabbed and killed his brother, Michael, and told the arresting sergeant: 'I loved him.' A group of lawyers in Brisbane had already noted a pattern: Aborigines on government missions in Queensland were killing those they loved best. As I wrote, they weren't killing bankers, or the people down the road, they were killing the people they loved: their nearest and their dearest. So these lawyers went to court to prove this was a syndrome caused by herding various Aboriginal clans into these isolated government 'reserves'.

When the court cases were all over I had a pile of transcripts on my desk forty centimetres high. It took eight weeks to write all four stories, while Harry Davis, efficient and dedicated, ran the bureau. Like this book, these articles were very difficult to write without getting into trouble: but I kept in mind something Evan Whitton had once told me: 'There is always a form of words.' Because I wrote nothing else, Steady Editor (not knowing what I was up against) rang and gave me—not for the last time—a bollocking. But I ignored all criticism from all sections of the paper and eventually handed over the four articles to the telex girl to send off to Sydney. As was my habit, I took her a cake from the French Patisserie in Brunswick Street to lighten the workload. A few days later Steady Editor came on the phone again. This time I was ready. I'd lost the windowed office and was now sharing a tearoom with no window in an old building out the back. So, come on.

'What have we done?' Steady Editor said with genuine anguish in his voice. 'What have we done? What have we done to our Aborigines?'

Steady Editor gave the stories huge play every weekend for a month. This unexpected display by the *Australian* had such an effect that the Aboriginal Treaty Committee in Canberra—chaired by Dr Nugget Coombs—at the end of 1982 published what they called 'these historic articles' in a yellow-covered book called *Four Stories,* which was sold around the country to raise funds and gain support for a treaty with Aborigines, something later promised but never granted.

That should have been the end of that for me, but when you interfere in people's lives it never is. Four years later, I came home late one night to my Taringa home to find a huge truck parked out the front and a large Aboriginal man sitting waiting on the front steps.

I knew it was him.

Larger than life itself, here he was, the baby boy. He was proud of the story of his parents, and he wanted his own copy of my 1984 University of Queensland Press book *Queenslanders* in which the story had been reprinted.

Then, less than two years later, he was back again.

This time his mother was dying in the Princess Alexandra Hospital. It was vital, he said, that I be there for her death, because I was the one who had told the story of her life.

Of his beginnings.

At the hospital, the dying woman's relatives filed silently out of the room on my arrival without looking at me. Though in a semi-coma and sweating profusely, this dying woman—who had been stopped in ripe life by a white government from marrying the father of her son—held my hand hard as her big baby boy wiped her brow and kept telling her over and over again:

'He's here, Mum. He's here now, the man who told your life. He's here.'

15 Nemesis of Evildoers

The first four years of the '80s saw five different Editors of the *Australian*. Mr One-Day Editor lasted just the one day: as if his career stood as a metaphor for the entire newspaper industry.

I have no idea why One-Day Editor got the flick, but I can tell you that Rupert himself had hired him the previous year as deputy editor. Apparently, one cold morning early in July 1981 Rupert was very unhappy that his *Australian* had missed the importance of an event in the then esoteric—nowadays exoteric—world of finance, and had not put the story on page one. Agitated, on his way to work, as I heard it, Rupert turned on the radio only to hear a brilliant dissertation on the significance of these economic events by a journalist with an English accent. Rupert had this man tracked down and found he was assistant editor of a business magazine and had worked on the *Times* and the *Observer*, as well as for the BBC. Rupert phoned the 44-year-old and hired him as deputy editor. Just over a year later he was promoted—briefly, as it turned out—to Editor.

One-Day Editor was followed by another Englishman, a knight of the realm. Sir Editor had been, throughout the '70s, a highly successful and famous Editor of Rupert's conservative tabloid the London *Sun*, but was not suited to a quality Australian broadsheet.

In fact, he wasn't suited to Australia.

Readers in England will have heard of Sir Editor—Sir Larry Lamb—who, when he arrived in Australia, was taken by Rupert for a Great Barrier Reef holiday on Rupert's own yacht. Ron Richards was there, and he recounted to me how Rupert was amazed that Sir Larry—who had happily taken on the biggest sharks, barracudas, gropers, snakes and jellyfish in English society—would not jump over the side and join everyone else in the warm, clear waters of the Reef. No way. According to Ron, on the last day of the trip Rupert and Ron ordered Sir Larry overboard for a dip in the still water above a very shallow reef. 'You could've read a newspaper on the bottom,' Ron said. They told Sir Larry (S'larry, as he became known to *Oz* reporters) it would be un-Australian not to have one swim on the Great Barrier Reef. Rather than be tossed overboard, S'larry relented, but said he would only go in the water if he was attached to the boat by a rope so that he could be hauled back in if anything went wrong. To Australians, this sort of behaviour was unheard of. But Rupert relented and, according to Ron, they hauled out the thickest rigging and, amid much hilarity, tied the rope around Sir Larry's white waist before he flopped over the side, making 'the biggest plop' Ron had ever heard. Sir Larry tugged, and twisted, and showed his teeth, as he plunged down and then rose up high out of the water while Rupert and Ron held on to the tackle like two big-game fishermen hauling in a Great White.

That swim of Sir Larry's was to closely mirror his Editorship of the *Australian*: neither lasted very long but a hell of a lot happened while Sir Larry was thrashing about.

During his few months as Editor, Sir Larry sacked a heap of reporters. Elsewhere, the figure has been recorded as thirty-nine. S'larry couldn't get me, because two months earlier—July 1982—I had temporarily transferred over to Rupert's brand new newspaper,

Brisbane's *Daily Sun*, after Ron Richards had asked me to help get it off the ground.

Ron was understandably nervous about taking on the entrenched *Courier-Mail* because he had argued for, and dreamt of, this moment—and now Rupert had given it to him. For more than a decade Ron had urged Rupert to let the popular *Sunday Sun* go daily, but Rupert didn't think it would work—even though the *Sunday Sun*, under Ron, had proven that it could compete with the *Courier-Mail*'s Sunday sister, the *Sunday Mail*, without benefit of flow-on readers and writers from a daily paper.

Rupert wouldn't give in to Ron, even though it must have irked him that the building, the printing presses, the managers, the reporters and the distribution were only being used to capacity once a week. But Rupert knew better than anyone how hard it is to get newspaper readers (not to mention newsagents) to change the habits of a lifetime. Exactly ten years earlier in 1972, Rupert had tried with our wrap-around. While it had added circulation to the *Australian*, the wrap-around failed to impact on the *Courier-Mail*, which people had to have if they wanted to buy or sell a house, a dog, a car, a holiday, a motel; to see who had died, been born or married; to find out who had been arrested or jailed; or even to put in for a government tender.

There was another dimension. Rupert had good reason to wait for the best moment, because of his family's belief that the *Courier-Mail* had been manoeuvred from their grasp. In the end, Rupert used Ron's intense desire as an incentive scheme. Ron told me Rupert had agreed to start a *Daily Sun*, but only when Ron had proven he could match the *Sunday Mail*'s sales on Sundays: a Herculean task. Between them, these two Brisbane Sunday papers sold more than three-quarters of a million copies every Sunday: the sort of total Sunday circulation that no other Australian city, except Sydney, could get anywhere near. So there wasn't much room for improvement. The intense rivalry meant that both papers lost millions of dollars a year; unlike in Adelaide, where the two losing Sunday papers (also owned by News and the

Herald) had years before done a 50–50 amalgamation to produce just the one paper, which then produced rich profits for both companies.

Ron accepted Rupert's challenge gleefully and he and Fatman lifted audited sales an incredible 46 000 per edition (which must surely be an Australian record) in the six months to March 1982, to rapidly narrow the gap with the *Sunday Mail*. So Rupert agreed to start a daily, with the first edition printed on 2 August 1982. The decision made, Rupert asked Ron how many papers a day the *Daily Sun* would sell initially. An enthusiastic Ron said he would be disappointed if more than 200 000 wasn't reached. Rupert replied that, up against the might of the *Courier-Mail*, Ron could chop that figure almost in half— and, in the end, Rupert was pretty spot on, with initial *Daily Sun* audited sales of 105 281.

I was glad that Rupert was taking on my old newspaper from cadet reporter days. You didn't have to be Einstein to realise that far too much power resided in the hands of a single, unopposed morning daily. The *Courier-Mail* was the only place where Brisbane people could read about each other every day, while also knowing that everyone else in the State was reading the same story too. It was the only place where any Queenslander's achievements could regularly be seen by everyone else. It was said that the ambitious and the powerful thought they weren't alive 'unless their photo is in the *Courier-Mail*', and that the only thing worse than being badly reviewed in the *Courier-Mail* was never to be mentioned at all. It was a syndrome— what Milton called 'that last infirmity of noble minds'—that conferred inestimable power on the *Courier-Mail*.

Since any story can be written positively or negatively, and be either displayed or hidden, the *Courier-Mail* had become Queensland's ulti- mate judge. Who was doing well? Who badly? What sins should be on the top of page one? Which on the bottom of page two? (Newspaper research shows that few people read page two.) Politicians, publishers, actors, schools, pilots, principals, judges, public servants, authors, shopping centres, miners, banks, airlines, universi- ties, farmers, theatre owners, chefs, sports stars, and everyone else in

Queensland with any power or importance were, sooner or later, judged successes or failures by the *Courier-Mail*. Thus this sole daily broadsheet was far more powerful than any government. A government might tax you, but the *Courier-Mail* could cost you your reputation and stop people from buying, as it were, your tickets.

While Ron and Rupert's *Sunday Sun* battled away once a week, screaming out for attention with large headlines (and the larger the headlines the less real influence a paper has), the visually staid *Courier-Mail* was the unseen daily porridge that bound up Queensland society: a glue that never came unstuck. It kept everyone, and everything, in touch with one another.

Thus were all the powerful groups in Queensland, including even charities and governments, forced to eagerly seek out the fellowship and favour of the *Courier-Mail* and its employees. Perforce, few ever dared publicly criticise the paper: the only organisation above review except, in 1982, for the police. (The power of the police came not just from carrying guns, but also from being the only source of many major news stories, plus photographs and security film surrounding robberies, rapes, drug-busts, traffic deaths, kidnaps, arrests, extortions and murders.)

All organisations with ambition, therefore, paid ex-reporters to help them seek the fraternity of the *Courier-Mail*. These ex-reporters—many from the *Courier* itself—are known as public relations officers (PRs for short) and most powerful people in Brisbane at that time had the full-time use of at least one or two. So much so that journalism, instead of being a career like in England and the US, had become a stepping-stone into PR. Journalists could remain in their union, get out of their shabby, stained, smoky, dented offices with mismatched, burn-marked furniture and drawers full of decades-old stories, and be paid more to present positive stories about their employer in publishable form to the *Courier-Mail*. And perhaps (incidentally) to other media. Many local stories on the nightly TV news are PR announcements organised by fellow journalists.

When I gave a lecture on journalism to doctors at Brisbane's Mater

Hospital in the early '80s, I wondered why they laughed as one when I pointed my index finger at the audience while emphasising the role of PRs in the media. It turned out that, to the doctors, PR and the right index finger meant something else entirely; they thought I was saying the media was controlled 'per rectum'.

Well, not that far out really, since PR operates out the back and away from the glare.

With basically all Queensland TV and radio stations controlled from down south or overseas, it was true to say that you couldn't successfully hold a reunion, put on a sold-out concert, get your wedding picture out to everyone, attack smoking or complain about the price of bread unless the *Courier-Mail* wanted to let you. So this was the sort of entrenched daily power Rupert and Ron were up against. Of course, there was always the ABC. But the ABC was in the same position as every other power group—especially as back then it was never prepared to use its muscle as a media watchdog. The ABC itself had to advertise in the *Courier-Mail*, and employed PRs to get daily publicity in the paper for its radio and TV programs. And, even then, the *Courier-Mail* sat in daily critical judgment on these programs, and, therefore, on ABC chiefs and their government-appointed jobs. It is probably for all these reasons that the ABC allows its broadcast stars to write for newspapers.

To make room in the building for the new *Daily Sun*, our Brisbane bureau was moved into the bottom of a dilapidated start-of-the-century building out the back while Ron Richards built me a new office at the *Daily Sun*. When I saw it was being built exactly in the centre of the building, bordered on all sides by uninterrupted views of varnished fake wood walls, I buttonholed him.

'Are you building me a bat cave, Ron?'

'Don't be like that.'

'But Rupert himself promised me an office with a window!'

'I wouldn't depend on that forever more,' advised Ron sagely.

I knew what Ron meant. Rupert's influence was becoming more and more remote as he got bigger and bigger overseas. Hadn't he just bought William Collins in Britain, which he'd merged with Harper & Row in the US to create HarperCollins, the world's biggest book publisher? So I let the issue slide. The next time I met Rupert I'd just let him know what had happened.

The in-phrase at News Ltd back then was 'the new technology', which meant all the typewriters were gradually being replaced by VDTs (video display terminals) or VDUs (Video Display Units)— computer word processors. Rupert was, naturally, way out in front in newspaper computer use in Australia. He was the first to use facsimile to send a newspaper to another city and the first to use computers to produce an Australian newspaper. He also started the first computer pages—though, with almost no illustrations available back then, the bloke running these pages in the *Oz* filled any holes with pictures of elephants. Unfortunately for Australia's future in an IT world, the elephants proved much more popular than the computer stories.

In 1979 I walked into our Sydney newsroom and realised something was wrong. There was no noise, no clanking of typewriters and no buzz of conversation. It appeared no one was at home until I spied the backs of all the reporters, who were sitting virtually inside space-age grey desk capsules with monitors built in before their eyes, every last one of them watching a small green light moving across a screen. Every time they typed an error there was a loud 'beep' which attracted disapproving looks from around the floor. Another typing error from machine number eighty-two!

Even from side-on, I recognised Charlie Wright: the slicked-back blond hair, the broad Mt Isa back, the wry grin which showed he'd had another wicked thought and which, luckily, reached all the way back to his ears. The only way I could get Charlie's attention was to stretch my arm into the capsule space and pat him on the shoulder— at which Charlie leaped backwards and out and swung around with his dukes up. 'Don't do that to me, man,' he said, before breaking into a mischievous grin when he saw it was the Brisbane bloke who had cleaned him up at ping-pong. 'I was being dragged further and further into that confounded machine by my eyeballs, Hughie. It sucks you in like a vampire sucking your toes.'

In 1982, these machines that screamed out in pain when a mistake was made arrived in Brisbane for the new *Daily Sun*. Ron, who was now in his mid-50s, never touched a VDU terminal, and he generously said that, because I was so old for a newspaper reporter (41), I needn't use one. 'You can ring a copy-taker and dictate your story over the phone from your office.' But I did use the VDUs, which were much easier and quicker than a typewriter.

While we had put up with cigarette smoke in the office for more than a decade, a huge red sign appeared outside the top-floor office where the computer mainframes sat: 'No Smoking in the Computer Room'. The computers were being treated better than the humans who used them.

A new Editor, John Hartigan, and a deputy editor, Col Allan, were flown up from Sydney to run the *Daily Sun*, which caused Ken Blanch to resign. Why would Rupert break up the Fatman and Robin team? Ron was still boss of everything in the building, but he wasn't the Editor. And just as Rupert had taken Rigby to London and then New York, the *Daily Sun* flew in Larry Pickering—obviously Rupert believed that the most vital employee on a newspaper is the cartoonist.

With brand new presses, Rupert's *Daily Sun* became the first newspaper in Brisbane to run colour pictures. There was a line-up of talent that included Sally Loane, Bart Sinclair, Kathy Davis, Bob Howarth, and Brian Hale as finance editor. Plus Paul McLean, John Newcombe, Wally Lewis and Keri Craig writing columns. Brigitte Bardot was about to turn 48, Andrew Lloyd Webber's musical *Cats* was getting rave reviews overseas, a couple of full-page advertisements in the *Daily Sun* promised satisfaction and quality in a mild cigarette, and the famous Valley Diehards were turning the first sod in their new clubhouse at Neumann Oval. (Twenty years later, with the Brisbane Rugby League competition killed off by the Sydney premiership, the Diehards were dead and their paddock was a cricket oval: the Allan Border Field.)

I attended the first news conference at the *Daily Sun*. As well as the new Editor and his deputy—both 30-something—the white-haired General Manager (Editorial) of News Ltd, Brian Hogben, was there, and the former Steady Editor was up from the *Oz* in Sydney to help. These Sydneyites started asking: 'What gigs are on in town?' Gigs? Gigs? I'd never heard that term in Brisbane.

'Who are your local film stars?' asked Brian Hogben. Well, actually, we don't have any film stars up here; the money for films is all kept down south.

'Then who are the stars of your local TV shows?'

'Well,' I said, 'we don't get to have our own TV shows, we get American, British or yours. The bloke who won the Logie here as Most Popular Local TV Personality for the last few years won it for reading out the six winning Lotto numbers on a Saturday night!' The Sydney blokes seemed taken aback. What strange country were they in?

'Then, since you haven't any movie stars or TV stars, we'll have to concentrate on your TV newsreaders,' Brian Hogben said.

'What about the Phantom?' I asked.

'The only really famous people are the Premier, Joh, and his government,' said Steady Editor, ignoring my comment.

'And while we're at it,' said Brian Hogben, 'let's get the Advertising Department out of the used-car yards! Is everyone in this town driving an old motor? I've got a great wheeze: let's have a new car as a giveaway prize for home deliveries.'

Brian Hogben was a tall, handsome, ruddy-faced man with a white moustache. I had never dealt with him before, since he was the highest-ranked journalist in the Australian arm of Rupert's company. A former Sydney Editor, I knew that he was well liked by News Ltd journalists. Even Charlie Wright said Brian Hogben was what we call all right (like 'not bad', high praise from an Australian). So I shouldn't have got upset when, one day, Brian pulled up a chair next to my VDU and said he would like me to preview a new Hollywood film, *ET*, 'and write how good it is'. That annoyed me, so I answered: 'What if I don't like it?' Which annoyed Brian.

'Then we won't run your story,' he said matter-of-factly, and stood up and walked away.

Luckily, I did like the film. In fact, I wiped away tears at one stage. And when my story appeared as a double-page spread, a woman cut the piece out of the *Sun*, wrote 'good work' across it, and posted it in to me. I've often wondered though: did I enjoy the film because the boss told me to?

Meanwhile, I decided that a story on the Phantom would suit the *Daily Sun*.

The Australian president and founder of the 700-member Phantom Comic Club was a local, 26-year-old John Henderson of Camp Hill. Queenslanders, John claimed, could relate best to the Phantom: 'because he stands for individualism, determination, wisdom, undying faith, belief in a cause and perseverance against impossible odds. And he doesn't hang around waiting for accolades.' Plus, I could have added, the Phantom doesn't get any say in the real world.

John Henderson occasionally turned up in the uniform of the Ghost Who Walks, and being a footballer, he was one of the few people who could fill the skin-tight grey body suit. One day, the Phantom arrived—black gun pouches and all—in the Botanic Gardens for the launch of one of my books. But, despite having the strength of ten tigers, he was jumped by some Special Branch officers. These officers were from the infamous Queensland police section whose job it was—before they were disbanded after the Fitzgerald corruption inquiry—to keep lists of people who dared write letters-to-the-Editor or who signed petitions to Parliament or who dissented at company AGMs. (State Special Branches were, in effect, privatised in the late '90s by corporations that now collate the data.)

'What kept you?' I asked Mr Walker when he turned up late.

'I had trouble with some roughnecks,' the Nemesis of Evildoers replied, as he adjusted his black eye mask and striped underpants. So I offered him a drink.

'A glass of milk and a bowl of water for Devil,' said the Guardian of the Eastern Dark.

The hardest day to sell the *Daily Sun* was on a Saturday because the *Courier-Mail* overflowed with classified ads and government jobs that day, and Rupert's *Weekend Australian* was sought after in the wealthier suburbs—which was the reason Ron never enjoyed doing the *Australian* favours. Ron came up with the idea of a full page of news and gossip about well-known Brisbane people—'Saturday People'—and page six was devoted entirely to this: no ads; a clean-skin page. After a few weeks, Ron said it hadn't worked, and asked me to write the page. I felt like the US comic strip character in the *Australian*, Doonesbury, who at that time was trying to become a top-shot newspaperman in Washington, yet had been assigned to write a gossip column.

Saturday People was similar (but with actual names) to a gossip page the *Sunday Sun* had successfully run for decades: 'Truth to Tell'. Ron told me that Rupert had queried the usefulness of Truth to Tell, saying it should be dropped. But Ron replied—quite rightly—that, despite the lack of names and the often-unlikely urban myth scenarios, it was one of the best read things in Queensland. Rupert said OK.

I ran into a problem on the *Daily Sun* when I wrote a feature on Brisbane's worsening air pollution problem (for the first time you could see the air). Not only did the cabinet minister in charge accost me, and wouldn't believe the figures were from his own department's annual report, but one of Rupert's Sydney Mahogany Row executives came up to my office to say 'we want positive stories'.

Soon after the *Daily Sun* started, Australia went suddenly into what was euphemistically called 'an economic downturn'. It should have been called a crash. Interest rates, as Rupert had predicted to me three years earlier, went through the roof. My solicitor and five other business partners were now paying 21.5 per cent for money we had borrowed to build some shops. Not one of these six, I knew, would be voting for the Fraser–Howard team at the 1983 election. Bill

Hayden was right: a drover's dog could have won that election, as Bob Hawke did...the man Rupert had told me would get the top job.

One day that September of 1982—in the midst of the crash—I wandered around the block from the *Daily Sun,* up McLachlan Street and down a few stairs to the *Australian's* new office in the bottom of No. 8: a building constructed in 1905 to manufacture clothing and hats. The huge single grubby room full of almost-adjoining desks, stacks of old newspapers, a score of metal wastepaper bins and overflowing ashtrays, had one tiny window so high up you could just see a bit of the sky if you stood in the right place.

Adrian McGregor wasn't in, and everyone else was standing around awaiting their weekly pay cheque. Instead, nine large white envelopes were delivered. Max Jessop, a Yorkshireman who was married with five kids and who loved the atmosphere of the Empire Hotel, beat everyone to the cheque—only to throw the envelope on the ground and burst unexpectedly into *The Red Flag.*

> *Then raise the scarlet standard high*
> *Beneath its folds we'll live and die;*
> *Tho' cowards flinch, and traitors sneer,*
> *We'll keep the red flag flying here.*

The greed-is-good era had just started, and Max was singing the workers' hymn. A life member of the ALP, Max, 43, had a tremendous tenor voice, and the little glass window rattled like a cage as he limped slowly around the office—hands outstretched, palms upwards—looking into each face from only inches away as he sang. Large tears, the biggest I've ever seen, rolled down from underneath his thick, horn-rimmed glasses as his voice dropped an octave:

> *The people's flag is deepest red,*
> *It shrouded oft our martyr'd dead;*
> *And as their limbs grew stiff and cold,*
> *Their life-blood dyed its every fold.*

Envelope after envelope hit the ground…five, six, seven, eight. And there was still an envelope for Adrian sitting on his desk.

They were all finished, paid off, unemployed, purged as of that moment. Thank you S'larry. Even a young finance reporter who had been sent up the previous week from Sydney was sacked: 'But I haven't got enough money to get back home to Sydney.' Even Harry Davis, who said he had been promised a job for life by Rupert when he had come over to be Editor of the wrap-around ten years and three months earlier.

No one could talk; no one joined in; they just stared as Max staggered like an ageing opera star in a modern tragedy—past the last of the rows of typewriters, which sat like cold metal monuments to Australia's past: Imperials, Royals and Coronas.

> It suits today the meek and base,
> Whose eyes are fixed on self and place;
> To cringe beneath the rich man's frown
> And tear our sacred emblem down.

Then Adrian arrived in his favourite brown corduroy jacket. We all watched as he opened his envelope to find his payout cheque. A sports feature expert, Adrian seemed disbelieving. 'But this can't be right. Brisbane's Commonwealth Games starts in just two weeks. It's the biggest sporting event since the '56 Olympic Games in Melbourne.'

Back at the *Daily Sun* I heard there might not be a job back at the *Oz* for me either: there was only one way to find out. I sent Ron a memo saying I wanted to return to the *Australian*. Ron took me to lunch at the Coronation Motel with one of the company's top accountants, Don Davies, and said he was very annoyed that I wanted to leave. 'I'm really worried about you, Hugh,' Ron said. 'I don't know where you're headed. We want you on the *Sun*. I'm afraid you're going nowhere. You'll end up like the Eagle.'

'Well, that's funny, Ron,' I said, 'because I'm worried about where you're headed and what's gonna happen to you.'

Don Davies, a gentleman, sensed the deteriorating situation and wisely turned it into a bit of a joke. 'So you think big wheels get into more trouble than little wheels?' Don said. 'Hugh has a point, Ron. You'd better watch yourself.'

Three months later, after Steady Editor had returned to replace Sir Larry, I got to return home to the *Australian*'s bureau to work with Liz Johnston, who had survived the purge.

Then, one day early in 1983, Brian Hogben unexpectedly found his way from Mahogany Row round the back and down the stairs into our ugly office. 'Hugh, could you come for a walk with me please?' Well, this was it. Ron was right.

We walked back up the stairs, right into McLachlan Street and around past the tiny park where some men sat and drank. As we walked towards what was to become the Chinatown Mall, Brian unexpectedly asked me how Harry Davis was going. Harry and Max Jessop, I understood, had tried to start a little paper south of Brisbane, but I'd heard it didn't work.

'We were too rough on Harry,' said Brian. 'We think Harry is a good man. We'd like Harry to come back to us. We'd like you to tell Harry we apologise for his dismissal, and we would be very pleased if he would come back and work for us at News Ltd as if we'd never told him to go.'

I couldn't wait. Harry's wife, Pat, would be so pleased.

Rupert had been busy late in 1982 starting up satellite TV stations in Boston and Chicago. But, as the Phantom would say whenever the drums of the pygmies rumbled through the jungle, 'a rumour can go round the world.'

The drumbeats of Harry Davis's sacking had finally reached Rupert, who eventually came through for him, as promised.

16 Rupert goes to the Ekka

It was pretty unusual for Rupert to turn up in Brisbane in March; it was too early in the year. But the bloke in charge of the *Sun*'s car pool always knew who was coming and who was going and, on Friday, 4 March 1983, he whispered to me the headline news that Rupert was in town.

This was the day before the federal election that saw Malcolm Fraser lose power to Bob Hawke. In the previous *Weekend Australian* I had written an article saying, 'Hawke is going to win,' so, given Rupert's intense interest in politics, I expected him to magically appear in our bureau at any moment.

If he could find us.

All day Friday I was ready to point out that I didn't have an office. But by five o'clock, nothing. I checked once again with my mate in charge of the cars—no news. As we stood chatting next to the bowsers at the local BP garage, which looked after all News Ltd vehicles, my mate suddenly said, 'Hey, I believe you are doing very well! Bloody well.' This caught my attention, because, being in charge of the cars, he overheard lots of conversations as he drove important people around.

How did he know I was doing very well?

'I saw you on television!' he said triumphantly. No wonder everyone in Australia works really hard to succeed so they can appear in television advertisements.

Much to my disappointment, just before six o'clock that Friday evening, my friend from the car pool told me that Rupert had departed for Brisbane Airport, driving himself. Since the *Weekend Australian* was ready to be put to bed, and since for at least twelve hours on Sunday I alone would be covering the results of the election in Queensland for Monday morning's paper, I went off to Friday night tennis, leaving our new young reporter, Ross Peake, on watch.

Shortly after six that pre-election eve, Ross was standing alone in the aisle of our isolated office, guarding the fort after an extremely busy week writing politics: bored, leaning on a low fake-wood partition next to some fading newspaper files, day-dreaming after having checked the ABC radio news.

Someone strode confidently into our large room up the other end, through the glass doors opposite the toilets, saying, 'Where is everybody?'

Ross looked blearily across several desks towards the man in the beautiful blue suit with the friendly smile on his dial, and wondered for a moment why someone should want to know. No one had ever burst into our one-room bureau and asked such a question before; hardly anyone ever visited since we'd moved here. Was he lost? He was certainly far too well dressed for this part of town. The creased pale jaw, the well-shaved chin, the twinkling brown eyes. This bloke looked like, looked very much like, was, Rupert!

'Well, where is everybody?' Rupert repeated jauntily, as he moved through the room towards Ross with the walk of a man with developed leg muscles: as if he owned the place. But Ross was briefly nonplussed. He didn't want to lie, but neither did he want to say the other two reporters in the bureau had gone home or, worse still, that one of them was playing tennis.

'Er...er...er...'

'I know where they are,' said Rupert, answering his own question.

'They're all out covering the federal election!' And Rupert strode happily back out into the dark of Fortitude Valley.

It was a strange month all round back then when Bob Hawke won that '83 election, causing the stone-faced Malcolm Fraser to almost break down in tears on national TV. The *Australian* had recently appointed a new Publisher, Geraldine Paton, and she flew to Brisbane just before the election and came around to our bureau to meet me. I, of course, didn't have an office, so I grabbed a chair for her and put it in the aisle opposite my desk up against a pile of papers. It was not a good time to be meeting the first female Publisher of the *Oz*. This was probably the most exciting federal election ever, and Ross, Liz Johnston and I were rushing in and out on stories, covering one-fifth of Australia by ourselves, and all the phones were ringing constantly. But Geraldine understood and, I noted, remained pert and serene in a cute little tilted hat as we were continually interrupted.

As Geraldine was discussing her particular vision for the *Oz*, a phone rang on the news desk. I excused myself and rushed over to answer. The news editor was on the line from Sydney. 'Hugh, you'll have to get over to the Crest Hotel and do the colour story on Bob Hawke. We flew Geraldine Pascall up to Brisbane, but she's been found dead in her hotel room.'

'No she's not,' I interrupted. 'Geraldine's sitting at my desk, in a little hat.'

There was a silence. Geraldine Paton looked up, smiling, unaware, while the news editor said: 'Are you all right? I'm telling you, Geraldine Pascall is dead.' Immediately I realised my macabre error with a sudden vision of arts editor Geraldine Pascall's big hair, long cigarette, flowing multicoloured Egyptian cotton outfits and extravagant, enormous dark glasses that she kept on indoors and out. How could I have mixed up the two lady Geraldines?

On the Monday morning after the election I had seven election articles in the paper, four with my name on: Senator Neville Bonner, an Aborigine, was close to winning as an independent after leaving the Liberals who had dropped him down their ticket to an unwinnable position; cabinet minister Jim Killen was in danger of defeat but he said, when I found him, that he was 'hanging together like an old gate'; Premier Joh Bjelke-Petersen had refused to help his fellow conservative Malcolm Fraser in the campaign and had shot through to Singapore where I found him in a hotel room; and a thousand-word overview.

When I was leaving the office at nine o'clock that Sunday night, an editor rang to complain they had not received the commentary for the Queensland TV Guide. So I wearily typed six hundred words: recommended *The Dismissal*, which had been postponed because of the election; said *Alien* was monstrous; and observed that James Bolan from *When the Boat Comes In* was miscast in a weak comedy.

Luckily I'd brought my wife, Helen, in that day to help me. She'd been a journalist on the *Courier-Mail*, and we'd married in 1981 when I was 40 years old after Helen promised to give up smoking. My father, Fred, had been right all along. He'd said since I was a boy, 'Hughie, I'll have to nurse you till you're 40.' And I'd always wondered what he meant.

When I first met Helen I was struck by her incredible likeness to the beautiful Jessie in *When the Boat Comes In*. The same dark hair and fiery brown eyes; the same indentations and dimples below wider cheekbones; the daintiness too. Coincidentally, she came from a famous journalist's family. And his name was Hugh, Hugh Dash, who had worked for Prime Minister Menzies for many years. She asked if I knew Buzz Kennedy, a veteran classy writer on the *Oz*, because he had worked with her uncle. I found myself having to concentrate really hard while she talked: not just because of her soft, gentle and low voice, but because I was entranced.

Yes, I knew Buzz.

Helen had just read a book about Errol Flynn's son, Sean. Yes, I knew Sean. I'd known Sean Flynn in Bali in 1969 before he went to Vietnam to cover the war and disappeared, forever, in Cambodia.

It was wonderful to meet a beautiful Brisbane girl with similar interests. Later we would sit in the alcoves at the Snuggle Inn at Milton and have welsh rarebit. We even both had Harry Chapin's single *Taxi* at home. We had a hell of a lot in common.

Having a journalist as a wife meant we could discuss stories and newspapers every night, which made me consider my actions, and those of the *Oz*, much more. Which led, occasionally, to me writing memos of complaint about my paper. One of the problems with complaining to your bosses is that you had then better not make a mistake yourself. Once I made an error in a story because I'd forgotten that the boundaries of Bill Hayden's seat of Oxley had changed. Next day the Editor rang: 'You're always ready to criticise us; so now I'm ringing to criticise you.'

On one occasion it seemed that Humorous Editor would be arrested because of a mistake by me. The story began innocently enough when a Brisbane lawyer told me that a judgment in a family law case had altered a basic tenet of our society. The *Family Law Journal* reported that a woman had been awarded sixty-five per cent of the family home in a divorce case because her husband was dying of cancer and had only six months to live. The court ruled he had 'limited future financial needs'. The man appealed, but the Full Bench of the Family Court dismissed his appeal. I quoted the lawyer as saying solicitors would now be asking clients: 'How ill is your spouse?'

We published a photo of the sick husband who, by the time his appeal had been dismissed (February 1982), had outlived the original judgment by six months. 'We are all dying,' he said. 'The judges are out of touch with reality.'

After my story appeared, Humorous Editor rang to say a couple of Federal Police were in his office. 'They've come to arrest me because it's against the law to name the people involved in family law cases.' This put me into a real panic. An hour later, I telexed the following to Sydney:

Since this judgment altered the very basis of divorce settlements in Australia, it seemed to me that all Australians had a right to know.

The case had already been widely published in the CCH *Family Law Journal*, a journal read by thousands of lawyers around the nation and, presumably, by others like myself. My story did not report the case itself, but dwelt on the significance of the judgment. A Brisbane lawyer, shocked by the finding, contacted our paper and said people should be warned of the consequences... This was not only a matter of considerable public interest and importance but was also an alteration, by precedent, to one of the most basic tenets of our society: that divorce partners do not receive more than half the property just because they are healthier, or younger, than their partner.

I sweated it out for the next few weeks. But I needn't have. Humorous Editor didn't go to jail, and he never mentioned the incident again. In fact, as you'll have guessed, Humorous Editor was a bit of a joker. Before he was promoted from Editor to Mahogany Row, Humorous Editor went on a trip around News Ltd's operations with Rupert. The party arrived in Brisbane in August during the Brisbane Exhibition, a huge agricultural show known here as 'the Ekka' and which most locals attend. Humorous Editor came to see me and, just before he left, he said, 'By the way, Rupert wants to go to the Ekka.' I wasn't surprised, since I knew Rupert was interested in everything, and I knew that he owned two bush properties himself, including Australia's largest Merino stud, Boonoke, 142508 hectares on the rich, flat, well-grassed Riverina plains of New South Wales near the Victorian border. I rang the Royal National Association, who went into a frenzy when they heard that Rupert Murdoch had asked to visit their Show. Special VIP tickets were arranged, car spaces set aside... Then I rushed breathlessly around the building to find Humorous Editor to tell him everything was in place.

He looked at me as if I were crazy. 'You believed me? I was only joking.' A few years later when I passed him in the narrow corridor of Mahogany Row, instead of saying hello, Humorous Editor burst out laughing.

However, he hadn't thought it was very funny when he was Editor and I wrote a column about Amnesty International (which defends prisoners of conscience around the world).

I'd joined Amnesty International after a Brisbane lawyer sought my advice because Amnesty had not been able to get any publicity for their cause. Putting on my per rectum hat, I said that if Amnesty wanted to make news, it had to present to the media something to film, and something to photograph: 'Build a jail in King George Square and put prisoners-of-conscience inside with signs on them like: "I was the wrong religion"; and "I wrote the wrong story".'

Amnesty asked me to be one of the prisoners, and—as it transpired—it was entirely appropriate that they asked me to wear the 'I wrote the wrong story' sign on my chest. Thrown into prison with me, as the 'I was the wrong religion' person, was a bearded Catholic priest, Father Jim Soorley, who has since been elected several times by a vote of the entire city as Lord Mayor of Brisbane. Thus did I become the only person in history who could claim to have been in love with one Lord Mayor of Brisbane (Sallyanne Atkinson) and in jail with another. At one election, I even had to decide who to vote for: my soul-mate or my cell-mate?

About a year after this I received Amnesty's newsletter from London to its 250000 members. Amnesty complained about all the usual suspects: South Korea, Argentina, Bolivia, Laos, Russia, Spain... and I was amazed to find Amnesty had condemned Britain for 'cruel, inhuman and degrading treatment' of an Irish prisoner in an English jail. Particularly as Amnesty had been founded in England exactly twenty years to the month earlier, when the British sense of justice and fair play was offended by the fact that three young men had been jailed in Portugal for drinking a toast to freedom.

This Amnesty newsletter arrived during the brief thirteen-month period on the *Australian* in which I had the privilege of my own weekly column, 'Sidelines'. Ever-mindful of Rupert's wise dictum 'we don't write serials', and knowing that most newspaper columnists tend to merely regurgitate the most interesting news story of the week, I tried to write on a wide range of subjects, to occasionally be amusing, and, most importantly of all, not to be predictable: antibiotic resistance; how finance companies tout for people to borrow money; child suicide; dentists; and that Greg Chappell will probably one day be best remembered for the special white cricket hat he designed.

I decided to write a column about Amnesty's report that an Irish prisoner had spent eleven months in solitary confinement with no exercise; no access to any person other than a minister of religion; no visits; no religious service; no use of his personal possessions, including his radio. (After all, even Hitler's officers let Steve McQueen take his baseball mitt and ball into solitary in *The Great Escape*.) I knew this wouldn't be a popular column and fully expected it not to appear. Australian newspapers had, not unnaturally, always reported Northern Ireland from an English perspective, since England's Queen is our Queen, and since most of our stories are provided by, or taken from, London newspapers or London-based reporters. And I knew from working for Reuters the difficulties of knowing what word to use to describe people who rebel against a government. There's a long hierarchy of possible words and here's my list: 'terrorists' if they have absolutely no chance whatever of ever assuming power and, more importantly, you don't want them to; 'dissidents' if they are having no impact; 'activists' if they have some small political support, and you're on the other side; 'rebels' if they're a slight chance one day, and your feelings are neutral; 'extremists' if you just don't like them; 'insurgents' if they're doing quite well and might one day become guerrillas; 'partisans' if they aren't doing well but you'd like them to; 'guerrillas' if they're winning some battles and there's a chance that you might soon have to do business with them instead of the current regime; 'the Resistance' if you're firmly on their side; and 'freedom fighters' once they become certainties to assume power.

In all Australian papers back in 1981—including ours—Irish rebels were terrorists.

The day after my column appeared, Humorous Editor phoned. 'OK, you've had your say on Ireland, now lay off.' My Sidelines shot had upset the British High Commissioner to Australia, who wrote a three-page complaint—though I was merely reporting what the respected Amnesty had said.

Humorous Editor let me keep my weekly column for a whole year after that incident, whereupon I left for the *Daily Sun*. He was the only Editor who ever allowed me a regular weekly column on the *Australian*—perhaps because he had a sense of humour.

There were many difficult judgments to be made in an isolated position like mine. For example, when Brisbane artist John J. Delahunty asked if he could paint my portrait as his entry for the Archibald Prize to be presented in March 1982 I wasn't sure whether to become involved. I had just got back from covering the 1981 rebellion against French rule in New Caledonia. From my Vietnam experience I had expected to go into the Pacific island on a Hercules loaded with reporters in flak jackets; instead, I went on a Boeing 747 full to capacity with Australian tourists. The tourists obviously didn't read the papers: they got irritated when told that heavily armed 'rebels' had set up roadblocks, delaying their travel from the airport to Club Med.

Happy to be back home—and not wishing to pre-judge an artist— I told Delahunty he could paint me as long as he didn't interrupt the office. Delahunty was true to his word and merged into our bureau on his first day as if he'd always been there: making tea, answering phones, cleaning paints, taking notes, running copy to the telex.

He was still there when I went home late that evening, and, next morning, big John Delahunty was already on the job at his wide canvas. But he was unshaven and looked like he'd slept in his shirt. 'I worked so late that I decided to sleep the night in the building,' he explained.

'But what about the nightwatchman?'

Delahunty had never been in our *Sunday Sun* building before the previous day, and over the years security had become very, very tight. Computers had been installed. Rupert's newspapers had irate readers and tough competitors. Three security guards now patrolled the building round the clock, and Delahunty couldn't be missed: he was a large man with big lips and an artist's attitude to authority.

'Nightwatchman?' said Delahunty with a questioning frown, as he reached for an imaginary Colt 45 high on his right hip. 'Oh you mean Gary!' he said, whacking an imaginary baton into his left palm. 'Gazza made me up a bed for the night on the couch in the ladies rest room.'

17 The lies we tell our readers

In 1985, both Rupert and I independently decided to visit China. During the '80s the 'Communist' and 'Red' tags had been gradually dropped as China came out to join the world of capital growth and corporate surplus. So, naturally, Rupert—whose company had now become not only multinational but also multimedia—wanted to be part of the action.

My reason for wanting to go to China was totally different.

As mentioned earlier, in 1965, when Australia didn't recognise China and I was a naive 24-year-old journalist working in Hong Kong, I had wormed my way into Peking and got inside the Forbidden City. When they had asked who I represented, I said myself. Which was true.

Twenty years later, when our paper was offered a free trip on the inaugural Qantas flight to Peking, I put up my hand. I pointed out to a section editor that I had been in Peking before the infamous Cultural Revolution, and would therefore be perhaps the only Australian journalist who could compare the old China with the new. Also, I had worked as a foreign correspondent in Asia for years.

None of this impressed this editor. 'Get in the queue, pal. There's eight people down here in Sydney ahead of you: and I'm one!' he said.

In the end, a Sydney journalist was sent and I didn't see any stories published as a result. What a waste.

I could see I'd have to resign again, which was a pity because it was champagne time. At long last the *Australian* was making an annual profit: just as Rupert had confidently predicted twenty-one years before. This profit would mean, no doubt, that soon the paper would at last start appointing the promised foreign correspondents to give an Aussie view of what was happening around us, instead of Australia's traditional total reliance on an American and English view of the world.

Rupert himself had by now become a sort of foreign correspondent. Aged 54, Rupert had moved to LA and had taken over the famous 20th Century Fox searchlights. He was now not only making Hollywood films, but had done what was considered impossible in America and started a fourth TV network, with Fox TV stations in Washington, New York, Los Angeles and lots of other major US cities. I thought Rupert could now take Australian culture to the world. But our man in LA wasn't even an Australian anymore, having taken out American citizenship in order to be allowed to buy their television stations. At least his company, News Corporation, was still registered in Adelaide, where it was founded.

The corporation was getting so big now that Ron Richards had been promoted to Chairman of Rupert's Sun Newspapers in Brisbane, and his successor in the Valley was former Adelaide journalist Frank Moore. Ron moved into a corporate office in the centre of the city. When I visited him, I looked out the window down on the GPO across Queen Street and exclaimed: 'Ron you've got an office with a window overlooking Queen Street!'

'Don't be like that,' Ron replied, smiling impishly and fiddling with his sock.

Though Rupert now lived in the US, I did get invited to his Elizabeth Bay apartment in August 1985 to see his wife, Anna. There was a large, wide, tree-and-lawn garden in front of the brick block, which had unspectacular partial Sydney Harbour views. I was surprised that the apartment itself wasn't luxurious; it was just like I imagined any ordinary neat harbourside apartment would be. I was there to interview Anna Murdoch about her first novel *In Her Own Image*.

Whenever there was a difficult writing assignment, a job directly important to Rupert himself, no one in Sydney seemed game to take it on. So they would fly in an outsider from one of the BAPH States, such as an expendable Queenslander.

Anna and I had several cups of coffee and discussed her book, and—as much as I dared—her husband of nineteen years. The interview enabled me to ask questions about Rupert and find out more about what sort of person he was at home. What did he think of his wife and the mother of three children becoming an author? 'Rupert was a big help once he accepted that this was what was going to happen,' Anna said. 'Once he saw it was going to come off, he was my greatest support.' So, I mused, this fellow Rupert was the type of man who had to believe something would work before he would put his weight behind it. Anna said that once Rupert decided it would work he even took over the role of mother, at one stage taking Lachlan, 13, and James, 12, for a holiday in the Colorado snow while Anna slaved to finish her book.

At home, Rupert took on the cooking.

Was Rupert any good as a cook? 'The thing is that Rupert has great confidence in whatever he does,' Anna said. 'He may not know how, but he attacks the task with great enthusiasm and confidence, and so fools everybody into thinking he can do it.'

Unlike many book reviewers, I had read the book and was thus able to carry on a conversation about the characters: which, I knew from having published four books myself back then, is a rare compliment to an author. Within the novel, the athletic, romantic, truculent hero, Harry, dominates the book and owns what is clearly Rupert Murdoch's grazing property. What did Rupert think of Harry—the bloke who was so sexy both sisters fell in love with him? 'Rupert read it in Rome when we were staying there at the American Embassy,' Anna said, with a revealing nostalgic air. 'When he finished the book, he put it down next to him, looked up at me, and said, "Who the hell's this Harry guy?" And I said, "It's all based on you darling!"'

Anna added that the book was, of course, fiction.

Would Rupert ever retire?

'No chance, ever,' Anna said.

My other reason for being in Sydney was another Rupert-alert assignment, to write a series of features for News Corporation's 1985 Annual Report. Traditionally much more lavish than any other Australian company report, this one looks like *Vogue* magazine. It not only goes to stock exchanges around the world and all shareholders, but is sent to world political leaders as well, including the US President and the British Prime Minister. It is designed and written to show the power and precociousness of Rupert's News Corporation Limited. Mahogany Row didn't like the fact that each year a photographer was flown out first class from London to take the Australian pictures, complaining: 'We've got hundreds of good photographers here!' But there was nothing they could do to change it.

I talked to Anna in between interviewing the New South Wales Sports Minister, Michael Cleary, about why he read Rupert's Sydney *Mirror*; Edmund Capon, director of the New South Wales Art Gallery, about why he read the *Australian*; and others on why they read Rupert's *Daily Telegraph* and his *TV Week*. I even drove down to the banks of the Georges River to interview a housewife, Betty Stubbings, who taught microwave cookery after reading a publication of Rupert's Bay Books: *Microwave Cooking Made Easy*. Then it was off to Melbourne to interview a businessman who said he loved flying on Rupert's Ansett Airlines, and a furniture manufacturer who chose to advertise on Rupert's Channel 10 because it was so effective. 'The more my ads irritate people, the more furniture I sell,' he said.

The idea, of course, was that I travel around Australia interviewing the interesting and successful customers who made News Ltd's wide range of assets so worthwhile to appear in, to invest in, and to lend to. But one national magazine in Melbourne went too far down that PR track. They needed a young, upwardly mobile employed homemaker to represent their female readership. But the 'typical reader' they presented me with kept turning and saying to the magazine's representative: 'How old am I supposed to be again?' and 'My boyfriend's a doctor, isn't he?' I stood up, told them that while the line between good PR and telling lies was fine, they had clearly stepped over it. This was one story that wouldn't be going in the Annual Report.

I wrote the Anna Murdoch story in the Melbourne Hilton that night on a portable typewriter and next morning, on the way to Adelaide, dropped off the three thousand words at Rupert's Melbourne *Southdown Press* to be telexed to Sydney for publication on the weekend. But, because I'd lost control of my story, the opening line with Rupert saying to Anna 'Who the hell's this Harry guy?' made it into a Melbourne newspaper column the day before the full story was published in our paper.

With Rupert now an American citizen and far away from the paper he had created, a whole new generation of younger, brighter, young men had popped up in Sydney, all battling aggressively for the top and all assuming they knew exactly what Rupert wanted. I got the impression some thought I should be pensioned off, now that I was in my mid-40s. Like the army, which recruits young people so that they will do exactly what they're told, Australian newspapers love young reporters; not just because they're cheap, but also because everything's news to them. So I went around pointing out that most of the American war correspondents in Vietnam had grey hair, which was why they did such a great job. After all, it's no use cabinet papers being released after thirty years if all the reporters covering the story are too young to remember the time.

I was also missing the philosophy and wisdom of my parents, Fred and Olive, who had died within two years of each other.

When I wrote a complaining memo to one of these new generation younger editors, he rang back with: 'Look, I don't want to have a pissing match up against the wall with you.' Another, who had the eyes of a travelling rat, got very annoyed when I said I couldn't go on a police helicopter looking for drug plantations because I had a perforated ear drum as a result of an operation the previous day under a general anaesthetic to remove concrete-hard wax (keratosis obdurans). Though this was my first sick leave ever, he hung up in my sore ear. A few weeks later, he flew up to Brisbane and spent two minutes of his working day in our branch office, staying just long enough to say, 'Just what have we got to do to make you happy?'

Well, where could I start? The only authority I had was over office journalists I'd personally hired for the job, because under union rules negotiated by News Ltd, my job as bureau chief was not an 'exempt' position, meaning I was required to be a member of the union and so did not have the power to fire staff. They could ignore me if they wished. Which was why over the years I had so much trouble with one of Rupert's rules: no grog in the office. At one time I bought a Café Bar out of the petty cash tin, and I felt chuffed as Max and Harry queued up for the first time for a coffee. I never used the machine, so it was a couple of years before I found out that the Café Bar's water tank had long since been filled with Star Wine, or a cheap sherry which Valley journalists called 'yellow death'. Another thing I was unhappy about was the money wasted on flying reporters up to Queensland since the nine S'Larry sackings in Brisbane. Why not have more reporters on the spot, particularly as one-third of the *Oz*'s circulation back then was in Queensland?

After Joh Bjelke-Petersen's government sacked hundreds of striking electricity workers in the mid-1980s, the *Australian* flew up a reporter to interview the Premier and write the definitive piece. This bloke was one of a new breed writing articles that would once have been anathema to the *Australian*—like articles denigrating teachers for not teaching children to spell. Once, the *Australian* carried a front-page headline 'THE LIES WE TELL OUR CHILDREN', which caused lots of irate phone calls from teachers. I was starting to learn that while some writers on newspapers are paid for their ability to make sense of a complex world, others make a living by taking a predictable view on every subject, from smoking to Aboriginal rights: a view which most often appeals to business managers and corporate advertisers.

A few days after this Sydney reporter arrived, the telex operators rang me from the *Sunday Sun* building next door: 'We've never seen anything like this. His article is hand-written, single-spaced, on foolscap, and on top of all that he can't spell. He hasn't spelt Bjelke-Petersen right once!'

I kept the sheets of foolscap: 'So there is Sir Joh, master of all he surveys, slayer of the union dragon, Emperor of Queensland, the little man's friend and the master politician...He represents the literally silent majority.' Well, Joh's party never got forty per cent of the vote in Queensland, let alone in Australia. But there's no law saying newspapers have to tell the truth.

And newspapers aren't geared to observe the small changes happening in our lives over months, years and decades either. For example, a signature, once sacrosanct, is not a signature anymore: rubber stamp signatures have become as common as the old 'CANCELLED' or 'PAID' rubber stamps once were. But I've never seen that written. Every organisation in Australia now aspires to a new logo, a slogan, and naming rights on someone else's building. If a company has 'Australia' in the title, it means it's owned overseas. Chairmen who get standing ovations from shareholders at AGMs might well be sending the company broke. When people say 'Look after yourself', it's one of the few times they actually mean what they're saying. Whereas 'I hear what you're saying' really means 'Shut up'. Footballers should be told that you can't transfer your loyalties: loyalty, by definition, is not transferable.

Perhaps I was making too many such observations, because by 1985 it seemed to be more difficult to get my stories published in the *Oz*. So I started to keep unused articles in a pile marked 'U'. Some of my stories were used but buried: like when I was tipped off that the University of Queensland was going to award Premier Bjelke-Petersen—a man once described by London's *Sunday Times* as 'anti-Abo, anti-Commo, anti-Eco, and anti-Homo'—an honorary doctorate. I knew this would send academics around the country crazy, so it should have been big news, especially for our newspaper. After all, the *Australian* had recently successfully lobbied all the vice-chancellors for their vote to get the *Higher Education Supplement*, which advertises most jobs for academics. (I had accompanied Steady Editor to see the vice-chancellors in Brisbane because Rupert had told him—correctly—that the future of our paper would depend upon beating the *National Times* to this supplement.)

'We've had Dr Who, and we've seen Dr No,' I wrote, 'and now, ladies and gentlemen, we're about to get Dr Joh.' But the paper inexplicably buried the story on page two. Sir Joh walked up to get his honorary doctorate while academics and staff protested, pushing so forcefully outside that they cracked sheets of plate glass in the exterior wall of the University of Queensland's Mayne Hall. Brisbane's Dr Ross Fitzgerald said it was 'like awarding Dracula a doctorate for plasma conservation'.

Because of this and other comments, I wrote a feature about Dr (now Professor) Fitzgerald, calling him 'the anti-Joh'. But he was so full of radical concepts (such as Orwell's 'In a state of universal deceit, telling the truth is a revolutionary act') that the story wasn't published. I added it to the U-pile, and told Ross it would never make the paper. So I was amazed when, several weeks later, my article suddenly appeared in the *Weekend Australian* across the whole top of a page, with a picture of Ross looking very handsome in his tailor-made white hat. It wasn't until the year 2000—fifteen years later—that Ross told me how it happened.

Ross was feeling very low in 1985 because volume II of his brilliant *History of Queensland 1915–84* had been recalled and pulped (it was later reprinted). So Ross mischievously rang the *Australian* at 2.00 a.m. one night in 1985 and shouted at someone on the other end of the line: 'This is the Chief Executive [Rupert's title] here. I want you to run Hugh Lunn's story on that fellow Ross Fitzgerald,' and hung up. The story appeared the following weekend.

Perhaps I should have been doing that myself.

Instead, I was breaking all those corporate rules: never complain, never explain, never resign, never pick your nose in the car park. Which meant that I had imperceptibly become more and more unpopular. Getting angry with one features editor I said, 'Look mate, I work here solely at the personal invitation of the Chief Executive.' I took more time to write because I wrote longer articles on more difficult subjects: like five thousand words on Sir Donald Bradman after the Don wrote back to me with his fountain pen to say why he didn't do interviews. Because editors are rarely former writers, they are unaware that the difficulty of writing a feature increases by the square of the number of words. Occasionally, I wondered if they knew the difference between writing and typing. To me, most of the things done on a paper were the mechanical, simple, automatic response of the experienced journalist: stuff I did as copy-taster for Reuters in London in the '60s. Thus I told Steady Editor once that I could sub the whole paper myself in a day: 'This is a good story; that's a bad story; this is page one; that's page three; this needs rewriting; that doesn't.'

Gough Whitlam has been the hero and the villain in the *Australian* at various times because, as my pastrycook father Fred observed when asked what he knew of newspapers, 'They write 'em up, then they write 'em down.' In November 1985 Gough was being written down. So when an editor told me to fly to Canberra and write a piece on the launch of Whitlam's book, I said, 'But you won't run it. You all hate Gough down there.'

On arrival at the National Press Club, Whitlam was accorded the sort of reception from the journalists, public servants and ambassadors that one would have expected for Bradman himself, and Gough scored boundaries with every stroke of his tongue. The room broke up when the former Prime Minister—so often accused of being imperious, arrogant and out of touch with ordinary people—began his speech: 'Fellow Excellencies'. Which reminded me of when, as a brand new Prime Minister, he told a dinner of frightened conservative businessmen in Brisbane: 'When I look at the powers available to me as Prime

Minister, I stand amazed at my own moderation!' My long story on Gough's launch, as I expected, made only a few sentences on page two. Yet in writing it I almost missed my own book launch in Sydney the next morning.

Seventeen years after I first wrote 'Gooks and Big Monkeys' (i.e. Vietnamese and Americans) my yellowing old manuscript had finally been published by UQP as *Vietnam: A Reporter's War*. It was launched in Sydney's Botanic Gardens Cafe and I was disappointed when the Editor of the *Oz* didn't bother to turn up. In fact, if Helen's Aunty Trixie hadn't brought along three of her best girl friends—Dulcie, Maggie and Alice (all four in hats and gloves and crystal-bead necklaces)—there wouldn't have been much of an audience when my old mate from Indonesian correspondent days, Sydney radio announcer Mike Carlton, got up to speak.

> Anyone who launches a book at the same time as Gough Whitlam and Ita Buttrose is certainly defying the odds in a courageous way. But not only did Hugh survive the Tet Offensive, he has also survived the Bjelke-Petersen government. Some have managed either, but not both. Ho Chi Minh and Flo Bjelke-Petersen: a lot to handle in one reporter's lifetime. Vietnam was one thing. But we all know how difficult and dangerous life in Queensland has become. The pubs and clubs are so full of poofters, child molesters, perverts, and southern AIDS carriers that the government has had to legislate against them, a fearful thing. But we are not here today to tell Queensland jokes. There are spies everywhere and the author is, himself, a loyal Queenslander born and bred, and he would not like it to get back to the Special Branch in Brisbane that he had been seen laughing at Queensland jokes south of the Tweed. There are people in Boggo Road [jail] for less...
>
> I worked in Vietnam for a bit myself. As they used to say, Vietnam was 'the only war we got. And I ain't even bullshitting'... Hugh has written about it, and he has written about it truly. Even the lies are true... [The book] is a valuable and timely antidote to the rampant

Rambo mentality. Suffice it to say that, while Hugh was watching US Marines die at Con Thien, Sylvester Stallone was teaching PE at a girls finishing school in Switzerland.

Naturally, Mike Carlton's long, clever speech went unreported.

In 1986, after my Vietnam book had been published in New York, I was absolutely sure the *Australian*, as a national paper, would print my report on Brisbane's first Writers Week. After all, they'd printed my preview. So I followed Australia's most famous book writers closely all week.

Using her considerable talent for fantasy, author Thea Astley impishly suggested Australia build an above-ground monorail linking every casino in the country. Helen Garner at dinner in West End pulled out a notebook and wrote down anything interesting she heard. Rodney Hall and Tom Shapcott recalled how they used to swim against each other at inter-school carnivals at the Valley Baths in Brisbane—and, it turned out, both had recited poetry while swimming. Trying to explain Queenslandness, Rodney Hall recalled that at Brisbane's old Museum there were two large, plate glass display cases side by side. One contained a stuffed kangaroo and joey, a stuffed possum and a stuffed platypus; the other contained the same. 'The first, in beautiful letters, pronounced "Queensland Marsupials"; and the other, in equally beautiful lettering, said: "Southern Marsupials". We could tell the difference. Ours were better, because they were ours.'

At filmmaker Gerard Lee's launch of *Latitudes*, an anthology of Queensland writing which included Sue Johnson's sexy piece 'Mango Man', Gerard said he always carried a banana in his coat pocket when down south hawking scripts. He said that when he told a Melbourne academic he was going to launch this book of Queensland writing, the academic had replied, 'That'd be a very slim volume.' 'Within seconds,' Gerard Lee told the appreciative Brisbane crowd, 'I pulled out my Cavendish and gave him a pistol-whipping he won't forget for a long while.'

That story never appeared. In a fit of pique I announced to Steady

Editor that I wasn't writing any more articles until the ones I'd already sent down were published.

At the same time, conversely and perversely, I often got the freedom and the time and the space necessary to write stories which other Australian newspapers would not have allowed at that time—though many might now. Like a feature on the hypocrisy rampant in Queensland back then.

Under a fundamentalist Queensland government that held every seat on the Gold Coast and which, publicly at least, was so straight that it condemned pyjama parties, I listed what was in truth happening on the tourist strip: the wet T-shirt contests, with ice in the water to make the young women's nipples stand out; the full-colour front pages of topless, bottomless teenagers in a weekly Gold Coast newspaper; the 'Minimal Dress' contest won by a Palm Beach High School girl who wore three pieces of adhesive unconnected material because she'd heard that another girl was wearing just six Band-aids; the 'Bikini Races' where girls inevitably lost their bikini tops; the Miss Teenage contest for girls from thirteen run by a bloke who had designed the 'bum-out cheekini bikini'; the ads for prostitutes in local papers (prostitution was supposed to be illegal); the nightclub act where a female was dragged on stage by a chain, bound on her hands and knees and whipped by another woman.

The *Australian* ran my pseudo-humorous sexposé over a full page. But the Queensland government managed to avoid the truth until *Courier-Mail* reporter Phil Dickie and then the ABC's Chris Masters brought it home much more starkly a year later, creating the Fitzgerald corruption inquiry into Queensland's official lies, which saw the Police Commissioner jailed.

Occasionally there was a story which more than made up for all those that went unused. Both Best Editor and Steady Editor backed me in difficult circumstances when I wrote a series of stories about a little boy called Robert Hoge who had been born with a large tumour in the middle of his face: a tumour that had pushed his eye sockets and nostrils five centimetres further apart than normal. The tumour had grown in place of his nose, and such a face—once the tumour was removed—ensured that little Robert Hoge would spend his life within an institution. It seemed only incidental that both Robert's legs were severely deformed. There was no chance that he could ever walk on them. His distraught mother, Mary Hoge, of Manly in Brisbane, at first could not accept Robert as her own. 'I went home prepared to forget about him,' she told me.

Yet all Robert was, was ugly.

Doctors at Brisbane's Mater Hospital promised Mary that if she would take her baby home, they would do all they could to learn new techniques being trialled in France to rebuild a face by cutting up the skull and moving it around. A Hoge family meeting with husband Vince and all the kids voted to bring Robert home, and wait, and hope...and be stared at.

Four-and-a-half years and a couple of overseas study trips later, the two Brisbane doctors were ready with five other specialists for a thirteen-hour operation they called 'cranofacial correction of hypertelorism and bifid nose'.

I called it: 'The Remaking of Robert Hoge'.

In the ensuing operation, Robert's eye sockets were cut out and moved four centimetres closer together, like two sides of an unjoined pair of glasses. His deformed legs were removed—one below and one at the knee—and were used to provide bone and cartilage grafts for large facial gaps created when the eyes were moved inwards. After the widely separated nostrils had been pulled together, the surgeons used Robert's big toe to make him a nose.

It was such a groundbreaking operation that I broke all the AMA rules and named the doctors. Or perhaps it was because of the high I felt when I visited Robert in his cot after the operation and, because Robert demanded it, read him his story about 'the cat in the big hat'. Robert now looked as good as most Rugby League players after a 1950s Queensland v. New South Wales match. Luckily, I ended up spending a few hours at the hospital because, before our photographer

Tommy Campion arrived, the nurses rushed to remove the cradle-cap bandage from Robert's head for the photo. I stopped them.

'Triumph of love—and medicine' was the headline on the front page and the paper backed me and published the names of the doctors which meant I was summoned to appear before the Queensland Executive of the AMA in Brisbane. Though most of these doctors disagreed with what I had done in naming the surgeons—'giving them publicity'—one made a passionate speech saying medicine needs heroes. 'It is not as if these doctors are going to corner the market in such an operation,' he said. The head nun at Brisbane's Mater Hospital, Sister Angela Mary, supported me. The *Australian* sold every paper it printed that weekend, and many people had to go without one. The story was later reprinted in a Rupert publication in the US.

Many people wrote to the paper in response, including my erudite Grade 12 English teacher, Brother 'Doc' Campbell:

> It was a pleasure to find on the front page a story which does ample justice both to a marvel of family faith and courage, and to a modern 'miracle' of surgical skill and dedication. You have enhanced the achievement by your account of it. I am glad you risked the displeasure of the AMA by naming the surgical team. *Prospere procede et regna.*

Mary Hoge wouldn't talk to any other media, so I wrote about Robert a number of times, in 1984 quoting from Mary's personal diary about Robert's days at primary school where, three times in the first week, he broke one of his artificial legs. Mary at first felt angry that Robert had been seated down the back of the class 'to keep him out of sight'. But later she realised: 'If he was at the front I might have thought they were parading him.'

On school sports day a few years later, Mary wasn't sure if Robert, with his two artifical legs, would be allowed to compete. Then she found out he'd entered himself for the sprint championship race.

She wrote in her diary, the one I had suggested she keep:

Robert wanted so much to take part I wasn't about to stop him. He lined up with about eight or nine children. *Bang!* The children start to run. Robert kept up for the first few paces then fell behind. About a third of the way he fell over. Quickly he got up again and once more started to run. Tears swelled in my eyes. My heart was bursting with pride. People were shouting 'Come on Robert!' He finished the race to shouting, cheering and clapping. Friends turned and said something, but I couldn't speak. I was crying again. The timekeeper said that none of the officials at the finish line knew who had won the race.

One of the kids watching said, 'It took a lot of kids to beat Robert, didn't it?'

18 Bad news

Every day for six weeks at the end of 1986 I predicted on the front page of the *Australian* that Queensland's 75-year-old Premier, Sir Joh Bjelke-Petersen, would be beaten at the State election after two decades of dogmatic rule.

I was wrong.

At the previous election, in 1983, I had been the only journalist in the country who had correctly predicted that Joh's gerontocracy would win power for the first time in its own right and would no longer need its Liberal coalition partner. This prediction had caused two things: I was interviewed in my office by more than twenty other media organisations, and I was blamed by some journos for Joh's 1983 victory. When one thousand cheering souls turned up to the fundamentalist Premier's election launch at the Crest Hotel, a fellow journalist leaned over to me and said, 'Now see what you've done.'

Until 1986 I'd never been wrong on an election. My 1983 prediction that Bjelke-Petersen would win alone was seen as so outlandish back then that a top News executive rang to ask if I really believed what I was writing. Perhaps the company wanted to know who to support in that election—Liberal, Labor or Joh—since newspapers love to support winners. And certainly, after winning power alone in

1983, Joh took all government advertising off the *Courier-Mail* and gave it to the *Daily Sun*, which had come out urging a vote for Joh (though a year or so later Joh took government business back to the *Courier-Mail*.)

So, when I said Joh Bjelke-Petersen would lose in 1986 (despite the fact that the 'Bjelkemander' had been further redrawn in his favour since 1983) I was widely believed. And for the first time for years my prediction coincided with that of most media pundits.

My stories that the most successful, most disliked State Premier in Australia's history would be beaten stirred up great interest. In fact, the story became so big that Steady Editor replied—when I complained a story of mine hadn't been given a big enough run— 'Where do you want us to run your election stories: above the masthead?' He had a good point.

Steady Editor got so excited that, for the first time, he wanted to be in the Brisbane tally-room at QE II stadium for the fateful night. Steady Editor and I had a sort of love–hate relationship, though I rarely saw him because I was so low down on Rupert's totem-pole. In fact, it had been so long since we'd met that when he arrived for the election he said, with a surprised look, 'You're going bald!' Well, I'd been going bald for a couple of years. With him he brought several of Rupert's top Sydney and Canberra journalists, including Paul Kelly and Jim Oram, one of the group's best writers. Other news organisations sent their top men north too, including Peter Bowers from the opposition *Sydney Morning Herald*. It was a long way from the State election nine years earlier when I had been the only journalist to interview the Premier face to face the day afterwards on his peanut farm outside Kingaroy.

What worried me was that so many media pundits down south were now also predicting Joh's defeat. They had been emboldened by my confidence: and I could well be wrong. It is often difficult to understand your own motives for doing something. Was I trying to get rid of a government too eager to use its unfettered power? Was I writing 'Joh will lose' because it was a great story? I examined my conscience and decided I was following a gut feeling that Queensland had had enough of their belligerent Premier whose narrow leadership reflected the fifteen years he had lived alone in a cow bail as a young man, where he said the hardest thing he ever had to do was to shoot his ageing horses.

With a week to go, business began to pour money in to help keep the leader they loved afloat; one edition of the *Courier-Mail* alone had eleven full-page advertisements for Joh's National Party.

The day before the election, Rupert's Newspoll was to release its findings. My job was to interview the pollster, Sol Lebovic, and write the story. Newspoll was on its way to proving it was the superior pollster in Australia. Sol Lebovic told me he would prove at this election that he could do what many said could not be done: he would poll a dispersed, diversified State like Queensland, over the phone, and predict the result.

Friday morning, Sol rang my office. Joh would win, he said, and predicted the result precisely. So I had to write this as the front-page splash in the *Weekend Australian*, contradicting everything I had written for the last six weeks.

The Saturday morning of the election, Allen Callaghan rang my house early: 'Hugh, don't go to the tally-room tonight. Joh's sure to have a go at you publicly.' But how could I stay away now that I had all my bosses flying up to witness the 'downfall' of a man who had personally doubled his party's vote in two decades? I kissed my wife Helen goodbye, and told her I was in for a long, bad night. 'I'll wait up for you,' Helen said, 'and rub your chest.'

In the tally-room I sat next to Steady Editor and his men as the results went up on a long wall. As each new set of figures was posted I could feel by osmosis how unpopular I was becoming.

Like an invading army driving through town on their tanks, accepting the flowers invariably presented to the victors, Bjelke-Petersen and his team were cheered into the tally-room a little after 10.00 p.m. and mounted the rostrum to claim victory. He looked down into the tangle of journalists, where he saw me. 'I see a guy down here in the middle,' he said, pointing, and Steady Editor's eyes, and those of everyone else in the room, followed the finger all the way down to my nose. 'I had better not name him because I might embarrass him. If I said whether he knew whether the sun was going up, or coming down, I wouldn't know. But he doesn't impress me very much.' Peter Bowers turned and said, 'Hugh, we can offer you a safe house, a nom de plume and a B grade in Sydney.' It was a terrible night which reminded me of a line written by grandfather Hugh Lunn when something not dissimilar happened to him: 'Those that loved me, fell away from me; and those that hated me, hated me still more.'

Even before that election I'd clashed with Steady Editor. I'd been seconded from the *Australian* for the second year running to work on Rupert's Annual Report: this time to do a series of features on 'A Day in the Life of News Corporation'—where I learned a bit more about Rupert's progress. Progress Press in Melbourne, where News Ltd printed million-circulation magazines and millions of brochures (junk mail), had started out as the newspaper of the local community Progress Association and yet now printed 364 days a year, twenty-four hours a day. The two house-sized presses stopped Christmas Day, but only for maintenance. Ken Catlow, the boss, told me that when the press was still tiny Rupert had asked him if there was anything he needed. 'Well, we could really do things if we had one of those fully computerised German printing presses, but they cost twenty million dollars each,' Catlow had replied.

'I'll get you two,' was Rupert's response. And he did.

For that 1986 Annual Report in August I flew Syd-Bne-Syd-Melb-Bne-Dwin-Gove-Crns-Tville-Bne-Syd-Melb-Bne without a day off and then wrote ten 700-word stories. Steady Editor didn't seem to realise what I'd done and rang to say my recent productivity had been 'appalling'. It hadn't helped that in May, June and July that year I had been on three months long service leave, a reward for fifteen years of service. As far as I knew I was the first reporter from the *Australian* who'd lasted long enough to get long service leave: so Steady Editor could be forgiven for forgetting where I was.

There was also aggro because I'd then spent a week in Townsville, where I addressed the Australian Universities Graduate Conference (AUGC) annual dinner and was a guest at the Association for the Study of Australian Literature (ASAL) conference at James Cook University. This caused one editor to ring our office secretary and say, 'What does Lunn do up there all day?' Well, if I'd been asked, I'd have said it was important for a national newspaper to spend the occasional week in the northern half of the country; that my visit made the front page of the *Townsville Bulletin*; and that the *Weekend Australian* published the full-page article I wrote on the ASAL conference, one of the most difficult I've written.

The morning after that terrible 1986 election night, Steady Editor handed out his riding instructions to each reporter and, lastly, turned to me. 'In your story you can be as up front as you like about being wrong,' he said, and didn't shake hands when he left that night. My story certainly wasn't run above the masthead next morning; it was buried on the inside on page four, a left-hand page:

> It was All Saints Day in Queensland at the election tally-room and—with Halloween night over—all the ghosts of the past, and all the things that come out of the dark, were supposed to be banished.
>
> But it didn't happen.
>
> It was, I can tell you, a terrible blow to us media pundits who were not only wrong but who really did want to see the end of a 'trick or treat' government. On TV interviews we looked like those Halloween pumpkin heads: a fixed artificial smile, a shaky glow, and as ugly as sin—at least to Joh and his euphoric National Party... [who] put out the bonfire that was going to scare all the ghouls away.

Once again, I wrote, the majority would be ruled by the minority: 'which means obeying laws passed by the few'.

However, within a year, Joh Bjelke-Petersen—a man once bitten by his own dog—was forced out of office by his own party, which then lost office.

My punishment, as I saw it, was to immediately be sent around the nation to cover the England v. Australia 1986–87 Test cricket series. The one thing I had grown to hate since getting married was being away from Helen. Yet more and more the *Australian* sent me out of town for long spells. Which made me recall Owen Thomson's dictum: 'If you want to get rid of someone, give them jobs they hate.'

When the government released the Petrov Papers about the 1954 defections of two Soviet Embassy officials in Australia, Vladimir and Evdokia Petrov, I was sent to Canberra. The media was shown to a room with a hundred desks and chairs in neat rows like a classroom, each desk with a thick bundle of photocopied selections from the files. Adjoining rooms were full of filing cabinets, each drawer crammed with Petrov files, and we were welcome to search these. Then we were shown down a dark tunnel to yellow fireproof rooms also full of Petrov Papers. We could read those too. A national TV reporter had brought a Petrov expert with him. I watched as the TV reporter arrived, positioned his man next to one of the desks, and waited for the camera to roll. 'So,' said the TV reporter, slapping the tall pile of photocopies that had just been released, 'what do you think of the Petrov case now that the secret papers have finally been released after thirty years?'

'They confirm everything I've always said,' answered the expert.

Within four minutes TV had its story, and they left. It took four days for my article to be unearthed and created: what Russia looks for in an Australian spy.

A trip to the Coburg Peninsula above Darwin was made more difficult when I collapsed in the heat, and in Adelaide for the first Formula One Grand Prix race in Australia I near collapsed from the noise. Most of the journalists covering the car race behaved and wrote like teenage groupies, not independent reporters, applauding as one when the hero-worshipped leading driver walked into the press conference after setting a lap record in the race for pole position. They had become ardent advocates for the sport that was providing them with a living.

Writing colour stories on Test cricket might sound like a nice easy mark, but it's not like spending a lazy afternoon watching the cricket. The sports writer can just write the scoreboard, while the colour writer has to watch the entire scene closely every second of the day for his story, which might come from anywhere. And it's harder still if you're not in the burgeoning club of cricket writers. I wrote of the last day of the Brisbane Test: 'Played in front of 20 000 empty seats…' and refused to call the matches 'the (cigarette brand) Tests', unlike almost everyone else. I'd worked out that smoking in Australia killed the equivalent of four cricket teams a day. As a result, when I turned up early in the press box for one Test, there were two shiny gold cartons of cigarettes on almost every one of the hundred or so desks. But not on mine.

Covering Test cricket is actually very boring. In Adelaide, I wrote about the English cricket writers sitting behind me playing Battleships in the press box during the match: 'B…5'…'Oh you got my destroyer, damn!' Next day, these reporters pulled me aside and warned: 'Don't you write about us.' Later that hot summer day, I slowly became aware of a strange slurping sound. I was in the front row of the press box and turned around to see—rising behind me—row-upon-long-row of cricket reporters eating deliciously cold chocolate-covered ice-creams on two sticks. Somehow, I'd missed out.

In Sydney, emerging from the smoke fumes of the enclosed press box at the SCG, I learned how much better it is to work near head office. While I queued up for a cab, I noted that each day the *Daily Telegraph* writer stepped into a chauffeur-driven company car outside the ground. Next day I ordered myself one of these airconditioned office limos, and it duly arrived, whereupon the uniformed driver jumped out and opened the back door for me. Clearly the fruits of Rupert's four consecutive years of record profits were paying off in the Sydney office, if not yet filtering through to Brisbane.

Rupert's 1986 profits had leapt 152 per cent, partly on the back of breaking Britain's ancient print unions by moving his four national London-based newspapers to a fully computerised plant at Wapping.

Thus Rupert had become, in 1986, the first global newspaperman who no longer needed typesetters.

But Rupert still needed writers like me.

Didn't he?

19 A real hamburger

In August 1987 I was summoned to the Sydney head office, post-haste, to rewrite Rupert's Annual Report, which had to be in the hands of stock exchanges around the world by the end of September.

The review of operations of each of News Corporation's interests was normally written in New York, but this time, I was informed, there had been a failure in New York to understand the enormity of Rupert's takeover that February of the giant Australian Herald and Weekly Times group. New York had dismissed this takeover in the body of the Annual Report, whereas almost anyone in Australia knew that this was News making news.

The first question I asked on Mahogany Row before beginning the rewrite was: 'Is this the biggest newspaper takeover in the English-speaking world?' They seemed surprised by this insight, but it was something Adrian McGregor and I had already discussed over lunch.

'Rupert will know,' came the guarded reply. As luck had it, Rupert was in town, and his answer was relayed back: 'Yes.'

To get just some idea of the size of this Aussie takeover you have to know that it added no fewer than seventy-five newspaper titles to

The News Corporation Limited (TNCL)—even after some news-paper divestments required by government.

This one step made Rupert, overnight, the largest publisher of newspaper titles in the world.

After starting out with the one afternoon daily in Adelaide, Rupert had become, in three decades, by far the biggest newspaper publisher in Australia, the country where his expansion had been so limited for so long. Now, for the first time, he had a major stake in Melbourne. Now, Rupert owned Australia's biggest selling daily newspaper, the Melbourne *Sun-Pic*, and papers in the Pacific Islands. Now, at the one stroke, Rupert had taken over the most influential newspapers in Melbourne, Brisbane, and Adelaide. Now, he published Sunday papers in each State capital. Now, Rupert was in charge of the biggest selling newspapers in five of the six Australian State capitals. Overnight, he had become by far the most influential person in Australia, owning two-thirds of the newspapers printed in the one country, including the national daily he himself had started, the *Australian*, which could now, as a consequence of the takeover, be printed locally in all five mainland State capitals instead of having to be flown around. This unique ability increased circulation, and the *Oz* soon reported record profits. Perhaps sweetest victory of all, Rupert had finally won his personal Battle of Brisbane. The Brisbane morning broadsheet *Courier-Mail*, the paper Rupert and Ron Richards had struggled together against from Fortitude Valley for decades and which his father had wanted to leave his only son, was now majority owned by Rupert and his family, with the rest owned by News Ltd. It must have been a sweet moment for Rupert

To achieve all this, Rupert could not let sentiment stand in his way. As one company wasn't permitted to own all the newspapers in Brisbane or all the newspapers in Adelaide, Rupert was required to divest the company of his old founding base the *News* in Adelaide and his Brisbane bulwarks the *Daily Sun* and *Sunday Sun*. But, as with the Melbourne *Truth*, once again Rupert's newspaper discards ended up being bought out and run by his former editors (this time in conjunction with a few key staff) who did not pose a potential threat. In complex deals, the Adelaide *News* went to its Editor while, in Brisbane, the two *Sun*s ended up with Frank Moore, the former finance editor who had been sent up from News Ltd in Adelaide a few years earlier to manage the papers. Ron Richards became Managing Editor of the *Courier-Mail* and *Sunday Mail*, the papers he had competed with since his days as a rugged, diminutive police roundsman in the 1950s, when he was extremely lucky to survive being dangled upside down from the roof of the infamous National Hotel by a detective called 'Buck' who was annoyed by a story Ron had written.

Bob Hawke and his Treasurer, Paul Keating, had made Rupert's overnight expansion possible when they changed Australia's media ownership laws to outlaw 'cross-media ownership' (stopping a media proprietor from owning a newspaper and a TV station in the same city). A side effect of this was to allow one person to control almost as many Australian newspapers as they could get hold of. The negative consequence of the change was that Rupert had to get rid of Channel 10 TV stations in Melbourne and Sydney—though they were worth much more now that the new laws meant national TV networks could be built for the first time.

As soon as Rupert heard, in December 1986, that the media ownership laws were about to be changed, he flew at once from the US to Australia with a few key men, at the same time telling top executives in Sydney to meet up with them at Melbourne's huge Regent Hotel to prepare for a takeover raid on the nearby Herald offices the moment the legislation passed in Canberra. Because of the need for secrecy—in case a potential competitive bidder heard Rupert was making a pre-emptive strike—all the News executives were told to book into the Regent Hotel under assumed names.

Everything went well, and everyone was in place in Melbourne ready to act.

However, there was one little unforeseen hitch.

No one had thought to tell the others what their assumed names were. So some of the shrewdest newspaper executives in the world, holed up in Melbourne's Regent Hotel ready for the biggest newspaper takeover in world history, at first couldn't find one another. As I heard it, for a few nervous hours Rupert-men sat fidgeting in various parts of the public foyer of the hotel, occasionally peering out from behind newspapers held close to their faces, watching out for their incognito comrades.

On arrival at head office in Sydney to rewrite the Annual Report, I was greeted by News Ltd General Manager Walter Kommer, a resplendent debonair man of Dutch extraction who said, 'This New York attempt at writing our Annual Report was a real hamburger.'

Walter showed me into the vacant office of the company accountant who always signed my weekly pay cheque. It was up some stairs from Mahogany Row in an adjoining building. Walter pointed to an IBM personal computer sitting unplugged on the desk. 'Rupert said you can use this. Anna has just finished writing her new book on it.'

But, but... I didn't know how to use a PC. I'd only ever used the VDUs where all you needed to know was how to type. Should I say I had no idea what this PC machine did? Should I say I didn't know how to turn it on, or what made it go?

'So this is a personal computer?' was all I could say.

'You got it!' said Walter, thrilled that I had no questions, and he walked away in triumph.

The perceived wisdom touted in those days was that no one over the age of 37 could possibly learn to use a PC. I was 46. I'd heard of word processing applications called *Word Star* and *Word Perfect*, but when I turned it on this PC had some application I'd never even heard of: *MS Word*. Someone told me it was the word processing system preferred by universities. I spent the next few days clicking on words at the bottom of the screen to see what they led to.

Surrounded by reports from all of Rupert's operations around the world—magazines, books, TV programs, records, computers, films, printing, distribution, an airline—I began with 'newspapers', and started that section with two pages on the successful, fiercely contested Herald & Weekly Times takeover 'making TNCL the premier publisher in its home country'. After explaining the width and breadth of newspaper titles captured in the raid—and the elimination of the major opposition commercial printer and distributor in Australia of brochures—I wrote that News had been forced by competition laws to sell its two TV stations: Channel 10 in Sydney and Channel 10 in Melbourne.

There were no confidentiality agreements to sign, but my work was closely monitored. When I got it wrong, Walter never complained. He just gave me the acceptable corporate language: in company annual reports you don't say circulation or advertising revenue is down, you say it is 'soft'. The company Chairman, Richard Searby, QC, an old school chum of Rupert's, called me in. 'You can't write that we "sold" the two Channel 10s: we didn't own them.' (When Rupert had become a US citizen less than two years earlier he could no longer own or control TV stations in Australia, so the two TV stations were put into a holding company, Network Ten Holdings Limited, which owned and controlled them, while News retained a financial interest.)

So what to write?

Richard Searby said it was simple: 'News divested itself of its limited holding in the two TV stations.'

Occasionally, I would ring up a branch of News myself to get more details on what sort of year they had had, if I felt not enough information had been supplied. Once Walter Kommer asked where I got the information on how one small offshoot was doing so extraordinarily well.

'I rang the boss myself,' I said.

'Don't listen to him! They're doing shocking,' said Walter. 'There's unsold stock all over Sydney! It's a real hamburger.' He said to ignore everything I'd been told and instead dictated words like 'slack' and 'subdued' and phrases like 'buyer resistance' and 'adversely affected'. Writing an annual report was much harder than it looked.

The hours were long and I missed Helen so much it hurt. Walter picked me up from the Hilton before eight each morning and, after nine at night, we walked through Mahogany Row turning out the lights. Most days I ate by myself in the staff canteen and never saw anyone from the *Australian* there. Occasionally, Walter took me out for lunch at a swish restaurant. He could have eaten in the board-room for free every day, but didn't like the healthy food. I could see why Rupert had picked Walter out and liked him so much, and relied on him to look after his personal mining interests—recorded in a long line of grey filing cabinets outside Walter's office. Walter was a flamboyant character who even dared to wear light-coloured suits. He loved finance, good food and newspapers. Unlike your normal successful corporate executive, who could never be described as outspoken or forthcoming, Walter was full of self-disclosure and spoke to the printers the same way that he spoke to fellow executives: accusing them all, at some stage, of making hamburgers. I liked Walter and wished I could have worked for him when he was the second Editor of the *Australian* (two before Owen Thomson).

Two American reporters had arrived supposedly to help on the Annual Report. I was stunned to see what beautiful gunmetal and Prussian blue suits they wore. Never in my 46 years had I seen such fine material. Their suits reminded me of the armour knights wore for protecting their vital organs, and their back. I started to notice that almost all the Sydney executives dressed in armour colours: charcoal, slate, black, steel blue, silver, grey, cobalt blue. This caused me, for the first time, to look in the men's room mirror at my now maculate brown herringbone wool jacket and to realise how far I had diverged from a corporate attitude over the years stuck down in Brisbane's Fortitude Valley. I'd read just that week that 'brown is a loser's colour', and I realised then why my jacket had been for sale at half price in Edward Street just eleven years earlier.

My father, Fred, had always quoted grandpa Hugh Lunn's advice to buy as good a suit as your purse would allow, but my purse wasn't allowing anything. The investments with my solicitor were doing so badly that every week all my wages went to pay the twenty per cent-plus interest. I had become, as my solicitor said, 'a millionaire...in debts'. It turned out that I had agreed to be 'jointly and severally liable' which, to my surprise, meant I was personally responsible for the debts of all six partners in the venture, even though I owned less than eight per cent. And most of these partners, it also turned out, were companies with no assets. I learned then why companies are 'proprietary limited'—because the debts of individuals are, under our laws, *un*limited.

I was going broke, but I wasn't alone. Rupert too, apparently, was in deep. I was told on Mahogany Row that he had been 'flying around Europe in a Lear jet seeing bankers'. Mahogany Row was worried and, as everyone now knows, the huge debts were to see Rupert's vast empire nearly crumble a couple of years later because interest rates had not fallen as he'd expected. Rupert had to do a deal with more than a hundred bank creditors, and only the quality of his assets, his personality and his persistence saved him.

One of the two American reporters in the good suits took off for Hong Kong a couple of days after he arrived and never worked on the Annual Report. The other wrote one paragraph, which Walter decided not to use because this was a writing job. But when I saw Rupert at the lift going off to address the Securities Institute investment lunch, both Americans were with him in their zoot suits without the drape shape. Which confirmed my suspicions since I'd arrived in Sydney that me and my brown jacket were being deliberately kept away from Rupert.

Once, Rupert arrived at Walter's office as I sat with my back to the door while Walter chatted as he signed hundreds of joined company cheques that had been spat out of a computer. I'd never seen Walter move so fast: out of his seat, around the huge desk, leaning in like a 400-metre champion round the bend, and across the carpet to the door before Rupert could get more than one pace into the room. Rupert spoke to him very warmly: in a way one might expect he'd speak to the closest of lifelong friends. There was no hint Rupert was the boss.

His ability to befriend such key executives was another reason for Rupert's success. But there was a downside. As I did my rounds along Mahogany Row I found a degree of frustration that a couple of people had made almost independent empires out of their editorial bailiwick, and little could be done because they were seen as friends of Rupert. 'It's because Rupert's more of a man than a corporation,' one executive explained. Rupert's motivation to keep expanding, I was told, was that he wanted to become the world's newspaper legend. Yet he was already that. I could see that I was working for a man with personality, prejudices and interests who, in a very old-fashioned way, worked for, owned and ran the company: right down to the lowliest writer. A man of whom everyone said: 'He knows what he's doing.'

My biggest surprise was that the offices on Mahogany Row, for one of the world's most powerful corporations, were not at all luxurious. There was no solicitor's green-marble reception area, no barrister's artificial leather bookshelves, no corporate Corinthian pillars, no dado of gold raptors around the walls—just a warren of hallways, bends and added-on steps through knocked-down walls. A former chocolate factory that had melted into the surrounding buildings.

My business partners had called a meeting in Brisbane re our burgeoning unpayable debts. I had to attend, even though I knew Rupert's Annual Report would struggle to make its deadline around the world. But this was almost life or death for me. I stood in front of Walter's desk and told him I'd have to go back to Brisbane for a day. Walter looked slowly up over his horn-rimmed glasses as if I were joking. I'd already told him over lunch a few times about my debt problems and Walter had tried to come up with ideas to save us, but he had to make sure the Annual Report was done on time.

'This is what you call a *real* hamburger,' Walter said, moving his head from side to side. 'A double whopper with the works.'

'If I don't go, I will be bankrupted,' I said.

Walter examined me closely, the large illuminated magnifier lamp that sat on his desk reflecting in the lenses of his glasses. He stared for a long time, and I watched his face change from bewilderment that he was even discussing such a request, to the mercy that lived forever in his guts, and which he could not escape.

'It's a real hamburger, Hugh, but you can go for twenty-four hours. Tell them I think a cash box company is their best chance.'

When I got back to Sydney next day there had been a last-minute hiccup when it was suddenly realised that News now owned Gordon & Gotch Limited, a multinational (Australia, UK, New Zealand, Canada and Papua New Guinea) magazine and book distributor, and Australia's largest retail bookseller. The reason it had been overlooked in the rush was that Rupert's nephew had been specially put in charge of reviewing this $300 million revenue organisation immediately after the takeover: it was just another prize for News shareholders. I visited the nephew, Matt Handbury, in his small office on the non-window side of Mahogany Row; he handed over his review and I quickly wrote some paragraphs into the Annual Report.

When I had finished the Review of Operations, Richard Searby called me in to where he was sitting at Rupert's small bare antique desk and said: 'Now I want you to write the Chief Executive's Review: three pages for the front of the report on how Rupert saw the year.'

'I thought Rupert would write that himself,' I said, amazed.

'Don't worry,' said Searby, 'he'll be watching what you write very closely.' I already knew Rupert watched the Annual Report closely— the previous year he had rejected the first cover because it included in a montage a photo of an Australian businessman who was noted for takeovers. 'People will wonder what he's doing on the cover of our Annual Report,' Rupert said.

Searby listed several major events which Rupert's Chief Executive's Review should include, especially the final settlement of 'the troubles' at Wapping in England and the Herald takeover. He said it was most important for Rupert to thank his 'strong, hard-working executive team' because of the executive structure where Rupert dealt directly with subsidiary heads 'in a worldwide and very large Group which operates without a big head office'. 'Flag it!' ordered Searby enthusiastically. 'It is enormously important, and very appropriate in these times.' I guessed he didn't want the stock market to perceive TNCL as a one-man band. But there had been no mention of this in the previous Annual Reports, I noted.

Still, Rupert was now going on 57.

Back at Anna's IBM computer, I started to write the Chief Executive's Review. Not only was I now up there with Rupert, I *was* him! Well, at least for the purpose of this one exercise, I had to become him, because that is the only way to write for someone else. So I sat at the keyboard pretending I was Rupert Murdoch and was surprised when out it came, no trouble at all: 'It was a year of great expansion for the company in the United States and Australia; of realisation of our aims in the United Kingdom; and one in which we gained our first major foothold in a fourth continent—with the purchase of the *South China Morning Post* in Hong Kong.'

Because Rupert often said how he loved 'challenging entrenched monopolies' and 'shaking up complacent competitors' I welcomed the arrival of the *Independent* in London as a result of Wapping and said I welcomed the competition for the *Times*. By the time I got to the end of the three pages I was feeling so powerful that I decided not to thank the executives too effusively.

I just didn't feel they deserved it.

Later that day, Walter came to my office and said Rupert would like a printout of his proposed Review. 'No problem Walter,' I said and clicked on the word 'print' as I'd done scores of times in the past three weeks.

Nothing happened.

'What's wrong?' said Walter, whose only failing was a lack of patience. 'Nothing,' I lied. 'The computer's just playing up a bit.' I hit 'print' again, but again nothing. This was strange because it had always worked when I was writing the rest of the 104-page Annual Report. Now, for just three pages, nothing was happening. I turned the printer on and off. Then I re-booted, getting that dreaded notice you used to get on PCs back then: 'Abort, Retry, Fail'.

'Retry' and 'Fail' had no effect. 'Never touch "Abort",' someone had once told me, so I left well enough alone.

'I'm afraid Anna's computer isn't working properly, Walter.'

'This is different to anything with which I have had to come to terms,' said Walter. 'Rupert is still waiting.'

Just as Walter was leaving to tell Rupert that, in fact, he couldn't have his Review, that it was lost somewhere in his wife's computer, I had an idea. The last printout I'd done was for pages forty-eight and forty-nine. Was it possible, just faintly possible, that this gadget was so dumb that it was looking for pages forty-eight and forty-nine when there were only three in this document? It was. I changed the numbers, and out came the Review from the silent dot-matrix printer on the white continuous-form paper.

'You got it!' said Walter, ripping off each page himself as it arrived, and disappeared in a blur. Then I printed one out for Richard Searby.

Next morning Richard called me around. 'You haven't given the executives the thanks or the prominence I asked for,' he said. 'You've put it right at the end! And you didn't flag it!'

OK, I said.

Sitting casually on my desk when I got back was the copy that had gone to Rupert. It was corrected in, of all things, pencil, in tiny, neat writing.

The first thing I noticed was that Rupert had corrected a spelling mistake with a tiny insertion of a fourth 'i' in 'initiative'. My reference to the *Independent* in London was crossed out, and so too was my more than generous praise for Rupert's executives. Rupert had replaced this with a last paragraph saying that at the core of the company's growth was a small team of talented executives: 'Without this experienced and proven team…we could not have reported such a successful year.'

That was more than sufficient.

Michael Rand, the man in charge of the *Sunday Times Colour*

Magazine, had been flown out to perform his magic on the Annual Report, as he did each year. He and two assistants had taken over an advertising office on the North Shore. When we dropped over in Walter's Volvo to see how it was going, Michael Rand said he had a problem with my Chief Executive's Review because I'd begun: 'It was a year...' Rand said he had designed the Annual Report so that the first letter of each section would be a huge dropped capital letter contained inside a square of four different coloured patterns. 'The letter "I" is uncomfortable in the square. It doesn't give the page the force we require,' he said, holding his stomach as if in agony. 'Can't you see it?'

Well no, not really.

'It's a real hamburger,' said Walter, looking at the anorexic 'I'.

'Well,' I said, 'how about an "F"?'

'An "F"?' said Rand in disbelief. 'That would be crisp! An "F" would look absolutely super. But where can we get an "F"?'

'Instead of "It was a year of great expansion for the company..." I can just turn it around and make it "For the company it was a year of great expansion...".'

'You got it!' said Walter. 'But first we'll have to check with Rupert.' I was surprised. It was such a simple change, and made absolutely no difference to the meaning or tone of the Review. 'Nevertheless,' said Walter, 'we will have to check with Rupert. It's in his name and it is the Annual Report.'

Rupert was in Taiwan looking at printing presses and I sat opposite Walter as he held the phone while people on the Chinese island searched for our boss. I didn't like it. Rupert would be annoyed that we were wasting his time on such a trivial matter. I just hoped he didn't blame the writer. But, listening to only half the conversation, it was obvious that Rupert was thanking Walter profusely for checking with him first.

Yes, we could change to an F, and the Annual Report could go to the printer on time. Rupert ran the company more closely than I'd ever imagined.

Although I hadn't got to see Rupert, there were a few high-up people who were apparently happy with my work. The boss of News Ltd, Ken Cowley, thanked me profusely; Walter thanked me generously; and the accountant said in his heavy accent, when he moved back into his office after my job was done: 'Everyone is saying, "Thank God for Hugh Lunn".'

But none of this helped me at the *Australian*. While I was writing the Annual Report, an editor rang and asked me to write a piece on the large numbers of Aboriginal deaths in custody, a major story at the time. Of course I had to knock him back.

Now that the 1987 Annual Report was out of the way I wished to resign. I hadn't talked to Rupert since he'd asked me to stay on more than six years earlier. I didn't like being given orders by a 24-year-old Sydney news editor who had been in grade one at primary school when I was working for the paper's survival. I was insulted they wouldn't trust me to write a column, while a heap of New Right wets and drys and TV celebrities did—even if they were part of a lobby group; even if they lived in England; even if they lived in New York. And all urging that we adopt the Asian economic model! To me, our paper had been ever so slowly opened up to an unkindness of writers, many of whom were on the side of the merciless. Long gone for sure were the days when we gave Australian of the Year to Nobel-Prize-winning author Patrick White or to John Sinclair for saving Fraser Island from sandmining. In 1985 the prize had gone instead to an American abattoir owner in Mudginberri who broke his unions. The change in the *Australian*'s tone was being noticed by other people too. One of them was David Hackworth, who was then living in Patterson Street, Auchenflower, Brisbane. In the mid-1980s Hackworth wrote an angry letter to the paper, cancelling his subscription.

> I speak frequently to large audiences...and without exception your paper is singled out as an example of what a free press is *not*. If your subscriptions fall off you might consider re-evaluating your one-sided

reporting...editors become victims of prejudices, blinkered views and narrow-mindedness just like soldiers.

It turned out that Hackworth was 'the most decorated US soldier in history'. Promoted to officer in the field in Korea and with three Vietnam tours during which he rose to Colonel, Hackworth later wrote a brutally honest war memoir, *About Face*, about how he changed to become an anti-war protester.

(Goodness knows what he would have made of the *Australian*'s headline in April 1995: 'Vietnam War: just and winnable'—the same headline we had all laughed at back in 1972 in the old Fairfax *Sydney Morning Herald*.)

I sent Hackworth's letter down to the Editor in Sydney with a note of my own:

If you want my feelings on this letter, our paper has to be very careful that it does not become so identified with the right that it loses its influence and only preaches to the converted. I think there is a need to balance the outpouring of (here I named two columnists) to give the other half of the population something enjoyable to read. Though often accused of being a conservative myself, I have found it neces-sary...to try to balance the book, as it were, by presenting an alternative view. It is, for example, a simplistic notion to blame wage earners for the economic problems. Business partners of mine— lawyers and accountants—tell me that Australia has lost thousands of millions a year because of tax evasion schemes...(if I didn't work for it) I must say that I would probably not buy the *Australian*.

Now that I was writing letters to the Editor myself, I realised I'd joined Owen Thomson's 'powerless punters'.

As usual, I turned to Helen who so often fortifies my resolve. (I'd learned a valuable lesson early on. Whenever we had relationship problems, Helen would stand in front of me and look up with strong brown eyes and say: 'We have to talk.')

'Resign,' she said, 'and write the book on your childhood. It's what you want to do and it's worth doing.'

'But we owe so much. Without my salary we'll go bankrupt,' I warned.

'Then let's go bankrupt,' Helen said.

'But such a book might only sell a thousand copies.'

'Even if only a thousand people read it, it will be worth it,' Helen replied.

So I took the big step and resigned, aged 46: 'I am not leaving to work for any other paper or magazine. I just want to write what I *want* to write.' I had in mind, as I performed the act of resigning from a very well-paid position, what my pastrycook father, Fred, used to say when he abhorred some unfortunate act that mankind was engaged in: 'I leave that to them that enjoys it.'

To my surprise I got an invitation from Managing Director Ken Cowley to spend a weekend at Rupert's sheep station, Boonoke.

It was an opportunity I just couldn't pass up.

20 Never trust a man in a black hat

My last job for Rupert, as I worked out my three months notice at the end of 1987, was to write daily colour stories from the Fitzgerald Inquiry. I was told to be there for the expected sensational appearance of the Assistant Police Commissioner, who had admitted taking huge monthly bribes from other corrupt police and had already sought indemnity.

No one knew when the Assistant Commissioner would be called. But he was expected to name those who had taken part for several decades in 'the Joke', the name corrupt Queensland police called their system of protecting prostitution, illegal casinos, and SP (starting price) bookies.

With the eyes of the nation watching—and with Quentin Dempster doing an acute, intuitive job re-creating the Inquiry with actors on ABC-TV every night (in the days when Queensland had a local *7.30 Report*)—the Fitzgerald courtroom was so packed with reporters that we were practically sitting on each other's laps, while a murder of barristers spread out across the other nine-tenths of the room: barristers not being as lean, or as hungry, as reporters.

At a high bench up front, which was the width of the wide court, sat the Commissioner, Tony Fitzgerald, alone. This was the man who had given up his job as a Federal Court judge in order to live permanently in his home town of Brisbane; the lawyer who had been given a six-week appointment to look into allegations of corruption and was to find so much public immorality that—at the end of two years—he decided to close the Inquiry and change the system rather than keep on jailing corrupt officials. Fitzgerald therefore created the anti-corruption Criminal Justice Commission to watch over police, public servants and politicians, and to investigate all complaints. Because of his pro-active Elliott Ness approach to corruption-busting, Fitzgerald was the man that everyone in the street now loved and admired above all others, so his reforms were adopted 'lock, stock and barrel'—though few powerful men wanted a CJC looking over their shoulder.

To the Queensland public, who had learned not to trust their police or their government, it was as if Fitzgerald had ridden into a lawless town from out of nowhere and cleaned up the whole place all by himself: 'Who was that wigged man?'

The day Tony Fitzgerald was appointed to run the Inquiry—while Premier Bjelke-Petersen was busy down south on his futile mission to try to become Prime Minister—I came home from work and said to Helen: 'The State government has just made an incredible mistake. They don't know what Tony's like. He's just not like any other judge: he's unclubbable.' Fitzgerald rarely went out, and spent all his spare time at home with his wife and three kids. As it turned out, Commissioner Fitzgerald seemed genuinely surprised to find that there were massage parlours all over Brisbane: though they all had large signs out front like 'Gentle Fingers'.

I knew Tony Fitzgerald as a tennis player and had drunk a lot of lime juice and soda water in his kitchen. In fact, I was in a difficult position as a journalist because he was now Australia's biggest story, and Adrian McGregor and I had been playing tennis with him on his backyard tennis court two evenings a week for six years. I never told the Sydney office that I knew Tony Fitzgerald. I didn't want to ruin our relationship.

It would have been easy to write a feature on Tony for the *Oz*.

Adrian and I had long-since discovered that people reveal their true character on the tennis court. In 1982, after a decade of trying, Adrian and I had won the Greater Brisbane Pennant Reserve men's doubles, and the University of Queensland A Grade men's doubles. We'd observed a lot of personalities along the way. Like the redheaded bloke who, as he shook hands with each of us over the net after losing to our hacking style, said slowly and deliberately: 'You two would be the two greatest perpetrators of rubbish I've ever seen.'

Aged 45 in 1987, Tony Fitzgerald was a year younger than me, and I knew from playing tennis with him that the crooked cops and politicians were in for some surprising moves, done at lightning speed. Tony's favourite tactic on the tennis court in doubles was, when you least expected it, to flash across the net in a blur of blue. Fifty per cent of the time, he dropped the ball softly a few centimetres over the net; the other fifty per cent he would hit the ball such a vicious blow that he often frightened me. I could see something in his eyes that told me he was after a result, not a playmate. Though Tony would say he knew exactly where the ball was going, I did a lot more dodging and weaving while playing against him than at any other time on a tennis court. He was a cheerful friendly character on court, keen at repartee, and mostly wearing a flashy red or blue sweatband around his forehead. His serve revealed much about his approach. The Commissioner would leap a foot off the ground to hit the first serve as hard and as flat as he could; if that missed, he very, very cautiously made absolutely sure of the second serve—knowing that, because the serve was so soft, his opponent would more than likely get over-excited and belt it out. But then, every now and then, Tony hit the second serve even harder than the first: usually on a big point, which is exactly when you wouldn't expect him to take the chance.

So I knew Tony Fitzgerald as a man who took big risks but then, given a second chance, next time would usually play safe: while still always willing to occasionally gamble it all on one throw of the dice. His favourite sayings on court were (when he arrived to see us playing) 'same old shots'; (when he was congratulated on hitting several winners) 'It won't last'; and (when he was unlucky) 'There's no justice!' To which my reply was: 'Well, you should know, Tony.'

When down and out at 0–5, love–40 he wouldn't give in. 'Let's play it a point at a time,' Tony would urge.

Once, I got a real insight into what those two years of listening to official lies was doing to him. We were standing on the side of the court stretching quads and hamstrings when Adrian McGregor put down his racquet and told us a story of how two people had given him totally opposite reports of an incident.

'One of them must be lying,' I said.

Tony Fitzgerald put on his headband, picked up his racquet, and turned and said as he walked away onto the court: 'Don't be silly, they'll both be lying.'

After the Fitzgerald Inquiry started, Tony came up to me on the tennis court one day and said not to worry if I saw some plain-clothes security police hiding in the garden.

'I haven't seen anyone,' I said.

'No, but they've seen you,' the Commissioner replied.

The next time, I noticed their mirrors. These sullen men were there to protect Tony from being killed, because he was playing for keeps against some of the most powerful men in the State—most of them armed. He and his family needed all the protection they could get. Tony still kept many of his tennis appointments, though his game, which relied so much on a quick eye and deft touch, suffered. And, while his Inquiry continued to unveil ever higher levels of corruption, there were times on the tennis court, which was surrounded by bushes, when a possum in a tree could make the whole court fall silent.

At the Inquiry itself, security was tighter than anything I saw while covering Nixon's or Johnson's visits to Vietnam, or Agnew's visit to Bali, or Suharto's appearances in Jakarta. There was one particular security man who seemed loaded down with handguns underneath his checked sports jacket. I guessed he was an Untouchable who'd been specially imported to the country, or the State, to protect Tony Fitzgerald. He looked like Jack Palance as the evil, heartless, apathetic, cruel gunfighter 'Wilson' in the 1950s movie *Shane*—and I expected that this security man, too, would pull on a black glove before shooting someone down.

Once, I broke a string on a day Tony was too busy to play tennis. Knowing there were several racquets on a wall in the Fitzgerald home, I knocked on the door and was taken aback when 'Wilson's' dark left eye appeared around the corner of a window. He wouldn't open the window to talk to me. However, no threat is great enough to stop a tennis player from trying to reach a racquet, or a ball, if he can see it. So I stood my ground while pointing stubbornly at the broken string, and then at the unblemished Fitzgerald household racquets on the wall inside the house. Reluctantly, with no change of expression, Wilson took a racquet off the wall with his left hand, opened the window just a crack, and, standing side-on as if he were about to draw, shoved it out. Wilson mustn't have known much about tennis, because he'd picked a child's racquet off the wall, one that was only good for a 10-year-old. After some hesitation, in which we eyeballed each other through the glass, I decided to play with the little racquet and lose.

I'd seen what Wilson did one day at the Inquiry to a brand new reporter who arrived from Melbourne and took a seat at the back of the courtroom. Wilson called him out of the row and told him to leave the court. The reporter protested about freedom of the press and showed his Melbourne media pass, but taciturn Wilson just pointed at the door saying the only words I ever heard him utter: 'I don't know your face.'

I'd been attending the Fitzgerald Inquiry for a few weeks, but there was still no sign of the Assistant Police Commissioner, who was expected to implicate other high-ranking officers, perhaps even Police Commissioner Terry Lewis himself—a man who had been appointed a Knight of the Realm by Premier Bjelke-Petersen (also the man who signed all our Queensland press passes).

It was by now the start of November: Melbourne Cup time. In Brisbane, buses are left abandoned in the road as the drivers—and everyone else on the bus—rush off down the street to watch the race. Cup parties are held in every hotel and club, every office has at least five sweepstakes, betting shops overflow and sittings of State Parliament are suspended.

Tony Fitzgerald had been listening to month after month of evidence of police corruption, including their regular attendance at all-night parties at massage parlours. So, not surprisingly, Tony was the only person in Australia who had forgotten that the Melbourne Cup was on. On the day before the big race, one man accused of being an illegal casino operator piped up in court to ask the question that was on everyone's lips: 'Commissioner, I presume the court will be adjourning tomorrow afternoon for the Melbourne Cup?'

Fitzgerald: 'And why would we do that?'

Accused (nonplussed): 'Well, my wife's got a big Melbourne Cup party on at our place.'

Fitzgerald: 'Have you remembered to invite the police?'

The Melbourne Cup was one club even Tony Fitzgerald had to join, and so he relented. The court adjourned for an hour the next afternoon for the running of the big race.

I'd followed the Melbourne Cup closely since I was a child at Mary Immaculate primary school where the nuns ensured that everyone got to listen to the race. So I joined all the lawyers and journalists in the pub across the road to watch the Cup on TV. But it didn't take long for the smell of cigarettes and stale beer to overcome my love of the horse race and drive me back out onto George Street. I made my way slowly down the deserted street—which usually bustled—buying an afternoon Brisbane *Telegraph* on the way. Then I had an idea: I'd walk back up the four flights of stairs to the courtroom and sit and read the paper until Tony's Inquiry cranked up again. I'd missed tennis for the last month, so I needed the exercise.

Clunk, clunk, clunk…my feet fell heavier and heavier as I tired near the top. The horses would be under starter's orders now. I turned the corner and started up the last set of a dozen stairs when there was rushed movement by a revolver of security guards above. Right before my eyes, the surrounded Assistant Police Commissioner was being hustled into the empty courtroom for his evidence. Tony Fitzgerald had made a sudden dart across the net to outfox all the crooks. He knew they would be too busy watching the Melbourne Cup to knock off the man who was their single most dangerous witness—the one witness Fitzgerald couldn't afford to lose.

One of the men leaped around to face the staircase with both hands disappearing across his chest and under his bulging jacket.

It was Wilson!

Was he wearing his black glove? Would he call me a no-good yellow-bellied deep-north Queenslander dingo dog...before gunning me down?

I held my hands up.

'Which way do you want me to go?' was all I could think to say.

Wilson motioned for me to go back, and I walked backwards down the stairs holding the *Telegraph* high above my head—grateful that he knew my face.

It was my closest call since the Vietnam War.

More than a dozen senior staff were going to Rupert's Boonoke property for the weekend to discuss the future of the *Oz*, and, Steady Editor said enthusiastically, Ken Cowley was going to ask me to stay on. I said I was definitely leaving, but if Ken was inviting me for the weekend then, out of politeness, I'd turn up. Ken wrote a nice letter saying he looked forward to meeting me there and would be 'delighted' if I could come. 'This weekend is to relax and discuss editorial opportunities. (It) will be informal and I hope you enjoy your stay.'

Early Saturday morning our special plane took off from Sydney, stopped in Canberra to pick up chief political writer Paul Kelly, and then headed south-west to the Riverina sheep-grazing plains. Ken Cowley, Rupert's boss in Australia, greeted each of us with a strong handshake as we alighted for morning tea on the homestead verandah. Being from coastal subtropical Brisbane I was surprised how flat and dry and treeless the high-grassed Boonoke sheep station was. But the area around the old brick homestead was green and treed, with a rose garden out front and, as promised, a tennis court. We shared rooms in the sprawling house and I ended up with the former Reporter Editor who, I was very surprised to find, was actually a lovely bloke when you got to spend time with him.

In small buses we traversed The Old Man Plain: mile after mile of high brown grass across Rupert's Ranch. At the ram shed his merinos were covered in a much thicker coating of wool than I'd ever seen on any Queensland sheep. Ken Cowley enjoyed talking to the ranch-hands and plunging both hands deep into the fleece on the backs of various rams, pulling it apart to show us the depth and aesthetic creaminess of the wool. A barbecue lunch under the homestead trees saw Paul Kelly and me telling funny political stories about Joh and Gough to John Lyons, a brilliant young journo who was the only one demanding these stories. I liked Lyons because, after the 1986 election fiasco the previous year, as Chief-of-Staff of the *Australian* he wrote me a letter ignoring the fact that my predictions were wrong and saying my six-week coverage was 'one of the best sustained pieces of journalism for a long time'. 'This view is shared by many people down here, both in journalism and outside,' he wrote. 'People from just about the whole range of the media down here have been commenting on the standard of the coverage, and I think your sustained performance over the last month has benefited the paper both for the short term—with a marked increase in sales—and the long term, in setting ourselves up as a dominating force.'

After lunch, it was on to Rupert's ant-bed tennis court for some executive-bonding doubles. Under a cloudless blue sunny sky I wore my black wide-brimmed felt hat because I'd had a skin cancer removed above the right eyebrow. This was the hat I'd worn out west when covering the Winton-to-Longreach horserace, where I was told an old bush saying: 'Never trust a man in a black hat.' So I wore the black hat reluctantly, and smothered my face in white reflective sunburn cream—which then leaked into my eyes. Tears rolled down my cheeks, creating tracks through the white cream until I looked like an evil character in a Peking Opera instead of the pink-cheeked hero I'd once been.

Worried what Ken Cowley might think, I sprinted off the court and up to the homestead to ask for some eye drops. But I couldn't get the drops in. A passing shearer offered to help and, before I could move, he picked me up, bent me backwards over his leg and, as if jetting a sheep, flushed each eye with the relieving liquid.

Back on the court in my untrustworthy Akubra, I kept forgetting that these journalists weren't Richmond Rovers or Jindalee Lemon, and that I didn't have to play so hard. Ken Cowley, who didn't play that day, fetched the many balls that ricocheted off racquets over the fence. But my form didn't impress one enemy in the camp: 'Is this what you do up in Brisbane all day?' I explained that a tennis player is, like a gunfighter, only as good as his technique. That tennis is a side-on, in-front game.

Instead of slinging off, Paul Kelly, a keen social player, said he was impressed.

As the sun set, Steady Editor took me for a walk in the rose garden by myself for a nice chat. I couldn't help but bring up the topic of cigarette smoking. Since I was leaving, I said that News Ltd would be very wise to do something about cigarette smoking in its offices. 'At the very least I'd get rid of the cigarette vending machines.'

Before dinner at the homestead, we drove as a group about thirty kilometres for a drink in a local hotel. Soon after we arrived, Steady Editor brought over the publican and his wife, saying they wished to meet me. They said they'd enjoyed my articles in the *Oz*.

Rupert's dining room at Boonoke was wide and long, with large paintings in ornate frames of each of the property's owners dating back to early the previous century. The first owner, if I remember, had the biggest portrait. He was a thin-faced, dark-eyed man from Ireland. Rupert's portrait was on a wall too—up high at one end, above the entrance door. But Rupert wasn't really into glory. He could have been a Lord in England, or a Sir in Australia, had he said the word. But he didn't. While the other owners were captured in oils,

Rupert was up there in a plastic and aluminium Kodak frame: a colour photo of him in shirt sleeves standing in front of a printing press with a newspaper tucked up under one arm.

As Rupert watched over our dinner, and as red wine was splashed around among the journalists, Ken Cowley called on various people to talk about the future of our now successful paper. He particularly thanked Steady Editor for all his 'excellent' work over the last two decades in various roles, always steadfastly helping keep the *Australian* going, through bad times and good. Then it became a bit evangelical, with a couple of younger editors leaping up to say what wonders they were going to perform in the future. One editor, an Englishman, said he was going to take our newspaper by the scruff of the neck and provide ever-greater circulation increases. He personally was going to make *the* difference, make the *Oz* work, and make sure great stories were written and produced. I'd never even heard of him before that weekend; he certainly hadn't been around for almost all my seventeen years. And wouldn't you guess: within a year this bloke had trans-ferred to another paper and, four years later, was back in England working for an opposition newspaper group.

After a dozen speeches I pointed out that it was interesting that only the three non-Sydney-based staff had not yet been asked to speak about our national paper. Ken Cowley replied that everyone would get to speak, if they had anything to contribute. I told how our office leaked when it rained, even though it was on the bottom floor. How we put rubbish bins on top of the three computers to stop water falling into them. The seven staff had to fight over these three computers, because only one had a printer and only one could send stories to Sydney. Ken said to Steady Editor that something should be done about that, and they both went off to bed.

The journos all stayed, breaking out the best Rupert wine they could find in a quick search of the homestead. It didn't take long for one *Oz* editor I'd clashed with previously to say, 'You should be on the front page all the time, but you're not.'

'I had front-page stories all summer while you were swanning around overseas,' I replied.

Before long, I was starting to feel in need of Ned Kelly's armour, or, at the very least, a good suit. Yet I had already resigned. I was a guest of Ken Cowley. Why was I copping this?

With great difficulty, I resisted the obvious temptation to point out my front-page story in the *Weekend Australian* that very morning. It was a story (illustrated by before-and-after photos) about a TV hostess who had been sacked after her face turned black. But then the world's top brain surgeon (a Japanese who was in Brisbane for a conference) operated on the pituitary gland at the base of her brain to turn her face back to its normal colour. Inside, I'd written a full page on this visiting surgeon. His waiting room in Japan was filled with people who had developed a facial tic in middle age, which contorted the face so violently that they could no longer appear in public. This surgeon would operate through a keyhole incision to separate a hardening artery from the seventh nerve in the brain, and the tic would magically disappear. We got hundreds of calls to our Brisbane office about that story, which arose simply because I didn't write the usual 'pawpaw injections for bad backs' story when covering the Asian–Australian Congress of Neurological Surgery Conference. After they read it, *Sixty Minutes* flew a team to Tokyo to do my story.

Then Paul Kelly performed one of his deep throat clearings, which made everyone shut up in deference to his intellect. 'All I can say, as a former Editor of the *National Times*, is that Hugh Lunn *is* the *Australian* and if you've got a problem with him, then the paper has a problem.' I hadn't expected anyone to have the guts to go out so far on a limb on my behalf.

The next afternoon we flew back to Sydney, and, in the event, Ken Cowley didn't ask me to stay on.

The circulation of the *Oz* had risen for each of the last five years I was there. The *Weekend Australian's* circulation was now 289000— nearly double what it was when Owen Thomson had telexed fifteen years before to say we'd soon all be drinking champagne out of our navels. I was one of the few who was leaving the *Oz* without being paid to go.

When an accountant asked 'What about your super?' I said I'd never joined the scheme.

'But it's compulsory,' he said.

'I was never optimistic enough to join Rupert's superannuation scheme,' I replied.

As I walked out of the Brisbane bureau for the last time at the end of 1987 I felt a bit like Alan Ladd as he rode off into the mountains at the end of *Shane*—sad, bleeding, leaning awkwardly to the left. Except that there was no one calling for me to come back.

But, as one who believed Shane lived, I was off to a better life having hung up my gun.

Ron Richards took me to lunch and was nice enough to offer me a job on what was now Rupert's *Courier-Mail*. I told Ron I'd finished with newspapers. I'd reached a stage where I knew I should be in charge, or not be there at all. I revealed I was going to write a book about my childhood.

'But where's the market for that?' asked Ron. 'We know publishing at News Ltd. There's no market in Australia for childhood autobiography.'

I said I thought people would be interested.

It turned out that, as a boy, Ron had made wire coat hangers for pocket money in Bardon, and, since I'd made meat pies in my father's cake shop on the other side of the river at Annerley, we got nostalgic about the old days. Ron related how, when he first joined the *Sunday Sun* in the '50s from Warwick, he didn't know anyone. A lovely older sub-editor, who owned a huge American convertible, took Ron for a couple of drives down to Redland Bay on a Sunday to buy strawberries straight from the farms.

'But Ron,' I said, 'you sacked that bloke a few years ago.'

'It was the hardest thing I've ever had to do in my life,' Ron replied, and I saw a look I'd never seen on his face before: it still lived in his mind. 'I really suffered for it. But it had to be done.' It was true that this sub-editor had become known as 'pot-an-hour' because he was always down in the Empire drinking beer. And Ron had kept him on for years despite this.

I looked at my old mate Ron, and he looked back at me. We knew now that there were things that we both had to do; that, as my friend Pham Ngoc Dinh told his Vietcong captors in Vietnam, 'Every man has his own situation.'

As Dinh said after the Tet Offensive: 'Time go, War finish.'

Postscript

RON RICHARDS died as I was completing this book. At Ron's funeral the mourners included Ken Cowley and Robin's courageous cohort, Fatman Ken Blanch. There was standing room only in the church as a specially penned message from Rupert was read out which said, in part: 'Ron was one of our shining stars, and a good friend.'

ADRIAN MCGREGOR wrote several bestselling sports biographies and was re-hired by the *Oz* a decade later. He still works there.

ROBERT HOGE, 23, married Sue Dodd, 22, in 1995. They invited me, Helen and the neurosurgeon at his operation, Dr Leigh Atkinson, to the wedding. I was proud that little re-made Robert Hoge—after reading all the articles I wrote about his terrible deformities—had, when he'd grown up, chosen to become a journalist himself.

JIM EGOROFF now lives in San Francisco. He recently designed and built an upright hyperbaric chamber with its own seat and phone for Hollywood actors recovering from cosmetic surgery.

TONY FITZGERALD left his hometown to live in Sydney after having risked his all to put Queensland back on the rails—which made me wonder if the law has its dreamboaters too.

THE WALKLEY AWARDS—for so long unheralded and mispronounced as 'the Wakelys'—are now a success: they're on TV.

THE BRISBANE *TELEGRAPH*, the afternoon paper, was shut down a year after Rupert's takeover of the Herald group. Frank Moore closed the *Daily Sun* a few years later and, on 12 April 1992—five years after Rupert sold it—Moore shut down the plucky *Sunday Sun*. Brisbane was thus left with just one daily newspaper: the *Courier-Mail–Sunday Mail*.

THE *SUNDAY SUN* building in Fortitude Valley, shaken by printing presses and splashed by ink for so many decades, became Sun Apartments. The leaking *Oz* office in the old hat factory at 8 McLachlan Street became a dance club with an eight-metre-tall dancing marionette suspended inside.

PAUL KELLY became Editor of the *Australian* in the early '90s and removed its sharp New Right edge. Rupert's creation—started when he was just 33 years old—must now be as successful as he wildly dreamed in 1964. It now has foreign correspondents in London, Washington, Bangkok, New York, Los Angeles, Tokyo, Beijing, Jakarta and Auckland. Staff purges ceased after Sir Larry Lamb's reign ended late in 1982.

NEWS LTD now advertises 'a smoke free environment' for staff.

THE BOOK I wrote on my childhood, *Over the Top with Jim*, was, in 1991, the year's number one non-fiction book. It is now Australia's biggest selling book about an Australian childhood. Its popularity spawned a host of successful Australian childhood memoirs.

MARK DAY, Best Editor, recently gave this good advice in the *Australian*: 'Never take on someone who buys ink by the tonne.'

AND RUPERT: Rupert, who turned 70 in March 2001, is still expanding his empire—although he has long since achieved what they called on Mahogany Row his 'old Adelaide ambition' of becoming the most famous newspaperman in history. Even Microsoft's Bill Gates describes this Australian as 'the most influential man in the world'.

Vale

Geraldine Pascall, 38   **1983**
Bruce Rothwell, 61   **1984**
Harry Davis, 59   **1986**
Brian Bolton, 51   **1987**
Brian Hogben, 64   **1990**
Max Jessop, 55   **1994**
Jim Oram, 60   **1996**
Owen Thomson, 65   **1998**
Ken Edwards, 47   **1998**
Harry Reade, 70   **1998**
Ian Moffitt, 74   **2000**
Sir Larry Lamb, 70   **2000**
Sir Ken May, 85   **2000**
Ron Richards, 71   **2000**

Over the Top with Jim

In 1950s Brisbane the Cold War was hot news and so were the buns at Fred and Olive's famous Annerley Junction cake shop. Enter one Jim Egoroff: tough guy Russian subversive agent and all of nine years old. Hugh Lunn's over-the-top adventures have become Australia's all-time bestselling family favourite.

Head over Heels

The bestselling sequel to *Over the Top with Jim* follows Hugh Lunn from late adolescence to his early misadventures as a cadet reporter and his obsession with his luminous fellow cadet, Sallyanne, who has no idea that the torch Hugh carries for her could light up Brisbane…

> 'Brilliantly witty…a wonderfully innocent, beguiling book.'—Ross Fitzgerald, the *Age*

More Over the Top with Jim

From the Gabba to the Ekka, from a day on the beach with Fred at 'Sufferer's Paradise' to a rainbow cake supper at Auntie Vera's country police station, Hugh Lunn tells more hilarious, over-the-top stories about his now famous Annerley Junction family.

Spies Like Us

What do you do when it's the swinging '60s and you've got the job as a reporter and the car, a Sunbeam Alpine, but lost the love? Hugh Lunn went to Hong Kong with his Wimbledon tennis-playing mate Ken Fletcher, who knew all about gambling and women.

A masterpiece of exotic locales and laconic charm.

Vietnam: A Reporter's War

Hugh Lunn's account of reporting from Vietnam during the perilous Tet Offensive, where he discovered that Vietnam was a war of words—and images—as well as bullets.

Winner of the *Age* Book of the Year Award for Non-Fiction